SIGNING ENGLISH

EXACT OR NOT?

A Collection Of Articles

Research Articles on
SEE, MCE, TC

Edited by
Gerilee Gustason, Ph.D.

Modern Signs Press, Inc.
P.O. Box 1181
Los Alamitos, CA 90720

© 1988 Modern Signs Press, Inc.

International Standard Book No.
Soft Bound 0-916708-18-7

Library of Congress Catalog No. 88-090953

Publisher
MODERN SIGNS PRESS, Inc.
P.O. Box 1181
Los Alamitos, CA 90720
(213) 596-8548 (V/TDD)

The publisher welcomes your comments and suggestions
on this and future editions.

Printed in The United States of America

NEW INFORMATION

It has been 16 years since the beginnings of Signing Exact English. That length of time was needed for growing children to get to a point where results became apparent. With all that past, independent researchers are beginning to study English results of using the various communication systems. Since the studies have not as yet been published, the full texts cannot be distributed. However, we do have permission to distribute a brief summary.

One area commonly receiving a lot of attention is reading scores. Studies (CADS, 1984) indicate that the average 16 to 18 year old deaf individual reads at slightly above third grade level. A recent study was made including all the students in one program in which Signing Exact English was used (Moeller, 1988). Twelve students ranging in age from seven to eighteen were included. Of that group, nine read at or above grade level. One student not at grade level was an 11th grader reading at 9th grade level.

A frequent comment is that Signing Exact English cannot be used effectively because of the "difficulty" in signing the full language. A study by Luetke-Stahlman in 1988 produced the following results:

> With a group of 25 teachers using Signed English or PSE, an average of only 70% of the spoken words and morphemes were signed. That same study with 21 teachers using Signing Exact English showed an average of 92% or words and morphemes being signed. With a sample of four teachers, as much as 100% of all the words and morphemes were signed using S.E.E.

A study done by Marmor and Pettito in 1979 is often quoted as evidence of inability to adequately sign complete English sentences. That study is based on a sample size of <u>two</u> teachers.

Another 1988 study by Luetke-Stahlman involved a sample of 116 students. Four tests of English literacy were used. Those tests were given to six groups of varying sizes indicated below.

> SEE 2, n = 26 students; SEE 1, n = 14; oral, n = 22; PSE, n = 17; ASL, n = 12; Signed English, n = 25.

The results were analyzed by comparing one group's scores with each of the other groups' scores. SEE 2 (Signing Exact English) scored significantly higher in more cases than any of the other communication systems. No group scored significantly higher than SEE 2 on any of the tests.

Bibliographical information is on the other side of this page.

Luetke-Stahlman, B. (1988a) A description of the form and content of four sign systems as use in classrooms of hearing impaired students in the United States. Submitted to American Annals of the Deaf.

Luetke-Stahlman, B. (1988b) SEE2 in the classroom: how well is English grammar represented? in Signing English in Total Communication: Exact or Not? ed. G. Gustason. Los Alamitos, CA: Modern Signs Press, Inc.

Luetke-Stahlman, B. (1988c) Instructional communication modes used with Anglo hearing impaired students: the link to literacy. Submitted to the Journal of Speech and Hearing Disorder.

Marmor, G. & Pettito, L. (1979) Simultaneous communication in the classroom: how well is English grammar represented? Sign Language Studies, 23, 99-136.

Moeller, M.P. (1988) Language skills of deaf students using Manually Coded English. Presentation at convention of American Speech-Language-Hearing Association, Boston, November, 1988.

Parkins, S. & Whitesell, K. (1985) Evaluating the manual communication skills of prospective teachers and currently employed teachers of hearing impaired children in two hundred and fifty four schools/programs for hearing impaired children in the United States. Submitted to the North Carolina Council for the Hearing Impaired, June 14, 1985.

Wodlinger-Cohen, R. (1986) The manual representation of speech by deaf children, their mother and their teachers. Paper presented at the Conference on Theoretical Issues in Sign Language Research, Rochester, NY, June 1986.

TABLE OF CONTENTS

INTRODUCTION

The following articles have appeared in various publications over the years. A few appear here for the first time. This collection focuses on providing an overall view of the use of Total Communication and various forms of Manually Coded English in general and the use of Signing Exact English in particular. The articles are meant to supplement the information provided in the introduction to the text, <u>Signing Exact</u> <u>English</u>.

During the past few years, there has been increasing interest in the question of sign communication facilitating the learning of English by hearing impaired students. Researchers have begun to focus more and more on this question. What type of sign communication is most effective in helping students learn English? Can teachers and parents sign everything they say? Do they? The articles collected in this book take hard looks at these and similar questions.

This collection is not all-inclusive. However, the references listed at the end of each article and those in the RESOURCES section should provide a starting point for further reading. Comments and suggestions are welcome.

PREFACE

Tom Spradley
(Co-author of DEAF LIKE ME, Random House, 1978)
and Louise Spradley

Each year in the United States several thousand parents are shocked by the discovery that they have a deaf child. When we learned that our infant daughter was deaf we directed all our efforts to helping her become "normal." This, we were told, meant teaching her how to lipread, talk, and use her residual hearing. We did not realize that what little speech she heard or saw on our lips did not contain the ingredients to start language growing in her mind.

Language is something that is caught, not taught, and deaf children can catch it as easily from signs as hearing children do from speech. Signing and talking are just two different indicators that language is growing in a child's mind. This fact eluded us for five years. For our daughter to be normal and catch language from us, we would have to learn to sign as clearly as we spoke.

Learning to sign seemed like an enormous task. Slowly, awkwardly, we began learning and using one sign at a time. To our delight, our daughter began to understand our signs and used them to express her own ideas. As we progressed we discovered that learning American Sign Language (ASL) was like learning a foreign language. Familiar words, when changed into signs, were often used in unfamiliar ways. Recalling the shape for each sign was difficult at first, but this problem seemed minor compared to the overall task of learning to sign, in the unfamiliar pattern of ASL, an idea we could express without a second thought in English.

When our ability to use ASL did not keep pace with our need to communicate, we took the signs we knew, and, quite unconsciously, put them together in the best English possible.

Finally, we accepted the fact that during the time we had available to pass on language to our daughter we would not become competent signers of ASL. She would have to catch this language from deaf friends, just as she caught English from us. In time we would learn to use many of the idioms and visual characteristics that make ASL such a unique and important language. But we could not wait. We needed to communicate now.

The first edition of *Signing Exact English* provided the help we sought. In it was a vocabulary selected for use with young children, and a method of putting signs together, to match our spoken words, that allowed us to concentrate on communication, while the language we already knew guided our hands into a spontaneous flow of explanations, stories, humor, and love. And in the process our daughter began to catch our language.

There remains an urgent need for innovative strategies that will help parents play the vital role, rightfully theirs, of passing on language to their deaf children. Hopefully, help will come from current research into sign language, and enable parents and their deaf children to become bilingual, able to use both ASL and English. The authors of *Signing Exact English* have made a major contribution to this cause. English-speaking parents will find this enlarged edition a valuable resource. On its pages are the tools for making their own language visible to their deaf children. We heartily recommend this edition, and express our gratitude to the authors for their accomplishment.

Reprinted with permission from *Signing Exact English*, 1980 Edition.

FOREWORD

Hilde Schlesinger, M.D.,
Director, Center on Deafness
University of California, San Francisco;

co-author of

Sound and Sign: Childhood Deafness and Mental Health
U. California Press, 1972

For those of you -- parents, teachers, and others -- who have had introductions to prior editions of this impressive work -- read no more. Undoubtedly, by now, you have gone through the many steps that lead to the exciting discovery that you can communicate with a deaf child or adult through an intricate system of movements of the body and face but more especially the hands as you continue to use spoken English. You have become an adept participant in dialogue in two modalities, through the hand and voice, through signs and words.

For those of you, however, who pick this book up for the first time -- pause awhile, and consider the following: What are the steps that have led to your interest in this book? A recent encounter? A novel experience? A successful (or unsuccessful) communication? A frequent reason is that of a recent encounter with an individual who, due to an impairment in the sense of hearing, depends to a large extent on his or her eyes for the acquisition or understanding of language. To meet an individual who acquires and uses language in a way unfamiliar to you leads to a novel experience.

Novel experiences can be exciting and rewarding or sad and fear-provoking. Most novel experiences combine all of these feelings to some extent. When the novel experience is related to the powerful human need to communicate, the feelings can become intense. Communication -- dialogue between human beings -- can and does occur in a variety of ways that are essential to our well being: the eyes through sight, the body through touch can convey a variety of meanings. Most human communication, however, is accompanied by or initiated through a very complex human achievement -- the language of the society wherein the child is born. A language can be seen as a system of symbols used with certain rules by which people have come to abide. The symbols and their rules of usage become the vehicle for dialogue between people. Yet there are other important features of dialogue-shared interests: shared focus, shared social rules, and shared functions of language are numerous and subject to considerable research and debate. There appears to be some general agreement that a number of thought processes and concepts can develop fully without language, that some are promoted by language, and that still others require language for full development.

Language provides freedom from the "here and now," ability to anticipate the future, to recall the past, to describe objects and events beyond the field of vision, to develop solutions to some problems, to share or maybe even to develop imagination and cultural products of imagination such as stories and songs. In addition, language enhances the ability to understand the complex relationships between people and the feelings of other people. Although almost all members of the human species develop competence in the language of a culture, they differ markedly in the way in which they use language. Some use it more freely to comment on or ask questions about the world, the relationships between objects, between people, between feelings and action, between cause and effect. Others are more taciturn and tend to use language (despite full competence in its usage) less frequently for the functions mentioned above. Yet other individuals use language at great length and with much fervor and skill primarily for special areas of human endeavor such as sports, mechanics, hobbies, etc.

The Deaf Child and Dialogue

Despite the fact that acquisition of language is a complex phenomenon, most children learn it easily and playfully and by age five have achieved a nearly adult level of linguistic competence. Children do not acquire language primarily through imitation of adults. First, they are the creators of a language that has childrenese words and childrenese rules. This exciting process of first creating a language and then somehow adopting the adult version of the language of society is also subject to much research and debate. It does appear, however, that human beings are preprogrammed to develop a viable means of communication and that a certain amount of exposure to a specific language is a prerequisite for competence. For many years there existed massive confusion between speech and language. Because most of our linguistic interchanges occur through speech, language and speech were seen as identical, and yet speech is only one of the ways that can be used by the participants in a dialogue.

Under previous conditions deaf children, although continuously "exposed" to language through speech, could benefit only minimally or perhaps not at all from this exposure. The language they saw on the lips of the people around them was extremely limited because only 40 percent of the English language can be seen on the lips. In earlier times, deaf children learned neither language nor speech playfully and easily from their parents, nor did most of them become proficient in the language or speech of their hearing parents. In earlier times, deaf children of hearing parents learned the language of the deaf community -- American Sign Language -- from their peers and from the few deaf adults permitted to be in contact with them. They learned English with great difficulty and with unimpressive results.

Even in those earlier times, deaf children of deaf parents learned the language of their parents easily, playfully, and with great proficiency. The language of the deaf parents was either American Sign Language, a language in its own right with a word order and syntax different from English (See the Introduction), or Manual English. The language of the deaf parents was expressed through symbols made by the hands with or without the use of voice. This early parent-child dialogue resulted in clear-cut psychological and academic advantages

Reprinted with permission from *Signing Exact English*, 1980 edition.

for the deaf child of deaf parents. Exciting changes have taken place in the recent past of deaf children and their hearing parents due in large part to the existence of this volume and its prior editions. Hearing parents observing the advantages that deaf children of deaf parents had throughout their lives wanted to share in the process that led to these advantages.

The process is similar and yet different in crucial ways. Deaf and hearing parents both can use the hands to express the symbols of language. Most deaf parents, however, have a language system readily available to them, with their deaf children. Although some deaf parents may choose to use American Sign Language with their children, others may choose to sign English and still others may want their children to know both and to alternate their usage.

Most hearing parents initially feel more comfortable in using an English version of sign language than in using ASL. This is because learning a new modality is easier than learning a completely new language, or perhaps they feel more comfortable because they want their children to know the language that they themselves know best, or perhaps they feel more comfortable because they can combine the sign and the spoken word.

Dialogue and the Deaf Infant

Our experience indicates that the most ideal situation for the deaf infant and its hearing parents include the following: early diagnosis, accurate audiological evaluation, appropriate consistent amplification, and appropriate emotional support during the time of the diagnostic crisis. None of the above can be obtained from this volume. You, who want to engage in a dialogue with a deaf infant most optimally, will need to seek out the most competent professionals in your area. But while taking those steps, you can become engrossed in this book. You can seek out the vocabulary items that you want to share with your infant, repeat them to your infant, and teach them to your parents and your friends to use with your infant.

The period before the exciting moment when the infant returns the first sign to you will seem interminable, but it will come. All infants -- even hearing ones learning sign language -- will reproduce signs before they can reproduce spoken words. The ease with which the deaf infant acquires language depends in a large part on the early introduction of signs, the comfort and competency of the parents learning the new modality, and the attitudes and competencies of the infant's teacher. The ease with which the deaf infant will learn the use of speech depends to a large extent on the residual hearing, the efficacy of the hearing aids and a combined use of sign and word.

You who start with the deaf infant have a distinct advantage. You can keep ahead of your infant in your acquisition of S.E.E. signs. You will experience the excitement of early language acquisition and of early dialogues. You will be spared the frustration of delayed language onset. Nevertheless, you must experience some of the pain and frustration of having a deaf infant: learning a new modality of English, meeting numerous professionals, resolving conflicting advice. It won't always be easy, but it will be easier than it was ten years ago. The deaf children we know who started S.E.E. signs about ten years ago are doing well. They learned English as their first language from their parents. They are using it in dialogues with their parents, their peers and their teachers. They are conducting their dialogues in a combination of signs and speech and they are doing well in school.

Children and parents who come upon S.E.E. signs in the early childhood years can benefit almost as well as the infants, *if* they begin to use signs before they have experienced a massive feeling of failure in communication and before they have been labelled failures by teachers and other professionals.

This book is useful for deaf children of all ages, but older children will usually have had experiences of failure with language and dialogue. Some may have developed an aversion to human communication, some may have developed a very personal system of communication, still others may have acquired American Sign Language as their first language. The feelings and language style of these youngsters must be respected before we require their acceptance of another language we want them to learn.

It is my hope that all these groups of deaf children will acquire the skills that will enable them to communicate happily and competently with a wide variety of people, and that they do not come to believe that one means or mode of communication should be used to exclude the possibility of any other.

WHY SIGNING EXACT ENGLISH WAS DEVELOPED

In January, 1969, a group of deaf individuals, parents of deaf children, children of deaf parents, teachers of the deaf, interpreters, and program administrators met in southern California to discuss appropriate, effective ways to represent English in a gestural mode. From this group developed three published systems, originally similar but now quite different: Seeing Essential English (SEE 1), Linguistics of Visual English (LOVE), and Signing Exact English (SEE 2).

As it was pointed out in the winter 1974-75 issue of *Gallaudet Today*:

> **The main concern of the original group was the consistent, logical, rational, and practical development of signs to represent as specifically as possible the basic essentials of the English language. This concern sprang from the experience of all present with the poor English skills of many deaf students, and the desire for an easier, more successful way of developing mastery of English in a far greater number of such students. (Gustason, 1975)**

The educational retardation of deaf students has been well documented over the years, and has caused deep and widespread concern. In 1965, the Secretary of Health, Education, and Welfare's Advisory Committee on Education of the Deaf stated in the Babbidge report that

> **...the American people have no reason to be satisfied with their limited success in educating deaf children and preparing them for full participation in our society...the average graduate of a public residential school for the deaf...has an eighth grade education. (Babbidge, 1965)**

Many studies over the past sixty years have reported the low English language skills of hearing-impaired students, with reading and English scores reported for older deaf students hovering around the level attained by fourth and fifth grade hearing children. In Wrightstone's 1963 survey, 88% of 1075 deaf students aged 15 1/2 and above scored below grade level 4.9 in reading. Boatner (1965) and McClure (1966) classified roughly one third of deaf students sixteen and older as functionally illiterate, or unable to read well enough to cope with ordinary circumstances in life. These findings were not new. In 1918, a fill-in-the-blanks English test given to 1098 hearing-impaired students showed the average for fourth grade hearing children to be higher than the average for any grade level of the deaf. (Pintner, 1918)

Yet research has shown that the intelligence range for hearing-impaired persons, with no other disability, is the same as in the hearing population. (Vernon, 1969) Given this level of intellectual ability among the hearing impaired, their low test scores in reading and English structure take on a new dimension, and it is not surprising that little correlation has been found between intelligence and such test scores.

At the same time that such studies were pointing out the normal intelligence range of hearing-impaired students and their problems with English, other researchers were studying normal language development in hearing children. Children exposed to English, they reported, mastered much of the structure of that language, including basic sentence patterns and inflections, by about age three. Language structures are fairly stable by age six, and extremely difficult to modify after the age of puberty. Between two and three years of age, children make a great jump in the use of prepositions, demonstratives, auxiliaries, articles, conjunctions, possessive and personal pronouns, and the tense, plural, and possessive markings. (See, for instance, Braine, 1963; Brown & Bellugi, 1964; Cazden, 1968; Weir, 1962; Labov, 1965; Penfield, 1964; Moskowitz, 1978.) What hearing children learn is the language of their environment, be it French, Chinese, standard American English, the English of Great Britain, or whatever language they perceive. Many children in Europe learn two or more languages with little or no formal instruction. Adults who know only one language, on the other hand, often experience great difficulty trying to learn a different language.

Studies focusing on the English problems of hearing-impaired children identified specific areas of weakness. These weaknesses included omission of necessary words or incorrect use of words. Sentence structures were simple and rigid, with those of 17-year-old hearing-impaired students comparable to eight-year-old hearing children. Lexical, or dictionary, meanings were learned more easily than structural meanings, and deducing the meaning of words from context was not a common skill. While studies with hearing children indicated consistent sequences of structures mastered in English language development, no such sequences appeared in the English skills of deaf children; what was learned first was what was taught first in school, and this varied from school to school. Hearing-impaired students used fewer adverbs, auxiliaries and conjunctions than hearing children. (See Myklebust, 1964; Heider and Heider, 1940; Hart and Rosenstein, 1964; Cooper, 1965; Simmons, 1962, for examples.) Many of these problems, especially discomfort with the idiomatic nature of many American English word meanings, are experienced by native speakers of other languages attempting to learn English, and indicate the difficulty of learning this complex language when the optimal language-learning years of childhood are past.

These problems are not surprising when it is remembered that input must precede output, that this input is most beneficial when it takes place during the critical language learning years before age six, and that the hearing-impaired child's perception of English is often very imperfect, depending on the communication mode.

Even a partial hearing loss cuts off some of the auditory input, and hard-of-hearing children have very real problems learning English. For the profoundly deaf child, the problem can be even more serious. Since 40% to 60% of the sounds of English look like some other sound on the lips (as in the old examples of pan, ban, man), it is not surprising that even the best speechreaders with a ready command of English must use educated guesswork and knowledge of the topic and the language to fill the gaps. The problem of speechreading for infants is compounded when it is remembered that

> **...young children do not ordinarily differentiate the parts of what they perceive, especially if the stimuli are unfamiliar or have no meaning for them. They perceive largely in terms of context. (Mussen, 1963)**

Although three-year-old hearing children, as noted above, are well on their way to mastery of tenses and function words,

> **...in lip-reading...the child does not perceive every word in an utterance, but rather, catches the key**

Reprinted with permission from *Signing Exact English*, 1980 edition.

words, or even only the root parts of words (e.g., BOY instead of BOYS, WALK instead of WALKED). The words that are ignored are words that are not understood, as well as the function words (e.g., TO, AT, THE, FOR) that tie the communication together. (Hart and Rosenstein, 1964)

Similarly, -ing and -ed are difficult to speechread. It is not surprising, then, that some older deaf students who have learned that -ed is used for the past and -ing for a present action believe that the movie was interested because they saw it yesterday, while they are interesting in TV because they are watching it now. It should be noted, also, that while hard-of-hearing children may pick up more vocabulary, many of these structural affixes are as difficult to hear as they are to speechread, and such students often have difficulty with -s, -ed, and the like.

Obviously dependence on speechreading as a means of providing clear and unambiguous English input is a very dangerous dependence. What was needed was some way to make use of an unimpaired input channel, a more visual mode of representing English.

Fingerspelling, or forming words by spelling the letters of the alphabet on the hand, is larger and easier to perceive than speechreading. However, there is still the perception problem for very young children, since the child's eyes do not fully mature until age eight (hence the use of large print in primary story books). Moreover, skilled adult fingerspellers normally spell at a 300-letter-per-minute rate (Bornstein, 1965) while the average speaking rate ranges from 120 to 270 words per minute (Calvert and Silverman, 1975). If the average word length is calculated at five letters, this would mean spelling 600 to 1350 letters per minute. Using fingerspelling and speech together would thus mean either the speech rhythm would be distorted or letters would be left out or distorted in the fingerspelling.

Speech alone is obviously the easiest mode for hearing persons to use with a hearing-impaired child, but it is too often unsatisfactory in terms of the amount of information the child is able to perceive. Fingerspelling, while relatively easy to learn (26 letters are, after all, not that many) is not easy to learn to use well, and still presents perception problems for a very young child as well as production problems if the parent or teacher wishes to speak simultaneously. (See Caccamise, Hatfield, and Brewer, 1978, for further discussion of research and problems with the use of fingerspelling alone and in combination with speech.)

Signs present larger, more easily perceived and discriminated symbols in communication than either speech or fingerspelling for young hearing-impaired children. With early visual input of signs, it is not surprising that deaf children of signing deaf parents, able to communicate from infancy, have been shown to enter school with an advantage over deaf children of hearing parents, and have tended to maintain this advantage throughout school.

However, it must be remembered that American Sign Language (ASL), which is used by many deaf adults, is a language in its own right and not a visual representation of English. Children who learn ASL as their native language from their parents have been shown to develop better English skills than those who were not exposed to sign language, while children of deaf parents who signed to them from infancy in English, mastered English to an even greater degree. (See Brasel and Quigley, 1975, for a report of such research.)

This introduces another factor, since adults who know only one language often have some difficulty mastering a second one. For parents, the problem of becoming fluent during the early language-learning years is a very real problem. Accordingly, it may be simpler for most hearing parents of deaf children to begin with a form of signing in English than to attempt to become fluent in a foreign language (ASL) during what is for many parents a psychologically trying period of adjustment to their child's deafness.

The important issue is that comfortable parent-child communication be established as early as possible in a language readily available to the parents and a mode clearly perceivable by the child. If the parents know and use ASL with their child, English is still needed at some point for maximal functioning in our society, and should be taught in a clearly perceivable mode.

Research to date has focused on the receptive abilities of older deaf students rather than younger, but has shown consistently that understanding is greater with the use of simultaneous communication (speech, spelling and signs used in combination) than with the use of speech alone, signs alone, spelling alone, or spelling and speech without signs. (See Caccamise and Johnson, 1978, for a summary of such research.) While there are, of course, individual differences, the rule seems to be that the larger the number of modes used, the greater the chances for reception and understanding. A summary of research on the effect of the use of signs on English and on oral/aural communication skills finds not only that signs can assist in the development of English, but that they may facilitate the development of speech, speechreading, and listening skills. If attention is not given these oral/aural skills, they may not develop, but if such attention is given, the use of signs is not a detriment. (See Caccamise, Hatfield, and Brewer, 1978; Weiss, McIntyre, Goodwin and Moores, 1975 and 1978, for more discussion of this research.)

Some individuals have expressed concern that the use of all modes and the inclusion of manual English signs for word-endings may overload the child. While we need much more research on language acquisition with hearing-impaired children, some studies are beginning to appear. Research with deaf children of deaf parents acquiring ASL as their native language has shown that these children are quite similar to hearing children in terms of increasing length of utterance and in their progressive mastery of structures of language. While studies of language acquisition by deaf children whose parents use manual English signs is still limited, the appropriate use of signed markers for past tense, plurals, and -ing has been reported in children at age three (Schlesinger and Meadow, 1972). Anecdotal reports of profoundly deaf children whose parents and teachers consistently used manual English indicates that children with no disability other than hearing loss have the capability for acquiring such markers. One study of preschoolers using manual communication reported that what the mother used at home had greater influence than what the teacher used at school, and that if the mother used markers the child developed skill in using them also. The ability to use signs does not automatically transfer to the ability to read and write, and there has been some question whether indeed signing English would result in better reading and writing skills. This is a legitimate question in need of much more research. Early evidence indicates that while the transfer is not automatic, children exposed to manually represented English in the early yeas are much better able to make that transfer than those who are not. Children profoundly deaf from birth have been reported reading at second grade level before the age of five, and writing clear, error-free, idiomatic English at ages ten to twelve. While these are individual reports, and many questions remain about the level of parent involvement and fluency needed, and the psychological-sociological impact on the parent-child relationship, the evidence is that, given a mode comfortable to parent and child, transmission of the parents' native language to the child is quite possible. (See Schlesinger, 1978, for a discussion of the bimodal acquisition of language.)

This stress on the importance of exposing the child in all modalities to English if we wish him to acquire the language easily must not be interpreted as a rejection of the American Sign Language (Gustason, Pfetzing, and Zawolkow, 1974). There are many ways in which these two languages can and should go hand-in-hand for a fuller educational and developmental experience for hearing-impaired children. Ideally, we would like to see teachers and parents comfortable with both ASL and English, who could combine and otherwise utilize the two types of signing both in and out of the classroom in a variety of ways to enrich the communication experiences of students. Our goal is for hearing-impaired children to become truly bilingual, at ease in both ASL and English. How best to accomplish this is still an open question, and again we solicit constructive suggestions from users. We consider Signing Exact English a means of manual expression for those who are speaking English while they sign, and an introduction to the richness and variety of signs for parents of young deaf children. We also consider it a teaching tool for use with students who know ASL and are learning English as a second language. We would like to see the best of both languages in as many hands as possible. (See Caccamise and Gustason, 1979, Caccamise and Johnson, 1978, and Gustason and Rosen, 1975, for further discussion of the roles of both ASL and English in the education and general development of hearing-impaired children, and communication with the deaf adult.)

Signing Exact English (SEE 2), is NOT a replacement for ASL and is meant for use by parents of young children and by teachers of English. Persons working with deaf adults should understand that SEE 2 is not widely used among adults, although "new" signs crop up in common usage. The study of ASL is important not only for those desiring to work with adult deaf persons, but for parents and teachers. ASL is a rich and expressive language, worth studying for its own sake, and many of its principles should be put to good use in using Signing Exact English. While there is still a shortage of trained teachers of both ASL and SEE 2, those who wish to learn either are encouraged to learn as much as possible about the other. Incomplete understanding raises the possibility of misunderstanding and personal/psychological/ sociological problems -- for parents, for teacher, and for the child.

Because we wish to see such problems minimized, we encourage a study of and acceptance of both ASL and manual English. In the following pages we list important principles of SEE 2, suggestions to follow in the development of additional signs, and some points to remember for clear, effective signing. In these, we have attempted to combine our knowledge of ASL and English to develop a sign system that can assist deaf and hard-of-hearing children in their development of English language skills. We present both theoretical principles and practical usage suggestions for the system. We recognize the dynamic nature of language and communication, and that any communication form must accommodate its users. Few language rules are strict, and exceptions to rules can be found in all languages. We are aware that some of the signs in this book may not seem consistent with the principles listed, but these exceptions are based on users, whose skills in language usage continue to go ahead of the knowledge of educators and linguists as to how languages may be used most effectively in various modalities (alone and in combination) for maximum communication and language development.

8

IMPORTANT PRINCIPLES OF SIGNING EXACT ENGLISH

1. The most important principle in Signing Exact English is that ENGLISH SHOULD BE SIGNED IN A MANNER THAT IS AS CONSISTENT AS POSSIBLE WITH HOW IT IS SPOKEN OR WRITTEN IN ORDER TO CONSTITUTE A LANGUAGE INPUT FOR THE DEAF CHILD THAT WILL RESULT IN HIS MASTERY OF ENGLISH. This means, for instance, that idioms such as "dry up," "cut it out," "stop horsing around" would be signed as those exact words, rather than as "quiet" or "stop" or "finish." It also means that inflections or markers must be shown, such as talks, talk**ed**, talk**ing**, govern**ment**.

2. A second important principle is that A SIGN SHOULD BE TRANSLATABLE TO ONLY ONE ENGLISH EQUIVALENT. Initialized signs contribute a great deal here, providing such synonyms as HURT, PAIN, ACHE, and so on. But this principle also means that only one sign should be used for such English words as RUN, which has a number of different meanings and a number of different translations in ASL.

These two principles have led to a number of problems and jokes. How does one sign "I **saw** you yesterday" or "he **left** home last week"? Is the sign for **saw** the same as in sawing wood, and the sign for **left** the same as the opposite of right? For that matter, what of right, rite, and write? In an attempt to come to terms with these problems, more principles were developed. Words were considered in three groups: 1) Basic, 2) Compound, and 3) Complex.

3. "BASIC WORDS" ARE WORDS THAT CAN HAVE NO MORE TAKEN AWAY AND STILL FORM A COMPLETE WORD (GIRL, TALK, THE, the noun SAW, etc.). For these basic words, the three-point criteria of sound, spelling, and meaning is utilized. If any two of these three factors are the same, the same sign is used. This covers multiple-meaning words such as RUN, which would have the same sign in:

The boys will **run.** The motor will **run.** Your nose will **run.** These are all signed differently in ASL. (See the following "points to remember for expressive signing" for suggestions on combining ASL principles with English words in such cases.)

To take a different example, a different sign would be used for WIND in:

The **wind** is blowing. I must **wind** my watch.

In this case only the spelling is the same; sound and meaning both differ, and since two of the three factors are different, a different sign is used. In the case of RUN, spelling and sound are the same, and meaning varies; since two of the three factors are the same, the same basic sign is used.

4. "COMPLEX WORDS" ARE DEFINED AS BASIC WORDS WITH THE ADDITION OF AN AFFIX OR INFLECTION: GIRLS, TALKED, the past tense verb SAW. Once such an addition has been made the combination is no longer considered a basic word. Accordingly, the past tense of SEE is added to produce the verb SAW, which is **not** the same as either the noun SAW or the verb to SAW (which would have past tense added to produce SAWED). An affix is added in signs if it is added in speech or writing, regardless of the part of speech. The suffix -s, for instance, is used both for regular plurals (GIRLS, SAWS) and the third person singular of verbs (RUNS, SEES, SAWS).

5. COMPOUND WORDS ARE TWO OR MORE BASIC WORDS PUT TOGETHER. IF THE MEANING OF THE WORDS SEPARATELY IS CONSISTENT WITH THE MEANING OF THE WORDS TOGETHER, THEN AND ONLY THEN ARE THEY SIGNED AS THE COMPONENT WORD. Thus UNDERLINE would be signed UNDER-LINE but UNDERSTAND, having no relation to the meaning of the words UNDER and STAND, would have a separate sign and would **not** be signed UNDER-STAND.

6. WHEN A SIGN ALREADY EXISTS IN ASL THAT IS CLEAR, UNAMBIGUOUS, AND COMMONLY TRANSLATES TO ONE ENGLISH WORD, THIS SIGN IS RETAINED. As pointed out previously, the sign for GIRL is the same in ASL and in this book. This is clearest with single meaning words. With multiple meaning words, while the sign may fit one ASL way of signing the word, ASL may have other signs for different meanings. This is handled by Principle 3 above. Principle 6 explains why signs are presented in this book for compound or complex words such as CARE-LESS, MISUNDERSTAND, BASEBALL, CAN'T, that could, by following the principles above, be signed CARE-LESS, MIS-UNDERSTAND, BASE-BALL, CAN-N'T. A single sign is borrowed from ASL when ease and economy of movement are possible with no loss of clear, unambiguous English. It is our hope that users will choose the way they prefer of signing such words, while understanding that others may choose a different way of signing it.

7. WHEN THE FIRST LETTER IS ADDED TO A BASIC SIGN TO CREATE SYNONYMS, THE BASIC SIGN IS RETAINED WHEREVER POSSIBLE AS THE MOST COMMONLY USED WORD. For instance, the basic sign for MAKE is retained for that word, while the sign is made with C-hands for CREATE, and P-hands for PRODUCE. In some cases, as with GUARD, PROTECT, DEFEND, users have experienced difficulty remembering which is the uninitialized sign since all three words are used relatively equally; hence all three are initialized.

8. WHEN MORE THAN ONE MARKER IS ADDED TO A WORD, MIDDLE MARKERS MAY BE DROPPED **IF** THERE IS NO SACRIFICE OF CLARITY. For instance, the past tense sign is added as BREAK to produce BROKE, but BROKEN may be signed as BREAK plus the past participle or -EN. Similarly, EXAM may be joined by -INE for EXAMINE, but EXAMINATION may be signed as EXAM plus -TION. Such dropping of the middle markers serves to keep the flow of the sign smooth and efficient, while retaining the identifying marker which shows what word is used. Dropping is not done if confusion might result; for instance, WILL plus N'T creates WON'T, WILL plus -D or past participle marker plus N'T creates WOULDN'T. Dropping the middle marker in this case would confuse the two words.

9. WHILE FOLLOWING THE ABOVE PRINCIPLES, RESPECT NEEDS TO BE SHOWN FOR CHARACTERISTICS OF VISUAL-GESTURAL COMMUNICATION. While sign languages vary just as do spoken languages, and what is possible in one language may not appear in another, awkward or difficult movements should be avoided whenever possible. For instance, English does not use the trilled R present in other spoken languages, and some phonetic combinations are not normal in English (e.g., WUG is a possible nonsense word, but PKT is not). The same is true of ASL, where simple hand shapes (A, 5, 1) are used much more commonly than more complex hand shapes (R, P, etc.). Small differences in shape or motion should not occur far from the visual center of attention. These points are addressed further in the next section.

Reprinted with permission from *Signing Exact English*, 1980 edition

SUGGESTIONS FOR THE DEVELOPMENT OF ADDITIONAL SIGNS

Experience and common sense both tell us that when manual English is used, words are sure to crop up that have no sign in this book. When this happens, we have several recommendations.

1. SEEK AN EXISTING SIGN. Check other sign language texts. Ask skilled signers in your community, especially deaf native signers.

2. MODIFY AN EXISTING SIGN WITH A SIMILAR OR RELATED MEANING. Generally, this means adding the first letter of the word to a basic sign.

3. CONSIDER FINGERSPELLING. This depends, of course, on the age and perceptual abilities of the child, and the length and frequency of use of the word in question.

4. IF ALL ELSE FAILS, AND YOU MUST INVENT, TRY TO STAY AS CLOSE AS POSSIBLE TO ASL PRINCIPLES. We realize that many individuals using manual English are not yet familiar with ASL. In an attempt to give some guidance in this area, pertinent guidelines are summarized below. These guidelines were developed for collection, evaluation, selection, and recording of signs used in educational and work settings under the direction of Dr. Frank Caccamise of the National Technical Institute of the Deaf. The summary of these guidelines is included here with Dr. Caccamise's permission. The persons involved in developing these guidelines were for the most part concerned with college age hearing-impaired students. Most of the guidelines are, however, equally applicable when considering younger children. Those that need special consideration are noted.

There are four major components of signs: A) position, B) handshape, C) movement, and D) orientations (the direction of the palm and the fingers). The guidelines discussed below are based on how these four components are combined is ASL signs, and they may be used in considering or assessing the acceptability or unacceptability of newly developed signs.

1) THE SIGNING SPACE. Signs generally fall within an area between the top of the head and just above the waist, within a comfortable, but not fully extended, arm's reach to the sides and ahead. The center of this space is the hollow of the neck. Signs do occur outside this area, as in theatrical signing and for emphasis.

2) THE VISUAL CENTER OF THE SIGNING SPACE is the nose-mouth area, and while many signs are made near here, they are seldom made within this center. Vision is sharpest near this center, and less sharp as you move away from the center. When reading signs people usually watch the face of the signer rather than the hands, and facial expression and lip movement are important. An effort should be made not to obstruct the mouth area when signing since this interferes with speechreading. In addition to speechreading, the mouth area should not be blocked because the face and mouth area are important for grammatical expression in ASL and can and should be effectively used in SEE 2 to enhance communication.

3) POSITION. Signs made near the center of the signing space can use smaller movements and finer distinctions among signs than signs made further away from the visual center (e.g., APPLE, FRUIT, VEGETABLE, etc.).

4) SYMMETRY. Signs made near the center of signing space often use one hand, while signs made further away tend to use two hands in symmetry (e.g., HEAVEN, RUSSIA). Signs made in the neck and face area generally use one hand. Signs made below the neck generally use two hands. If both hands move, the handshapes should be the same.

5) DOMINANCE. For two-handed signs in which only one hand moves, the nonmoving or passive hand should have one of the seven neutral handshapes (1-A-S-B-C-5-0) or the same handshape as the moving hand. Ordinarily one attends to the moving hand. (Note: This need not occur when the moving hand brings attention to the nonmoving hand, as in GOAL, AIM, OBJECTIVE, TARGET, COMMENCE, INITIATE, etc.).

6) NUMBER OF HANDSHAPES PER SIGN. Most signs in ASL use only one handshape on each hand. Some signs require a slight handshape change, as in MILK or PRINT, but do not involve more than two handshapes. Accordingly, invented signs should use no more than two handshapes. (Note: Markers or inflections may be added to a sign already having two handshapes.)

7) SIGNS INVOLVING CONTACT. Four major areas of contact in signs are the head, trunk, arm, and hand. ASL signs are systematic in that signs made with double contacts are made within the same major area (e.g., INDIAN has both contacts on the head, WE has both contacts on the trunk, etc.). Exceptions to this are signs derived from compounds, as DAUGHTER from GIRL-BABY, etc.

8) SEMANTICALLY RELATED SIGNS. Signs which are related in meaning are often related in formation. For instance, the basic concept of a group is initialized to represent CLASS, GROUP, TEAM, and the like. (As stated previously, such related signs are grouped as "families" in this book.) This type of structural relationship should be considered in the development of new signs.

9) MOVEMENT AND WORD-TYPE: NOUN-VERB PAIRS. In ASL, some signs may have the same handshape, position, and orientation, but differ in movement, with nouns having short repeated movement and verbs having hold or continuous movement (e.g., AIRPLANE and GO-BY-AIR-PLANE). (Note: This guideline may be applicable in terms of effective signing, as listed in the next section. Signing Exact English does not rely on this principle to distinguish between or among English words. See, for example, CHAIR and SIT.)

10) COMPOUNDING SIGNS. There are two kinds of compounding, lexical and grammatical. Lexical compounding refers to signs made up of several reduced signs; e.g., FRUIT in ASL may be signed APPLE-ORANGE-BANANA, etc., with shorter and assimilated movements. Grammatical compounding

Reprinted with permission from *Signing Exact English*, 1980 Edition.

connects several signs to form a new one; e.g., LET-TER-NUMBER for ZIPCODE, or HEART-STUDY for CARDIOLOGY. (Note: This type of compounding is clear to ASL users, and some signs derived from compounds -- e.g., daughter -- are used in manual English, but this guideline is at variance with the first principle of Signing Exact English, that we attempt to sign exactly the words we say. Relying on a slight difference in movement, as in Guideline 9 above, or on a compound sign, may not provide a clear, unambiguous representation of the English word as spoken/written. This is a criticism of neither ASL nor English, but a recognition of the difference between the two.)

11) ITERATIONS. This refers to the number of times a sign is repeated. Some signs in ASL are limited to one repetition (e.g., the singular form of a noun such as GIRL). Signs needing at least two repetitions do not distinguish between two or more than two repetitions.

POINTS TO REMEMBER FOR CLEAR, EXPRESSIVE SIGNING

As stated previously, we believe ASL principles should be incorporated into English signs for more effective simultaneous communication. While the suggestions and guidelines listed before relate to the development of new signs, such guidelines can also be considered as an aid in production. Following are examples of this integration of principles or characteristics with SEE 2, and other points to remember in sign production.

1) Always speak when you sign, and let facial expressions and body English aid communication.

2) Affixes, and word-endings for tense, person, and the like, should not be made as signs separate from the sign for the basic word itself, but should flow from the base sign for the word. Similarly, signs for word endings should not be made with an emphasis equal to that for the sign of the basic word. Be guided by the practice of spoken English. You do not say "swinging" or "swingING" but "SWINGing." This may be compared to syllables in spoken words: they are not pronounced as separate words, but flow into each other. Similarly, combined words (compound words) should flow together. INTO should be signed INTO, not IN TO.

3) The past tense sign does not actually need to be made over the shoulder. A backward flip of the hand at the conclusion of the sign for the verb suffices to indicate the past tense (or the addition of -d, if preferred, for regular past tenses such as WALKED).

4) When adding a suffix to a two-handed sign, keep the left hand in the position of the sign (do not drop hand) while the right hand signs the suffix. This helps indicate that the suffix is part of the word and not a separate word.

5) Raising the eyebrows and freezing the hands in the air, or holding the end position of a sign instead of letting the hands drop, are ASL techniques for indicating a question that can be answered yes or no. A slight frown is often used with "WH" questions (What, Who, Where, When, Why, How). These expressions can and should be used in conjunction with Manual English signs. A question-mark sign is only for emphasis.

6) When making a negative statement, as in "I don't think so," "She isn't here," and the like, shaking the head from side to side aids in clarifying the negative.

7) With many signs, clarity can be added by making the sign in the appropriate place. This is true not only of multiple meaning signs such as BOW tie (signed at the neck), BOW and arrow (signed in the position of a bow), and hair BOW (signed at the hair), but of signs such as PAIN (in the neck? in the side?) and BUTTERFLY or BUTTERFLIES (in the stomach?). Of course in the latter examples the entire phrase should be signed, and the sign executed in the appropriate location. In showing fear of something to your right, do not make the sign on your left.

8) When signing pronouns, if the person referred to is present, sign HE, SHE, HIM, or HER in the person's direction, or sign and point. If the person is not pre-sent, it helps to set him or her up in a specific location and orient your signs to that location when talking about him or her. When talking about more than one person, setting them up in different locations aids immeasurably in clarifying to whom you are referring. Try putting one of them on your right, the other on your left.

9) Body, eye, and hand orientation help! When signing LOOK, the motion should move toward where you want the person to look: at the sky, the floor, out the window, etc. If you are signing a dialogue between two characters, turning slightly to the left when one is speaking, and slightly to the right when the other responds, helps to indicate who is speaking. Looking up or down can indicate relative height.

10) Some verbs should show the **direction** of the action -- towards the direct object. GIVE, for example, may be signed from the giver to the receiver, as can TEACH, SHOW, TEASE, and other such verbs. When you are the receiver, these signs can begin in front of you and move towards you, in a sort of mirror image of the sign.

11) Some signs can be made more than once when you are talking about plural nouns: e.g., make the sign for GIRL more than once before adding -s, or for BOOK two or more times before adding -s. Repeating the sign also shows an action that is ongoing, as in I AM PAINT-PAINT-PAINTING a picture or one that is very difficult, as in I AM STUDY-STUDY-STUDYING VERY HARD.

12) Some signs can very in size...a big dog is not as large as a big dinosaur, and BIG can be signed accordingly.

13) Signs can also vary in intensity, or be modified in their execution. A slow, thoughtful WALK should differ from a businesslike WALK; SYMPATHY can be more or less intense as shown by the motion; I LOVE YOU can be sincere or sarcastic depending on motion and facial expression.

14) Ham it up! Use facial expression and mime to help get the message across. You will find ASL a treasure trove of graphic and expressive signs, and you will find most children are natural hams.

15) ENJOY YOUR COMMUNICATION, AND ENJOY YOUR CHILDREN.

Selected References

Babbidge, H.D. (1965). *Education of the deaf in the United States*. A report to the Secretary of Health, Education and Welfare by his Advisory Committee on Education of the Deaf. Washington, D.C.: U.S. Government Printing Office.

Boatner, E.B. (1965). The need of a realistic approach to the education of the deaf. Paper given to the joint convention of California Association of Parents of Deaf and Hard of Hearing Children, California Association of Teachers of Deaf and Hard of Hearing Children, and the California Association of the Deaf, Nov. 6.

Reprinted with permission from *Signing Exact English,* 1980 Edition.

Bornstein, H. (1965). *Reading the Manual Alphabet.* Washington, D.C., Gallaudet College Press.

Braine, M.D.S. (1963). The otogeny of English phrase structure: the first phrase, *Language*, 39:1-13, Jan-Mar.

Brasel, K. and Quigley, S.P. (1977). Influence of certain language and communication environments in early childhood on the development of language in deaf individuals. *Journal of Speech and Hearing Research*, 20, 95-107.

Brown, R. and Bellugi, U. (1964). Three processes in the child's acquisition of syntax. *Harvard Educational Review*, 39:133-152, Spring.

Caccamise, F. and Gustason, G., eds. (1979). *Manual/Simultaneous Communication Instructional Programs in the Educational Setting.* Washington, D.C.: Gallaudet College Division of Public Services.

Caccamise, F., Hatfield, N. and Brewer, L. (1978). Manual/Simultaneous Communication Research: Results and Implications. *American Annals of the Deaf* 123:7, 803-823, November.

Caccamise, F. and Johnson, D. (1978). Simultaneous and manual communication: Their role in rehabilitation with the adult deaf. *Journal of the Academy of Rehabilitative Audiology,* 11, 105-131.

Calvert, D. and Silverman, S.R. (1975). *Speech and Deafness.* Washington, D.C.: Alexander Graham Bell Association for the Deaf.

Cazden, C. B. (1968). The acquisition of noun and verb inflections, *Child Development*, 39:433-448, June.

Cooper, R. L. (1965). The ability of deaf and hearing children to apply morphological rules. Unpublished doctoral dissertation, Columbia.

Gustason, G. (1973). The languages of communication. *Deafness Annual III.* Silver Spring, MD: Professional Rehabilitation Workers with the Adult Deaf, 83-95.

Gustason, G. (1974-75). Signing Exact English, *Gallaudet Today.* vol. 5, #2, 11-12, winter.

Gustason, G. and Rosen, R. (1975). Effective Sign Communication for instructional purposes: Manual English and American Sign Language. *Proceedings of the Convention of American Instructors of the Deaf.*

Hart, B. O. and Rosenstein, J. (1964). Examining the language behavior of deaf children, *The Volta Review*, 66:679-682.

Heider, F. and G. Heider. Comparison of sentence structure of deaf and hearing children. *Psychological Monographs,* 1940, 52:42-103.

Jordan, I. K., Gustason, G. and Rosen, R. (1976). Current Communication Trends in Programs for the Deaf. *American Annals of the Deaf*, 121:6, 527-532.

Jordan, I. K., Gustason, G. and Rosen, R. (1976). An Update on Communication Trends at Programs for the Deaf. *American Annals of the Deaf.* 121:6, 527-532.

Labov, W. Linguistic research on nonstandard English of Negro children, 1965 Yearbook, New York Society for the Experimental Study of Education, pp. 110-117.

McClure, W. J. Current problems and trends in the education of the deaf, *The Deaf American,* 1966, 8-14.

Moskowitz, Breyne Arlene. The acquisition of language. *Scientific American,* December 1978, 92-108.

Mycklebust, H. R. *Development and Disorders of Written Language:* Volume One. Picture Story Language Test. New York: Grune and Stratton, 1965.

Penfield, W. The uncommited cortex: The child's changing brain, *The Atlantic Monthly,* 77-81, July 1964.

Pintner, R. The measurement of language ability and language process of deaf children, *The Volta Review,* 20:755-766, 1918.

Schlesinger, H. The acquisition of bimodal language in *Sign Language of the Deaf,* ed. I. M. Schlesinger and L. Namir. New York: Academic Press, 1978.

Schlesinger, H. The acquisition of signed and spoken language in *Deaf Children: Developmental Perspectives,* ed. L. S. Liben. New York: Academic Press, 1978.

Schlesinger, H. and K. Meadow. *Sound and Sign: Childhood Deafness and Mental Health.* Berkeley, Calif.: University of California Press, 1972.

Simmons, A. A. A comparison of the type-token ratio of spoken and written language of deaf and hearing children, *The Volta Review,* 64:417-421, 1962.

Vernon, M. Fifty years of research on the intelligence of the deaf and hard of hearing: a survey of the literature and discussion of implications, *Journal of Rehabilitation of the Deaf,* 1:1-11, 1968.

Vernon, M. Sociological and psychological factors associated with hearing loss, *Journal of Speech and Hearing Research,* 12:541-563, 1969.

Weir, R. *Language in the Crib.* The Hague: Mouton and Company, 1962.

Weiss, K. L., C. K. McIntyre, M. W. Goodwin, and D. Moores. Characteristics of young deaf children and intervention programs. Research Report #91, Research Development, and Demonstration Center in Education of Handicapped Children, University of Minnesota, Minneapolis, 1975.

Wrightstone, J. W., M. S. Aranow, and S. Muskowitz, Developing Test Norms for the Deaf Child, *American Annals of the Deaf,* 108:311-316, 1963.

THE LANGUAGES OF COMMUNICATION

Geri Gustason, Ph.D.
Assistant Professor of Education
Gallaudet College, Washington, D.C.

Any consideration of communication with hearing impaired persons runs at once into the question: Communication with whom, about what, and in what situations?

It is easy in our thinking to polarize society into a hearing majority and a deaf minority, and impose the majority's mode of communication, the aural-oral mode, on the minority. It is also relatively simple to speak of the rights of the minority to its own form of communication, the sign language most of the deaf in the United States use in conversing with each other. It is far less simple to determine what mode or modes of communication would be most useful in different situations with individuals with varied amounts of hearing impairment and with varied backgrounds. A senior citizen losing his hearing has different communication needs from those of a moderately hard of hearing teenager and the requirements of both are different from those of a deaf-from-birth preschooler with no language training. But perhaps the chief question is: In what educational or social contexts do we wish to communicate? Quite apart from the questions of how much usable hearing an individual has, the visual perception problem of depending on speechreading alone, and the speech-teaching problem with children who will never hear, we need to consider the purpose of this communication, and the cultural group with which the individual is, has been, or will be associated.

Those who favor the aural-oral method of communication can point, and justly so, to students in residential schools for the deaf who have minimal hearing losses, but, whether by virtue of placement in such a school or of association with deaf family members, "function" as deaf persons. In written language, in sign language, perhaps in speech and speechreading abilities, and in social contacts their performance is indistinguishable from that of a profoundly deaf student. Hard of hearing students, or those with good English and speechreading skills, may be discouraged from entering Gallaudet College by being told that attending a program exclusively for the deaf "will turn you into a deaf person." The presumption seems to be that there is something inherently bad or inferior about being a deaf person, and that only hearing people who know sign language are capable of mixing comfortably in both hearing and deaf society. Relatively few deaf adults are in this position because they are unable to meet hearing society on its own terms. But is there any reason we cannot educate deaf children to give them some way to communicate with anyone, and to assimilate with both deaf and hearing people, and to choose their mode of communication accordingly?

That there are two cultures -- deaf and hearing -- is, or should be, an obvious fact (Rainer et. al., 1963; Vernon, 1969; Mindel & Vernon, 1971). There are national, state, and local organizations of the deaf, for instance, and 95% of deaf persons marry deaf persons. The existence of these two cultures need not, however, be a negative fact, with an "either- or" connotation. The problems they have in common do bring deaf persons together, but just as all hearing people do not share the same interests, neither do all deaf people. Shared interests can bridge cultural gaps, as can a shared language. In the past, language has been a barrier between the deaf and hearing;

problems in English, and the use of sign language, have been shared by many deaf individuals. When we attempt to make a deaf child as much as possible like a hearing person by denying him access to deaf culture -- whether in the form of deaf friends, acceptance of manual communication as the blind accept Braille for those who need it, or of appreciation of the theatre, dance, and other accomplishments of the deaf -- we are asking him to become a person he is not, and are denying the person he is. Why should communication mean one medium only -- speech, speechreading, English, or sign language? Let it mean all of these.

It is sad but true that success for a deaf individual is usually measured by how closely he conforms to the hearing standard. Most of the national leaders among the deaf are not merely extremely literate, but also have speech and speechreading skills that enable them to function with a hearing person. The further a deaf individual is from possessing a hearing person's abilities in language -- whether speech, understanding speech, reading, writing, using the telephone, functioning alone in a hearing group, or what have you -- the less successful he is likely to be. Because he can hear and react to an announcement over a loudspeaker, a hearing retardate often seems to be smarter than the most successful deaf person. Few of our students will say to hearing society, "Hey, I'm deaf. I didn't understand you." Without denying the value of the abilities that enable one to function in a hearing society, to help hearing society communicate with us, can we not begin to emphasize functioning with whoever we are with? If we are to fully respect individuals, can we not learn to communicate with the blind, the deaf-blind, the hard of hearing, or anyone else in whatever mode we can mutually establish? Most deaf adults use the American Sign Language. Anyone who wants to reach them socially, educationally, or psychologically should at the very least respect and accept this language.

Linguists these days are making much of the rights of an individual to the language of his culture. Studies of Black English indicate, for instance, that it has definite, logical grammatical rules that just don't happen to be the same as standard American English (Alatis, 1970; Fasold & Shuy, 1970; Dillard, 1973). To function effectively within his group, an individual must first, implicitly or explicitly, define that group. Achieving rapport in a ghetto area may, and probably does, involve the use of a quite different sort of language from that needed for assimilation in a middle class, upward-moving neighborhood. If you want to assimilate with a group, you must speak its language. It's as simple as that. In the old Ugly American days, we expected people of other countries to learn English. We refused to bother to learn their languages. French and Spanish are both established, recognized languages, but where they are not given respect, as in parts of Canada and our Southwest, children with these language backgrounds have shown poor educational achievement. This imposition of a "superior" language, a "superior" culture, is precisely the problem we face when we consider communication, education and social assimilation for the deaf. Learning English should not mean negation of other languages or other

Reprinted from *Deafness Annual III*, 1973, permission of American Deafness and Rehabilitation Association.

cultures, including those of the deaf.

Most educators of the deaf, and most parents of deaf children, have hearing. It is not surprising, therefore, that all through history the objectives of education of the deaf have centered around the assimilation of the deaf into the hearing world, usually on the hearing world's terms. We can go back to the German Heinicke and the French De l'Epee, for early examples of conflict over the best means of education, and the best modes of communication. Heinicke, an oralist, held that speech and speechreading were of paramount importance, and we may deduce that to him assimilation meant becoming a part of a hearing society, with the language of that society being used in the same manner as by a hearing person -- that is, speech. De l'Epee, on the other hand, agreed that using the language of the hearing society was important, but believed the mode was not. Accordingly, he set to work to develop signs for the inflections and grammatical markers of French, and to add these to the signs he found already in use by the deaf in France. The quarrel between these two gentlemen was thus one of mode rather than of language. Which would assimilate better? De l'Epee's students would theoretically be more conspicuous by their manual gestures, but language would be more visible and thus more easily learned. Their arguments (see Garnett, 1968) are echoed today, modern studies pointing out the difficulty of lipreading (Lowell, 1957-58, 1959; Vernon, 1969), and the superior achievement and adjustment of deaf children with the early use of sign language (Schlesinger & Meadow, 1971; Rainer et. al., 1963; Stuckless and Birch, 1966; Stevenson, 1964; Quigley & Frisina, 1961) and so on.

Yet, old as the argument is, if we look at communication in the education setting as being training to understand the language of the majority society, it is no secret that education of the deaf in this country has been anything but a howling success. The Babbidge report (1965), and the reports coming from the Office of Demographic Studies at Gallaudet College, merely add to the data indicating that deaf students can barely read and write. These statistics do not indicate a new phenomenon attributable to an upsurge of multiply handicapped deaf children, much as some educators of the deaf might like to use such a theory as an excuse to get themselves off the hook; unfortunately, research on the deaf has shown the same thing for a least fifty years (Boatner, 1965; McClure, 1966; Furth, 1966; Pintner, 1918; Pugh, 1946; Goetzinger & Rousey, 1959). The Babbidge report attributes this failure in education to a failure to find a way to teach language successfully. Studies have pointed out how much of English inflections and structure is indistinguishable on the lips (Hart & Rosenstein, 1964; Vernon, 1968), invisible in signs (Stokoe, 1970; O'Rourke, 1970; Gustason, 1972; Anthony, 1971; Blanton, 1967), and poses a real problem to deaf students (Thompson, 1936; Heider & Heider, 1941; Reay, 1946; Walter, 1955; Stuckless, 1963, 1964; Craig, 1964; Myklebust, 1965; Hart & Rosenstein, 1964; Cooper, 1965; Garber, 1967; Simmons,

1962; Cohen, 1964; Blanton et. al., 1967; Stuc... 1969; Gunderson, 1965).

An early approach to this problem of presenting... needed for successful assimilation in a hearing English-s... ing society was the Rochester method (Rochester Scho... 1963). Its use of fingerspelling, but not of signs, makes it possible to render visible every letter of the English language. It is interesting to speculate whether this method would have developed if Thomas Hopkins Gallaudet, who brought the language of signs from France to America, had not been learning the French sign language for use with English, where De l'Epee's inflectional signs would be useless.

Another approach to the presentation of unambiguous language clues is that of Cued Speech, which supplements the visual cues of speechreading with hand positions to eliminate ambiguity (Henegar & Cornett, 1971). The emphasis here is on the development of communication skills that are more nearly like those of the hearing society, and are more readily transferable to communications with hearing persons who use neither the Cued Speech handshapes nor the manual signs of sign language. The fact that speechreading is the hardest mode for profoundly deaf individuals to learn (Klopping, 1972) probably has something to do with the paucity of deaf adults who support it as a mode of teaching English.

In the past few years interest has grown in a form of sign language which takes its incentive from De l'Epee and creates signs for English inflections, vocabulary, and structural forms to add to the existing vocabulary of sign language (Anthony, 1971; Wampler, 1971; Gustason et. al., 1972; Bornstein, 1972; Washington State, 1972). The proliferation of signs in these various groups has confused many individuals. Which is THE right way?

At the same time, the value judgement that English and speech are good, and that signs used by the deaf are bad, is one that some deaf and hearing individuals are beginning to challenge. Those who discuss sign language are now forced to define what kind of sign language they are talking about. In the past, when one went to a sign language class, he learned signs for specific vocabulary items and put them together himself into English word order, without, however, the inflections or tenses of English. This approach led to what is called Signed English by some (Stokoe, 1970; O'Rourke, 1970; Gustason, 1972) and Manual English by others (Fant, 1972; Bornstein, 1972). The extent of the sign language spectrum (Stokoe, 1970; O'Rourke, 1970) ranges from the American Sign Language, Ameslan, or ASL through ASL sign in English word order but without inflections as defined above, to various forms of sign that add verb endings, inflections, and new vocabulary to more closely approximate English. The latter form is termed Manual English by those who use Signed English as the label for the middle form, and Signed English by those who call the middle form Manual English -- a confusing state of affairs.

SIGN LANGUAGE SPECTRUM

American Sign Language	Signed English (Stokoe) Manual English (Fant)	Manual English (Stokoe) Signed English (Fant)
structure different from English	English word order, no verb endings	English word order, adds endings and inflection

15

y linguists to the language of signs
_____ America and in other countries.
_____ beginning to realize that the reason
_____ he signs is not necessarily because the
_____ igning faster than the "hearies" can read.
_____ they are using a different kind of sign lan-
_____ form of signed English that accompanies
_____ multaneous communication." Now linguists are
point___ __t that the American Sign Language, Ameslan, or
ASL, as used by deaf adults, has all the elements of any spoken language, including structure, grammar, tense markers,
and regional dialects. In fact, its structure resembles Chinese
more closely than it resembles English (Stokoe, 1969-70; Bellugi, 1972; Bergman, 1972; Woodward, 1971). The National
Theatre of the Deaf, with its combination of ASL and mime,
has brought to hearing audiences the realization that this language is vivid, expressive, graphic, beautiful, and graceful,
and that the deaf performers are highly talented actors. The
kind of sign used in such a dramatic production differs from
that used in everyday dialogue -- as is true, of course, for any
spoken language. And while hearing audiences, new to the
language of the deaf, can appreciate its beauty with a running
translation in spoken English, many deaf individuals themselves retain the ingrained value that places English, the language of the hearing, at the top of the totem pole. Few deaf
individuals will sign to a hearing person the same way they
sign to another deaf person. Most shift into their best signed
English, perhaps with a few ASL idioms thrown in. Ask them
to define Ameslan or ASL, and you will find that many have
never heard the term. Give some examples, however, and you
may get "low verbal," "poor English," "bad English," or "broken language." Watch a typical deaf teenager telling a story in
ASL, and you will find expressiveness, clarity, grace. Ask
him to tell the same story in English. He can't. Ask him to
translate a sentence from English into ASL. Even when he
understands the English sentence, he often can't make the
translation. Tell him hearing people have trouble with their
English, and he won't believe you. Tell him not all hearing
people write well, and he won't believe you. Ask a hearing
person to tell a story in ASL. Few can. One extremely bright
deaf student said her sister was smarter than she was. Why?
"Because she's hearing."

With this bad image of sign language and the value of
English, of speech, and of speechreading and hearing, it is not
surprising that many deaf students from oral backgrounds find
life extremely difficult. The same is true of many hard of
hearing students who come to Gallaudet College because they
couldn't cope with a hearing university. They are "failures" in
a hearing society because they couldn't make the grade in the
hearing world of a hearing college. Some cling to their search
for success on a hearing person's terms and insist on talking to
their hearing teachers, resisting or rejecting any request that
they sign for the benefit of the deaf students who cannot
understand them. Some become bitter about their rejection by
the ASL-signing deaf students, who may make fun of their
poor sign language abilities These "Hearing" deaf or hard of
hearing students find assimilation difficult in both hearing and
deaf societies. The ASL-signing deaf students, however, generally have assimilated with the deaf world that many educators either refuse to recognize or try to combat. But these students have had years of education in the belief that English is
the be-all and end-all, and that speech and speechreading are
vital. As a result their self-concept leaves much to be desired.
Under these circumstances, it is hardly surprising that studies
show deaf children of deaf parents, who accept their children's
language as a valid, important, normal means of communication, are better adjusted than are other deaf children
(Schlesinger & Meadow, 1971; Stuckless & Birch, 1966).

It is for all of these reasons that we are hearing more and
more about "deaf pride," half joking references to "deaf
power," increasing pressure for the teaching of Ameslan and
for the teaching of English as a second language, and perhaps
an increasing militancy on the part of some deaf youth -- in
short, an attitude of "I'm deaf, so what? Wanna make something of it?" attitude. Assimilation into a hearing world, on
the hearing world's terms, is beginning to be a questionable
goal, but few yet have the nerve to say to hearing parents of
young deaf children, "Your child is deaf. He will never be a
hearing person. Don't try to make him one."

Yet no one is arguing that deaf individuals do not have to
live in a hearing world, or that they should live in self-contained communities in a kind of "let-them-go-back-to-where-
they- came-from" philosophy. Accordingly, at the same time
that sociologists, psychologists, and linguists are getting louder and louder in their recommendations that sign language be
acceptable, and that the deaf child be treated and educated as a
deaf child, there is increasing question as to how to teach him
English. Many are groaning, "Now that we've got many people to accept signs, we have to confuse them with this battle
over which kind of signs."

While the new attention that is focusing on sign language is
helping make it, and the deaf society it represents, more
respectable, the variety of sign language modes being taught is
wreaking havoc in sign language classes. Should ASL be
taught? Signed English or one of the new creations, and if so,
which? Many of those concerned with the acceptance of Sign
and the deaf child are afraid that the lack of harmony among
those advocating it will dilute and dissipate their efforts, and
that eventually they will lose out to the "nonsigning" group.

Certainly a primary duty is to define objectives -- to suit the
type of Sign taught to the type needed by the student of Sign.
Do you want to learn Sign to communicate with adult deaf?
You need a class in ASL. Is your interest in teaching English
to young deaf children? A class in some form of signed
English would probably be better for you. It makes no sense
to learn something which those with whom you want to communicate will not understand or which will not help you attain
your objectives. Ideally, of course, you should learn all forms
of Sign.

But the acceptance of the use of Sign should not turn into
fanaticism. Some hard of hearing and deaf individuals do not
sign. Whether they want to learn or not, they live in a world
with other people, and they and whoever wishes to communicate with them, must find mutually acceptable means of communication. No one way is THE way.

Compounding the problem is our tendency to assume that
communication, however it is established, will cure all ills; to
think, for example, that because hearing teachers have no
problems communicating with hearing students, they, therefore, are good teachers. An ability to communicate does not in
itself make a good teacher. Hearing people have family problems, psychological problems, educational problems, writing
problems, and no communication mode can remove these for
the deaf person either. We are not going to solve all these
problems for anyone, be he hearing or deaf, by using any specific communication mode, by improving his English, or by
making him a militant. True, we need effective communication. But we also need self-respect, self-acceptance, and

acceptance of the other guy. Far too many educators appear to be in special fields there because in those fields they can feel superior. In deaf education it is especially easy to communicate with other hearing people in the presence of a deaf individual while leaving him out, to be an "expert" to an inquiring hearing parent or other interested hearing person without including the deaf, to excuse one's failure to educate deaf children because their very failure to become literate precludes their telling just what is wrong with their education.

So while it is important to define one's objectives in communication according to the person and the situation, perhaps the chief obstacle to effective communication is one of attitude. If you really want to get an idea across to someone, and to understand him, you BOTH must try. If you do not respect him, neither of you will try very hard, and communication will be poor, regardless of the mode employed. Perhaps I don't normally use the same mode you do, but unless I am more interested in you, in your ideas and in your human "beingness" than I am in a specific mode, there will be no true communication. The same is true of your attitude. Which is more important, the person or the mode? Respect must come first, regardless of individual differences, regardless of mode. If respect is there, the differences can be overcome. If it isn't, why bother? And if it isn't, aren't we saying something very important about ourselves?

BIBLIOGRAPHY

Alatis, J.E. (Ed.). (1969). *20th Annual Round Table. Monograph Series on Language and Linguistics.* Washington: Georgetown University School of Language and Linguistics.

Anthony, D. A. (1971). *Seeing Essential English Manual,* Anaheim, California: Anaheim Union High School District.

Babbidge, H. D. (1965). *Education of the Deaf, A Report to the Secretary of Health, Education and Welfare by his Advisory Committee on the Education of the Deaf.* U.S. Department of Health, Education and Welfare.

Bellugi, U. & Klima, E. (1972). The roots of Language in the sign of the deaf, *Psychology Today,* pp. 61-64, 76, June.

Bergman, E. (1972). Autonomous and Unique Features of American Sign Language, *American Annals of the Deaf,* 117:5, 20-24.

Blanton, R. L., Nunnally, J.C. & Odom, P. (1967). *Final Report: Psycho-linguistic Processes in the Deaf.* Research Grant No. RD-1479-8, Vocational Rehabilitation Administration, Department of Health, Education and Welfare. Department of Psychology, Vanderbilt University.

Boatner, E. B. (1965). The Need of a Realistic Approach to the Education of the Deaf. Paper given to the joint convention of the California Association of Parents of Deaf and Hard of Hearing Children, California Association of Teachers of the Deaf and Hard of Hearing, and the California Association of the Deaf, November 6.

Bornstein, H., Director. (1972). *Little Red Riding Hood* (& other publications in Signed English). Washington: Gallaudet College Press.

Cohen, S. R. (1964). Redundancy in the Written Language of the Deaf: Predictability of Deaf and Hearing Story Paraphrases. Unpublished doctoral dissertation, Columbia.

Cooper, R. L. (1965). The Ability of Deaf and Hearing Children to Apply Morphological Rules. Unpublished doctoral dissertation, Columbia.

Craig, W. N. (1964). A Comparison of Two Methods of Teaching Written Language to Deaf Students, *American Annals of the Deaf,* 109-248-256.

Dillard, J. L. (1972). *Black English: Its History and Usage in the United States.* New York: Random House.

Fant, L. (1972). The CSUN Approach to the Training of Sign Language Interpreters. *The Deaf American,* 25:56-57.

Fasold, R. W. & Shuy, R.W. (1970). *Teaching Standard English in the Inner City.* Washington, D.C.: Center for Applied Linguistics.

Furth, H. G. (1966). A Comparison of Reading Test Norms of Deaf and Hearing Children. *American Annals of the Deaf,* 111-461-462.

Garber, G. E. (1967). An Analysis of English Morphological Abilities of Deaf and Hearing Children. Unpublished doctoral dissertation, Ohio State University.

Garnett, C. B. (1968). *The Exchange of Letters Between Samuel Heinicke and Abbe Charles Michel De L'Epee.* Washington, D.C.: Vantage Press.

Goetzinger, C. P. & Roussey, C.L. (1959). Educational Achievement of Deaf Children, *American Annals of the Deaf,* 104:221-231.

Gunderson, A. N. (1965). A Linguistic Analysis of the Written Language of the Deaf. Unpublished doctoral dissertation, Northwestern University.

Gustason, G., Pfetzing, D. & Zawolkow, E. (1972). *Signing Exact English.* Rossmoor, California: Modern Signs Press.

Hart, B. O. & Rosenstein, J. (1964). Examining the Language Behavior of Deaf Children, *The Volta Review,* 66:679-682.

Heider, F. (1946). On the Construction of a Language Usage Test for the Deaf, *The Volta Review,* 48:742-744.

Heider, F. & Heider, G. Comparison of Sentence Structure of Deaf and Hearing Children, *Psychological Monograph,* 52:42-103.

Henegar, M. E. & Cornett, R.O. (1971). *Cued Speech Handbook for Parents*. HEW Contract #OEC-0-8-001937-4348 (019). Washington, D.C.: Gallaudet College.

Klopping, H. (1972). Language Understanding of Deaf Students under Three Auditory-Visual Stimulus Conditions, *American Annals of the Deaf*, 117-389-392.

Lowell, E. L. (1957-58). *John Tracy Clinic Research Papers III, V, VI, VII*. Los Angeles: John Tracy Clinic.

Lowell, E. L. (1959). Research in Speechreading: Some Relationships to Language Development and Implications for the Classroom Teacher, *Report of the Proceedings of the 39th Meeting of the Convention of American Instructors of the Deaf*, pp. 68-73.

McClure, W. J. (1966). Current Problems and Trends in Education of the Deaf, *The Deaf American*, 18:8-14.

Mindel, E. D. & Vernon, M. (1971). *They Grow in Silence*. Washington, D. C.: National Association of the Deaf.

Myklebust, H. R. (1965). *Development and Disorders of Written Language. Volume One: Picture Story Language Test*. New York: Grune & Stratton.

Office of Demographic Studies. *Annual Survey of Hearing Impaired Children and Youth*. Washington, D. C.: Gallaudet College, 1968-1972.

O'Rourke, T. J. (1970). *A Basic Course in Manual Communication*. Washington, D.C.: National Association of the Deaf.

O'Rourke, T. J. (Ed.). (1972). *Psycholinguistics and Total Communication: The State of the Art*. Washington, D.C.: *American Annals of the Deaf*.

Pintner, R. (1918). The Measurement of Language Ability and Language Process of Deaf Children, *The Volta Review*, 20:755-766.

Pugh, G. S. (1946). Summaries from Appraisal of the Silent Reading Abilities of Acoustically Handicapped Children, *American Annals of the Deaf*, 91:331-349.

Quigley, S. (1969). The Influence of Fingerspelling in the Development of Language, Communication, and Educational Achievement in Deaf Children. Urbana: University of Illinois.

Quigley, S. P. & Frisina, R. (1961). *Institutionalization and Psychoeducational Development of Deaf Children*. Council of Exceptional Children, Research Monograph, Series A, #3.

Rainer, J. D., Altshuler, K. Z., Kellmann, F. J. & Deming, W. E. (Eds.). (1963). *Family and Mental Health Problems in a Deaf Population*. New York: New York State Psychiatric Institute.

Reay, E. E. (1946). A comparison between deaf and hearing children in regard to the use of verbs and nouns in compositions describing a short motion picture story, *American Annals of the Deaf*, 91:453-491.

Rochester School for the Deaf. (1963). *The Rochester method of instructing the deaf*. Rochester, New York: the Alumni Association, Rochester School for the Deaf.

Schlesinger, H. S. & Meadow, K. P. (1971). *Deafness and Mental Health: A Developmental Approach*. Final Report, Grant #14-P-55270/9-03 (R.D.-2835-S), SR 5. San Francisco: Langley Porter Neuropsychiatric Institute.

Simmons, A. A. (1962). A comparison of the type-token ratio of Spoken and written language of deaf and hearing children, *The Volta Review*, 64:17-421.

Stevenson, E. A. (1964). *A Study of the Educational Achievement of Deaf Children of Deaf Parents*. Berkeley: California School for the Deaf.

Stokoe, W. C. (1970). CAL conference on sign language, *The Linguistic Reporter*, April.

Stokoe, W. C. (1969-1970). Sign language diglossia, *Studies in Linguistics*, 21:27-41.

Stokoe, W. C., Casterline, D. C. & Croneberg, C. (1965). *Dictionary of American Sign Language*. Washington, D.C.: Gallaudet College Press.

Stuckless, E. R. (1963). Programmed instruction and errors in the written language of deaf adolescents. Unpublished doctoral dissertation, University of Pittsburgh.

Stuckless, E. R. (1964). Development and correction of the language of deaf children through programmed instruction, *Proceedings of the International Congress on Education of the Deaf*. Washington, D.C: U.S. Government Printing Office, pp. 889-893.

Stuckless, E. R. & Birch, J. W. (1966). The influence of early manual communication on the linguistic development of deaf children, *American Annals of the Deaf*, 111:452-462.

Stuckless, E. R. & Glover, M. (1969). Procedures and preliminary findings from a study of the post secondary student's ability to identify structural units and his language proficiency. Unpublished report. Rochester, New York: National Technical Institute for the Deaf, Rochester Institute of Technology.

Thompson, W. H. (1936). An analysis of errors in written composition of deaf children, *American Annals of the Deaf*, 81:95-99.

Vernon, M. (1969). Sociological and psychological factors associated with hearing loss, *Journal of Speech and Hearing Research*, 12:3, 541-563, September.

Walter, J. (1959). A study of the written sentence construction of a group of profoundly deaf children, *American Annals of the Deaf*. 104:282-285.

Walter, J. (1959). Some further observations on the written sentence construction of profoundly deaf children, *American Annals of the Deaf*, 104:282-285.

Washington State School for the Deaf. (1972). *An Introduction to Manual English*. Vancouver: Washington State School for the Deaf.

Woodward, C. (1971). Implication for sociolinguistic research among the deaf. Paper presented to the Linguistic Society of America, St. Louis, December.

THE DEAF CHILD'S RIGHT TO COMMUNICATE

Gerilee Gustason, Ph.D.
Assistant Professor of Education
Gallaudet College
Washington, D.C.

Roslyn Rosen, M.A.
Communications Specialist
Model Secondary School for the Deaf
Washington, D.C.

Statement: Every deaf child has several basic communication rights:

1) to full and free communication with his family, his peers, and his society,
2) to learn the language used in his environment,
3) to use any communication mode with which he is comfortable in a given situation.

In the context of this paper, we are defining a deaf child as one whose hearing impairment necessitates his placement in a special education program, and we are concerned with this child from the moment he becomes deaf -- whether this hearing loss takes effect before or at some time after birth.

While we support the development of aural-oral skills to the greatest degree possible -- the training of residual hearing, the use of speech, and practice of the art of speechreading -- we are first and foremost interested in the acquisition of language. Because children's eyes do not fully accommodate until approximately age eight, materials used with young children in the schools stress large and easy to perceive symbols. The printed word is used in large form, for instance. Later, when the child has learned to read and his eyes can accommodate to smaller items, he has no problem reading normal size type. We suggest that the visual cues of speechreading a language are too small for easy comprehension by infants and toddlers. In addition, not all the sounds of the spoken language may be visually clear and unambiguous. In English, for instance, approximately half the sounds look like some other sound on the lips.[1] Some languages, also, have a less than perfect correspondence of sound with printed word: **gay, weigh, fail**, for example, all represent the same sound in English.

Moreover, linguists report that normal hearing children have mastered the most basic patterns and inflections of their native language by the age of three, have internalized its basic structure by six, and have pretty well "set" their own language habits by puberty.[2]

Accordingly, we suggest that the use of manual cues, larger and more readily perceptible than speechreading, would greatly simplify the deaf child's task in learning his language at a very young age. Such cues do not replace, but rather supplement, aural-oral stimuli in the interest of unambiguity, ease of perception, and comfort.

How do we teach the deaf to communicate? By teaching him speech and signs? We must remember that the purpose of communication is to share ideas and feelings, and that communication is an articulation of mental activity. Then clearly the responsibility of the parents and teachers is to enable the child to acquire and share concepts and experiences, and to communicate in a code that is visual and understandable to both parties. This becomes the base for building language and communication skills.

Thus, input precedes output. For the deaf, this input must be visual and clear. Because of its visual nature, the language of signs is becoming widely accepted as an effective means of communication with the deaf.

The problem, as some see it, is making a natural language of signs represent a spoken language accurately for instructional purposes.

We would like at this point to differentiate among three basic forms of manual communication, which in actual practice often overlap. This overlap is natural, but it is important to distinguish among these three forms -- and accept all three, as the deaf child has a right to them all.

First, there is a form of manual communication we refer to as "in-group" signing. This includes natural gestures that develop to aid communication outside a standard language system. These can take several forms:

1) Gestures used between strangers not speaking the same language -- akin to mime (sometimes used by hearing parents of a deaf child). (Examples: no smoking, I'm hungry, etc.)
2) Gestures developed by deaf children or families to communicate their wants, in the absence of adult models. These may be understood by:
a) only his family, or
b) his classmates,
depending on the situation in which they develop. Some of these signs may become school signs, to facilitate communication among the children in the same school.

While such school signs may develop at least partly because of the lack of an adult model to expose them to more "standard" signs, they may also be likened to teenage slang -- a special jargon that may be incomprehensible to parents. The deaf child has a right to this jargon of belongingness, as well as to the language of his parents.

Second, there is the form of manual communication used by the deaf adults in the child's country. This language is usually a graphic representation of a thought which is not necessarily related to the structure of the country's spoken language. The degree of such a relationship may vary according to the educational level of the user, the speech-readability of the country's spoken language, and the degree of acceptance of manual communication by educators in that country. As a visual medium, it is capable of things which the spoken language cannot do. It can, for instance, as a three-dimensional medium, indicate directionality of an action:

teach   give

Reprinted from *World Congress of the Deaf,* 1975, with permission of the National Association of the Deaf.

It also serves as a visual substitution for vocal intonation. It can add emotional impact, "tone of voice," or degree of intensity:

no   walk   rain

Because of the dependence deaf people have upon visual stimuli, they often develop this expressiveness in manual gestures to an art. The deaf child has a right to be encouraged to develop in this same expressive art, and he has not only a right but a responsibility to accept his own and others' deafness and communicate with other deaf people in this communication mode which they can use so well. He has a right to be proud of himself and his language.

It is not always understood or accepted that the sign language of a deaf adult can vary greatly from the language of his hearing countrymen and have specific syntactical rules of its own, idioms of its own, a grammar of its own. In the United States, study of American Sign Language is turning up these rules of grammar, which are not related to the grammatical rules of English. For example, we have negation (don't know, don't want), and the establishment of pronouns by placement of persons (Mary met John yesterday. She liked him very much, but he didn't like her.).[3]

However, because the vast majority of his countrymen will be hearing, the deaf child also has the right to learn the language spoken by the majority in his country, to use in communicating with these people in whatever mode the situation warrants -- manual communication if he desires with those who understand it, speech and speechreading if he has the ability, and writing if he does not.

To learn this language at the age at which a hearing child normally learns it, the deaf child needs a clear, unambiguous visual representation of the target language, repeated in his environment as constantly as possible -- at home, in school. This is not to say that the home must or should become a school, but that family and teachers should communicate with him as fully and naturally as they do with a hearing child, using the native language represented by manual symbols. Such a manual representation of the language would need to be developed if it does not already exist.

People who take the existing signs in a country and use them in the syntax of that country's spoken language may think they are using a manual representation of that language. This is not necessarily the case. For example, in English we might sign

I will be go to the class for five day.
The lecture was very interest.
Yesterday we go several place.

In a full manual representation, all inflections would also be clear:
I will be going to the class for five days, etc.[4]
For maximum clarity and best articulation with the signs already used by the deaf adults in a given country, these deaf adults should be included in such developmental activities. If such a communication mode is taught by the schools to parents and teachers, and consistently used with the child, he should have a much easier time learning the language that is his right.

Our suggestions, then, are several:

1. Value the child and what he has to say more than any one communication mode.
2. Make all modes available for him to learn, including all the forms of manual communication.
3. Persons wanting to work with the adult deaf have the responsibility to learn the mode and form they use.
4. Develop a manual representation of the spoken/written language of the country, with input from deaf adults.
5. Respect, and teach the child by example to respect, all forms of communication.
6. Provide deaf adult models in the schools
7. Schools should provide classes for parents and teachers in manual communication, and explain what form is being taught and why.

In summary, we want to say that the deaf child has the right to be given every opportunity to be able to communicate with as many different people as possible in as many different situations as possible. The deaf child has the right to an education equivalent to that of his hearing peers and to master the languages as spoken by the majority of hearing people as well as signed by the deaf people in his country. Above all, he has the right to be accepted for himself, what he is and can do. We who work with the deaf child must first remember that he is first of all a human being and second that it is not his ears (or mouth) but what is between them that is important.

REFERENCES

Bellugi, U. (1972). Studies in sign language. In *Psycholinguistics and total communication: the state of the art*, edited by T. J. O'Rourke, 68-84. Washington, D.C.: National Association of the Deaf. (3)

Bellugi, U. & Fischer, S. (1972). A comparison of sign language and spoken language. *Cognition*, 1-2/3. 173-200. (3)

Bergman, E. (1972). Autonomous and unique features of American Sign Language. *American Annals of the Deaf*, 117-2, 20-24. (3)

Braine, M. D. S. (1963). The otogeny of English phrase structure: the first phase. *Language*, 39, 1-13. (2)

Brown, R. & Bellugi, U. (1964). Three processes in the child's acquisition of syntax. *Harvard Educational Review*, 39, 133-152. (2)

Cazden, C. B. (1968). The acquisition of noun and verb inflection. *Child Development*, 39, 433-448. (2)

Gustason, G. & Woodward, J., eds. (1975). *Recent Developments in Manual English*. Washington, D.C.: Gallaudet College. (4)

Hockett, C. F. (1950). Age-grading and linguistic continuity. *Language*, 26, 449-457. (2)

Labov, W. (1965). *Linguistic research on the nonstandard English of Negro children*. 1965 Yearbook, New York Society for the Experimental Study of Education, 110-117. (2)

Markovin, B. V. (1963). Helping the deaf child toward adequate language and speech. *Journal of Rehabilitation.* (2)

Penfield, W. (1964). The uncommitted cortex: the child's changing brain. *The Atlantic Monthly,* 77-81. (2)

Slobin, D. (1965). Grammatical development in Russian speaking children. In *The Development of Language Functions,* edited by Klaus F. Riegel. Report #8, University of Michigan Center for Human Growth and Development, 93-102. (2)

Stokoe, W. C. Jr. (1960). Sign language structure: an outline of the visual communication system of the American Deaf, *Studies in Linguistics,* occasional paper #8. (3)

Velten, J. V. (1943). The growth of phonemic and lexical patterns in infant language. *Language,* 19, 281-292. (2)

Vernon, M. (1969). Sociological and psychological factors associated with hearing loss. *Journal of speech and hearing research,* 12, 541-563. (1)

Weir, R. (1962). *Language in the crib.* The Hague: Mouton and Company. (2)

THE RATIONALE OF SIGNING EXACT ENGLISH

By Gerilee Gustason, Donna Pfetzing and Esther Zawolkow

In all the discussion of American Sign Language, or Ameslan, and new sign systems, and in chance encounters and remarks, it is increasingly clear that there are a number of misconceptions or misunderstandings about the various new sign systems and the people who teach them. We would like to clarify the philosophy and goals of Signing Exact English, in connection with frequently heard statements, and make some additional comments. Let us take some typical remarks:

1. "New signs are causing problems." Yes, we agree. It is a problem for teachers of sign language classes to know what to teach. It is especially confusing if students meet a variety of signs for the same word, with no guidance as to which one they are supposed to learn. The situation is aggravated when individuals take the position that only one sign is right and all the rest are wrong. A complete barrage of new signs would confuse a deaf adult who never saw any of them before. However, we do not advocate that those who wish to communicate with adult deaf, whether as friends, co-workers, interpreters, counselors or whatever, learn new signs. We do not advocate that anyone learn ONLY new signs. We agree there are problems, but the problems come not from the signs but from the manner in which they may be taught or used.

2. "Words like understand and forget are broken up and signed as under-stand, for-get, car-pet, butter-fly." This is not true of Signing Exact English. One of our principles is that if a word consists of two or more smaller words, it is signed as these smaller words only if the meaning is consistent with both. Accordingly, we do sign cow-boy, baby-sit, under-line. But understand has no relation to the meaning of the words under or stand, so we retain one sign for the entire word -- the traditional sign. This is also true of words like secretary, where the traditional sign is retained. It is true that other new sign systems may sign this as "secret-ar-y" but this is not done in Signing Exact English. Generally, when a traditional sign is unambiguous and only one English word translates that sign, the sign is retained -- as in such words as responsible which we do NOT sign as "response-ible." Not all new sign systems are alike, and it should not be assumed that what one system does all the others do also.

3. "If a deaf child learns new signs, he will not be able to talk to deaf adults." This is a very general statement, and one with which we tend to disagree. First, our children do not necessarily talk to each other in the same way they talk in the classroom or to English-signing adults. Also we do not feel that Ameslan should be relegated to the playground or the bathroom. If both Ameslan and English are recognized as valuable and beautiful languages, and both are taught, there is no reason our children cannot grow up bilingual, their usage determined by the situation and the person with whom they are talking. This leads into the next statement, that...

4. "Hearing parents of a deaf baby should learn Ameslan first." With this we would like to ask why. These parents experience enough trauma learning that they have a deaf baby and learning about deafness. Their language as normally spoken in the home is generally, in this country, English. As Roslyn Rosen, Communications Specialist at the Model Secondary School for the Deaf and deaf mother of three hearing

impaired children, pointed out recently at the Seattle Convention of the National Association of the Deaf, if you discovered you had a French baby would you make a great effort to learn French when you and the majority of citizens in this country speak English? What we would like to see is parents and teachers who treat both Ameslan and English with respect, who use their own native language, be it Ameslan or English, with the child, and actively encourage him to learn both.

5. "People who go to new signs classes are not aware that deaf adults do not sign this way." This is, unfortunately, true in many cases. We believe in, practice and actively encourage the clarification as to what kind of signs will be taught in a class and an explanation as to the types and uses of different kinds of sign. In our classes, we have always asked why people enrolled, and those who wished to learn to communicate with a deaf adult co-worker or friend have been referred to classes in traditional signs or, where they exist, classes in Ameslan. A great deal of harm and misunderstanding can and has been done when such explanations are not given.

6. "The new sign systems eliminate the use of fingerspelling." This is definitely not true of Signing Exact English. We do not attempt to develop signs for every word in the dictionary but rather signs for the words or parts of words (tenses, word endings, etc.) that give structure to English and for commonly used words. Fingerspelling is indispensable.

7. "People who use new signs want to eliminate the use of Ameslan." This is definitely not true of us. We would, as previously stated, like to see our deaf children grow up able to function freely, effectively and fluently in both Ameslan and English. Most of us use a mixture of both, what Bernard Bragg has labeled Ameslish (American Annals of the Deaf, December 1973, pp. 672-674). This mixture is comfortable conversationally, more so than attempting to use pure Ameslan without any influence of English or pure English without any Ameslan idioms. We regard Signing Exact English as one more tool to add to the educational repertoire but we certainly regard Ameslan as such a tool also. Both, however, are more than tools. They are the way we talk. A person should definitely not be ridiculed for or discouraged from using Ameslan but neither should he be ridiculed for or discouraged from using English. We are after comfort with both languages.

8. "New signs destroy the beauty of sign language." This is really a matter of opinion. It is also a matter of signing ability. Not all users of traditional signs or Ameslan make these signs look beautiful; certainly not everyone signs beautifully. Similarly, some signers chop up new signs so their signing style is jerky, forced. This is not the fault of the signs but the signer. It is natural not to like what is not understood, but if the signs are known and if they are done with fluidity and expressions, they are capable of as much beauty as Ameslan. People who speak English can murder that language with their speech if they are colorless, monotonous, staccato and so on. This does not mean the words themselves are lacking in beauty of expressiveness. The same is true of signs.

9. "Many good signs are changed for no reason." We do our best not to do this. As previously stated, if a sign is clear, unambiguous and has only one English translation, it is

Reprinted from *The Deaf American*, September, 1974, with permission from the National Association of the Deaf.

retained. Modifications are done to create synonyms, such as using the initial letter of the sign "hurt" for pain or ache.

10. "If we use new signs, deaf children won't learn to spell." There is nothing automatic about learning to spell, no matter what kind of signs are used. Signing Exact English attempts to build a structure of English syntax within the child's linguistic system, not to teach him spelling per se. This is similar to what happens with the use of any sign. A sign exists for a word: The child needs to learn to spell it. Children always have name signs for teachers and counselors; they need to learn how to spell these names. They need to learn to spell, period.

We are delighted with the increasing amount of study being given Ameslan and look forward to the combination of Ameslan and English in the classroom and the home. We are less than delighted with those who study and advocate Ameslan and attack new sign systems without ever having sat through an explanation of these systems or visited a school where they are used. Many misconceptions are spread by these people. We would like to see more mutual support and a recognition that communication skills in themselves, while of vital importance, are not the only element in good teaching.

In an article, "Why Ameslan?" in the June 1974 issue of the California News, Louie Fant brings up a number of points suggesting several evils in the push for new sign systems or English. These dangers, as he sees them, are:

1. An insistence that all deaf children communicate only in English. We make no such insistence. We wish to see the child able to communicate in a variety of ways, INCLUDING English but by no means limited to it.

2. English, according to Fant, is a language in which only a small percentage will be fluent. This depends on what is meant by fluent. Comparatively few hearing people who are comfortable with English are fluent speakers or writers or readers of Shakespeare. We believe our deaf children are equally capable of utilizing informal English and believe the questioning of this capability a great underestimation of their inherent abilities.

3. So much time is spent on English that little is left for other essentials. This is, of course, possible and is partially what we meant by saying that good teaching is more than

communication skill. Are all hearing children well educated, either in academic areas such as history or math or science, or in non-academic areas such as responsibility, creativity, social behavior? It is, of course, true that the teachers of older students must determine how much English is needed in content areas such as math or science, but it is likewise true that some English is helpful in reading the directions on a box of cake mix, for instance. With younger students, who have been exposed to both English and Ameslan, we do not believe this problem will exist in anywhere near the same degree.

Fant states that "Ameslan insures the deaf child against mere training. It vouchsafes his right to an education." Insofar as Ameslan implies an acceptance of the person and his individual self-expression, the desire to understand what the child says, the willingness to get across in any way that works, we would agree that Ameslan contributes to the makeup of a good teacher. But as a means of communication Ameslan can be no such insurance, any more than French or German or Chinese or English. Good teaching is far more than a language. Insistence on Ameslan alone would be just as restrictive and limiting as an insistence on English alone. If one denies Spanish to a Chicano child he does him a great disservice but to insist on Spanish alone in a country where the majority language is English is also a disservice. To obtain a position at a relatively high level in this country, some command of English is essential. Would the supporters of Ameslan relegate the deaf children to the lesser jobs because Ameslan is their heritage? It is true that a person can be quite content in a position in which English is not needed -- witness the university president turned trash collector -- but this must be a matter of choice, not lack of opportunity.

Ideally, we would like to see the best of both languages, Ameslan and English, in use. There is nothing wrong with the idiomatic sign for a running nose, but neither is there anything wrong with English because it expresses this concept with the words, "Your nose is running." There is a time and a place for different usages. If one helps explain the other, great. Let's teach acceptance, understanding, awareness, respect and pride -- for BOTH English and Ameslan, or Ameslan and English, whichever comes first and naturally to the parent and child.

EFFECTIVE SIGN COMMUNICATION FOR INSTRUCTIONAL PURPOSES

MANUAL ENGLISH AND AMERICAN SIGN LANGUAGE

Gerilee Gustason, Ph.D.
and
Roslyn Rosen, M.A.

A few years ago, when life was more simple, we could talk about "sign language." In recent years, the upsurge of interest in visual media and modes, including signs, for communicating with the deaf child has led to studies of what exists in manual communicating with the deaf child and what could be provided for better communication and better education.

Accordingly, it is no longer enough to speak of "signs" or "manual communication." We need to clarify what type of manual communication we are talking about, and determine what we wish to use in a given situation, with a specific deaf child or adult or a specific group.

Although many people have their own labels for different types of signs, and variations are the rule rather than the exception, we have found it helpful to speak of a sign language continuum because there is no sharp division between elements or modes. Briefly, the elements are: Pantomime, In-group signs, American Sign Language, Sign English, Manual English and Fingerspelling.

1. **Non-verbal communication or pantomime**: This means the natural use of the body and hands and utilization of facial expressions and moods.

2. In-group signs:

a.) Home signs may be defined as those signs that follow natural gestures and often develop within the family unit for basic communication purposes, if no formal sign model is available -- or as family "secret jokes" or references outsiders would not understand. These may refer to people, places of actions. (e.g. McDonald's, grocery shopping)

b.) School signs often develop within a school program for adult-child communication, to a greater or lesser degree depending upon the amount of exposure the child has to standard signs. Such signs may not be understood by the deaf adult community in the surrounding area if there is little or no contact between the two groups.

c.) Local signs refer to vocabulary that varies depending on the area in which one lives. In English, we may speak of a sandwich as a grinder, a submarine, a hoagie, a hero. In signs, there may be similar variants depending on geographical area, (e.g. football, goat, recess, chocolate.)

3. **American Sign Language, Ameslan, or ASL** has come in for an increasing amount of study in recent years aimed at analyzing the rules of grammar that exist in this language. Research is turning up definite grammatical principles that are often completely unrelated to the grammatical rules of English -- such as reduplication (of nouns to show plurality, of verbs to show continuing or habitual action), directionality (to indicate the subject-verb-object relationship, for instance), and word order (e.g. chronological order to the placing of the most striking feature first).

4. **Sign English:** Most of us use the traditional signs of Ameslan but in simultaneous communication which is based on English, we sort them out according to English word order. This becomes a sort of pidgin language, taking its vocabulary from Ameslan and its structure from English, and we will refer to this as **Sign English**.

5. **Manual English:** We come now to the reasons for the development of new signs, and systems known variously as **Signed or**

Manual English.

The basic rationale for these systems comes from dissatisfaction with poor educational showing of many deaf children, the need for input before output can be expected, and the lack of ease and clarity in the presentation of English through other visual modes. Regarding the poor educational showing, we should note a few typical research findings concerning the reading and language abilities of deaf children over the years:

Reading achievement scores and language test scores for the deaf have been uniformly low for at least fifty years, those of older deaf students hovering around the level attained by fourth and fifth grade hearing children. (Wrightstone, Aranow, and Muskowitz, 1963; Office of Demographic Studies, 1969; Goetzinger and Rousey, 1959, Pugh, 1946).

Some thirty percent of deaf students aged sixteen and older were classified as functionally illiterate by Boatner (1965) and McClure (1966).

It is interesting, also, to note the areas in which deaf children exhibit English problems:

1. They omit necessary words and use wrong words, these errors comprising approximately half of their syntax errors (Thompson, 1936; Myklebust, 1965).

2. They use sentence structures simpler and more rigid than those of hearing children, those of 17-year-old deaf students comparable to those of 8-year-old hearing children (Heider and Heider, 1940).

3. They learn lexical meanings more easily than structural meanings (Hart and Rosenstein, 1964), indicating their ability to deduce meaning from context.

4. No consistent pattern of development is exhibited by deaf children in the mastery of inflections or structure (Cooper, 1965) and they use fewer adverbs, auxiliaries, and conjunctions than do hearing children (Simmons, 1962).

Compare this to studies on normal language development in hearing children: These children have mastered a great deal of the structure of English, including basic sentence patterns and inflections, by the age of three; their language is fairly stable by age six, and language habits are extremely difficult to modify after the age of puberty. Between two and three years of age, a great jump is made, including the development of prepositions, demonstratives, auxiliaries, articles, conjunc-

Reprinted with permission from *Proceedings of the Convention of American Instructors of the Deaf,* June 1975.

tions, possessive and personal pronouns, the past tense suffix, the plural suffix, and the possessive suffix. (Braine, 1963; Brown and Bellugi, 1964; Cazden, 1968; Slobin, 1965; Velten, 1943; Weir, 1962; Penfield, 1964; Hockett, 1950; Labov, 1965; Morkovin, 1963.)

A child learns the language of his environment as he perceives it -- be it French, Chinese, Russian, standard or non-standard English. The question then was how to present clear, unambiguous standard English to the learner.

Speechreading, while a valuable tool for communicating with a hearing world, involves considerable educated guess-work. Problems include:

1. 40-60% of the sounds of English look like some other sound on the lips

2. Words ignored or missed are often structure of function words -- verb endings, articles, etc.

3. It requires a knowledge of language to fill in the gaps caused by the two problems above.

Reading and writing lack spontaneity, portability, and naturalness. In addition, since a child's eyes do not fully accommodate 'til age 8, (as evidenced by large print readers for the young) there's a perception problem.

This perception problem also affects fingerspelling. In addition, fingerspelling is often monotonous and fatiguing to watch, has little visual imagery to compare to tone of voice and involves fine muscle control infants do not develop for some time.

Sign English, as noted above, does not present a clear, grammatically complete version of English. Accordingly, in varying degrees, new sign systems attempt to provide manual signs to supplement already existing signs and increase the input to the child of both vocabulary and English markers, word endings, pronouns, and other structural elements. These additions take several forms:

1. word endings, affixes, verb tenses

2. the creation of signs for English words previously having no signs, (fruit, vegetable, parent, toy)

3. the use of initials with base signs (family, begin, make) and the creation of sign families for words similar to meaning and sharing a common traditional sign. One of them will retain the traditional sign, the others will be given a new hand shape. (**happen**, luck, chance, **event**, **occur**, result; **think**, reason, wonder; **friend**, acquaint, **mate**, **neighbor**, relate; **class**, group, family, **team**, **organize**, social, **forum**, workshop, **town**, city, village; and so on.)

The philosophies followed by various new sign systems include greater or lesser adherence to what may be called a one sign-one word rule, and differences in degree of departure from traditional Ameslan signs. We have neither the space nor the intention here to go into the difference among the various new sign systems but mention should be made of four major published systems:

1. The Gallaudet Preschool Signed English Program

2. Seeing Essential English

3. Linguistics of Visual English

4. Signing Exact English

In the summer of 1973 the Gallaudet Department of Education sponsored a two-week workshop on these four systems, and principals involved in each contributed papers detailing their philosophies and principles. These have been published under the title "Recent Developments in Manual English," available from the Gallaudet bookstore.

It is our contention here that the hearing impaired child

should have access to every means of communication that he can. Accordingly, we stress his right to speech and speechreading training, to "ingroup" signs relating to family and peers (much like teenage slang), to a clear representation of English, and to the rich heritage of visual graphics presented by Ameslan. In actuality, the elements of the continuum are rarely used in isolation or to the exclusion of the other elements. We call this spectrum of available modes or the combinations, the Communication Consortium. We believe that a total involvement in communication can draw upon them all and will enrich the child's communicative and language growth, and that Ameslan, besides being a vivid language in its own right, can add color, visuality and clarity to manual English. We would like to see child, parents, and teachers learn them all.

COMMUNICATION CONSORT

Effective communication requires an under_____ ___ __ deafness, the roles and interplay of the various _____ation modes and the skills of relating these to the abil___ __ __eeds of the other person and his/her situation. The d__ ___son is visually oriented and dependent to a large degr__ on facial expressions and movement in absence of vocal _ntonation to receive the finer shades of meaning. Vivid action or key words and inflection in terms of rate, size and directionality, make a greater impact on the deaf person that do English words, some of which do not directly carry weight or enhance understanding (such as articles, word endings, and such) especially when strung together by a poker-face speaker with dead hands.

What we would like to touch upon now is effective visual communication for the deaf, applying components of basic ASL principles to Manual English, to have the best of both languages available to the deaf child.

Here are some examples:

1. Combination of ASL concept visualization with manual English one word -- one sign principle: The English word "run" has dozens of different meanings and an equal number of ASL signs. The deaf child often is not aware that these different signs are linked to one English word; on the other hand, the rigid use of only one English sign fo all contexts may lead to misunderstandings or cut down on the rate of learning and effective communication since

the incidence of words input is lower for the deaf. We suggest that the teacher sign all the words and dramatizes, either in pantomime or ASL, the key concept. For example, "Your nose is running." The teacher can use both the Manual English (ME) sign (run-ing) and then dramatize with the traditional ASL sign of a dripping nose. "My car is running (run-ing) smoothly now (ASL-engine purring away)." "John is running (run-ing) for President (ASL-applying or racing)." "My stocking has a run (run) (ASL-rip)."

2. Combination of ASL repetition for plurality, habit, difficulty, and duration with Manual English word ending: The sign can be repeated but the word is usually said once.

Examples:

Plurality: The stories (story-story-s) are good.

Habit: My father always watches (watch-watch-s) TV.

Difficulty: I worked (work-work-ed) hard yesterday.

Duration: I am learning (learn-learn-ing) a lot in this course.

3. Utilization of three-dimensional qualities of ASL directionality and sight-line when using Manual English:

Directionality: John gave the book to me. ("give" is signed from the giver to the recipient.)

Sight-line: John sees Mary who is sitting in a chair. ("see" is signed from John at eye-level to Mary at chair-level.)

4. Utilize the ASL inflection to show size, rate, intensity, continuity, and as a substitute for vocal inflection: Position, location and expressiveness of the sign must correspond to or approximate the concept being conveyed. Example: "He lives in a big house." (big may be emphasized by an exaggeration of the sign and/or an accompanying facial expression.) "He ran for dear life." ("ran" is signed very quickly and in the appropriate direction.) "He talked and talked..." ("talk" is repeated and repeated, the rate relating to speaker's speed and listener's level of interest.) Other important ASL elements include setting the stage and establishing positions, adhering to logical or chronological time sequences, knowing ASL signs, and idioms, and so on.

The above illustrates only a few examples of how an understanding and proficiency in ASL principles will lead to effective English communication skills for and with the deaf.

So far we have spoken in terms of young hearing impaired children. These elements of a communications consortium would be equally helpful, although the degree and manner of use would very, in teaching English to older deaf persons. In this case, it has proved very helpful to make use of English as a second language technique.

We do not advocate wholesale teaching of new sign systems to those who work with deaf adults, but we do urge that those involved with education of the deaf become aware of the entire continuum, and decide what they wish to use with whom and why.

Thus we cannot de-emphasize the importance of knowing and feeling comfortable with both the American Sign Language and Manual English. This will lead to better communication skills on the part of both parents and school staff, and afford the deaf student increased educational opportunities and greater flexibility in social interaction. Bilingual education for the deaf is highly desirable, but since this is a relatively new idea on the school level, many questions and possibilities surround bilingualism in terms of educational principles, programs, procedures, and implementation. We educators of the deaf have ahead of us an exciting and challenging new field open for exploration and discovery towards the goal of helping the deaf student to become a truly bilingual person.

CURRENT COMMUNICATION TRENDS AT PROGRAMS FOR THE DEAF

I.K. Jordan, Gerilee Gustason, and Roslyn Rosen
Gallaudet University

A survey was done of communication modes presently used in schools and classes for the hearing impaired to determine frequency of use of various modes, both as the primary mode of communication and as a supplementary mode in special situations. Any recent change was reported as previous mode, present mode, class level affected, and year of change. The 796 responses (82% of those surveyed) indicate a large and continuing trend, with more than 64% of the reporting classes now using total communication. Questions were also asked about the provision of classes to teach sign language, the sign language book considered the primary reference, and whether standardization of signs was considered within the program.

In the education of deaf people in the United States today, there appears to be three general methods of communication most widely used: 1) the oral/aural method, 2) the Rochester method, and 3) the total communication method. In addition, Cued Speech is used in some programs.

Much discussion has taken place in recent years about the use of these communication modes in schools and programs for the hearing impaired, but little if any hard data have been available on how many programs use what mode -- total communication, the oral/aural approach, the Rochester method, Cued Speech, and so on.

Although the *Annals* directory published annually in April lists most known programs, their enrollments, the number of staff, and whether the program is day or residential, no mention is made of the school's communication philosophy. Likewise, the annual survey of hearing impaired children, conducted by the Office of Demographic Studies at Gallaudet College, includes a wealth of information about the young deaf population of the United States, but does not include information about the mode of communication used in individual school programs.

The recent proliferation of new sign systems designed to represent or encode English manually has added to the questions about communication. What system is used where and how widespread are attempts at standardization within programs are typical questions. Additionally, there is the question of whether programs offer formal instruction in signs to their deaf populations.

In an attempt to provide a hard data base for answers to these questions, and perhaps the eventual publication of a directory to aid those seeking programs using a specific mode in a given geographical area, a national survey of schools and classes for the hearing impaired was done during the 1975-76 school year.

For the purposes of this survey, we defined the four communication methods as follows: 1) Oral/Aural -- the use of amplification and speechreading without manual cues. 2) Rochester -- the use of fingerspelling in conjunction with speechreading and amplification. 3) Total Communication -- the use of manual signs, fingerspelling, speechreading and amplifi-cation.* 4) Cued Speech -- the system of hand cues utilized with speech for speechreading developed by Dr. Orin Cornett of Gallaudet College.

METHOD

Using these definitions and questions as a starting point, a questionnaire was constructed which asked what primary mode of communication a program used with classes at each level: preschool, elementary, junior high school, and high school. Also asked were the number of classes within each level; what, if any, secondary mode of communication was used; whether or not a recent change in communication mode had taken place (and if so from what to what and when); whether or not classes in Cued Speech, fingerspelling or signs were offered, and to whom. The questionnaire also asked what sign language book, if any, was used as a primary reference, and whether the program had been or planned to be involved in any attempt at standardization of signs.

The questionnaire was mailed October 1☒ 1975 to all 970 programs on the Office of Demographic S☒☒☒es mailing list. On February 9, 1976, a followup letter an☒☒☒ second copy of the questionnaire were sent to those prog☒☒☒ ☒hich had not yet responded. By June, 1976, the total n☒☒☒☒☒☒ of responses was 796, which represents a response fro☒☒☒☒☒ of the programs surveyed.

RESULTS

The responses were coded by the Offic☒☒☒☒ ☒ographic Studies and entered on a computer for anal☒☒☒☒☒☒ first analysis was a simple count of the number of ☒☒☒☒☒eporting use of the various modes of communication ☒☒ ☒☒☒☒☒t school levels (see Table 1). By far the most frequen☒☒☒☒☒☒☒ meth-ods were Oral/Aural and Total Communicati☒☒☒☒☒ ☒o com-munication modes together make up ove☒☒☒☒☒☒ ☒☒☒ pro-grams responding. (The total number ☒☒☒☒☒☒☒☒cation

Figure 1. Number of Programs Reporting a C☒☒☒☒☒☒Com-munication Each Year.

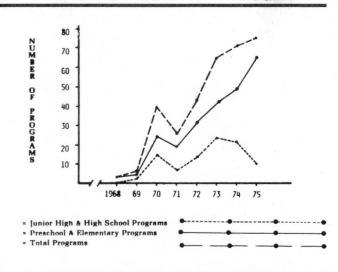

Junior High & High School Programs ....
Preschool & Elementary Programs ————
Total Programs — —

Reprinted with permission from *American Annals of the Deaf*, December 1976.

Table 1. Total number of programs reporting primary use of the 4 modes of communication at different school levels.

	Preschool	Elementary	Junior High School	High School
Total Number of Programs With Classes at Each Level	552	625	369	305
Cued Speech	9	8	6	7
Oral/Aural	284	341	195	148
Rochester Method	10	13	9	6
Total Communication	324	411	212	192
Total	627	773	422	353

Table 2. Total number of classes reporting primary use of the 4 modes of communication at different school levels.

	Preschool	Elementary	Junior High School	High School
Cued Speech	10	14	6	7
Oral/Aural	522	1,240	359	249
Rochester Method	38	72	33	12
Total Communication	689	2,196	688	1,046
Total	1,259	3,522	1,086	1,314

modes at each level is greater than the total number of programs reporting classes at that level because some programs use different primary modes in different classes at the same level.) Since many programs are very small, perhaps a better indicator of the frequency of use of each mode is the number of classes involved. Table 2 presents this information. The predominance of the Oral/Aural and Total Communication modes is even more pronounced here than in the data reported for programs (Table 1). It is noteworthy, too, that the number of classes reporting the use of Total Communication as a primary mode is far greater than the number of classes reporting the use of the other modes combined.

In addition to primary communication mode, programs were asked to indicate what, if any, supplementary communication modes were used; for example, the use of Cued Speech to teach a foreign language. Ninety programs reported the use of an additional communication mode, as shown in Table 3. Again, the majority of programs reporting indicate the use of either Oral/Aural or Total Communication.

In order to try to detect any trends in the field regarding communication modes used in classes, the survey included a question about whether or not any recent changes in communication mode had been made by each program. Changes were reported by 343 programs or 43% of the responding programs. The number of programs changing to and from the different communication modes is presented in Table 4. (The totals of the previous and present modes do not always match, because some programs reported only the new mode.) From those programs which reported a change, a clear pattern appears. The trend is toward Total Communication.

The number of programs reporting change year by year is presented in graphic form in Figure 1. It can be seen that there has been a large and continuing increase in communication mode changes in recent years, with the majority occurring at the preschool and elementary levels.

Related to the trend toward Total Communication is the question of instruction in manual communication. Programs were asked to indicate whether they offered or participated in formal classes (and for whom) in fingerspelling, signs, and/or

Cued Speech. Table 5 presents the number of programs reporting formal classes. It should be noted that 308 programs state they offer or participate in formal instruction in signs to hearing impaired students. This finding is at odds with the widely held belief that schools might use signs, but none formally teach signs to hearing impaired students.

Next, programs using Total Communication were asked to indicate which sign language books they considered their primary reference source.

This question was included in an attempt to determine what form of manual communication was used by those programs reporting the use of Total Communication. The lack of agreed-upon definitions and the problem of terminology (i.e., Sign English, Signed English, SEE I, SEE II) precluded a simple question in this area. Therefore, all books which we judged best known and most widely used were listed, and respondents were asked to check the one book they considered their primary reference source at each level. To check for oversights (e.g., the omission of a frequently used book or the emergence of a new one), an "other" category was included, and those checking that category were asked to specify the name of the book. No additional, single book appeared often in this category. Most of those programs indicating use of another book were using a locally produced manual. Table 6 shows the number of programs reporting the use of each book at each level. (Since some programs checked more than one

Table 3. Number of programs reporting use of a supplementary mode of communication.

Mode	Number of Programs
Cued Speech	9
Oral/Aural	33
Rochester Method	10
Total Communication	24
Other	14
Total	90

Table 4. The number of programs reporting changes from (previous) and to (present) the different communication modes.

	Preschool Prev.	Preschool Pres.	Elementary Prev.	Elementary Pres.	Jr. High School Prev.	Jr. High School Pres.	High School Prev.	High School Pres.
Cued Speech	2	0	3	0	1	0	1	0
Oral/Aural	90	3	131	1	44	1	37	0
Rochester	1	1	1	0	1	0	0	0
Total Communication	5	97	2	138	1	52	0	46
Other	4	3	2	1	4	0	6	0

Table 5. Number of programs offering or participating in formal classes.

	Finger-Spelling	Signs	Cued Speech
Hearing Impaired Students	244	308	20
Hearing Students	174	212	7
Teachers	232	300	12
Parents	245	318	6
Staff	217	283	5
Others	122	171	3

book, the total number of books used does not equal the total number of programs using Total Communication.)

In order to better compare the different books at each level, the percentage of the programs reporting use of any book at a given level was calculated. These percentages, shown in Table 7, were calculated by dividing the number of programs reporting the use of each book at a given level (e.g., preschool) by the total number of programs at that level using Total Communication. Since some programs reported the use of more than one book at the same level, these percentages sum to more than 100. It appears, from an examination of Table 7, that a large percentage of books at the preschool and elementary levels are those which present one of the newer systems of manual English. The total percentage of the Anthony, Bornstein and Gustason books at the preschool level, for example, is greater than the total percentage of the other seven listed books. Additionally, many of those programs marking "other" were using local material of similar nature. Related to this, a look at Table 4 will show that most of the reported changes to Total Communication were at the preschool and elementary level. It is safe to assume (and a look at the individual responses bears this out) that many of

Table 6. Number of programs reporting books as a primary reference source at each level.

Book	Preschool	Elementary	Jr. High	High School
Anthony: Seeing Essential English	44	54	22	17
Bornstein: Signed English Series	45	36	9	8
Fant: Ameslan	9	22	10	
Fant: Say it with Hands	27	39	23	
Gustason et al: Signing Exact English	119	159	59	
Madsen: Conversational Sign Language II	3	2	4	
O'Rourke: A Basic Course in Manual Communication	80	116	69	
Riekehof: Talk to the Deaf	22	33	19	22
Stokoe, Casterline, Croneberg: A Dictionary of American Sign Language	2	4	1	3
Watson: Talk with your Hands	37	54	28	30
Other: Please specify:	36	38	26	28

Table 7. Percentage of total communication programs reporting the use of each book, within levels.

Book	Preschool	Elementary	Jr. High	High School
Anthony: Seeing Essential English	14%	13%	10%	9%
Bornstein: Signed English Series	14	9	4	4
Fant: Ameslan	3	5	5	7
Fant: Say it with Hands	8	9	11	9
Gustason et al: Signing Exact English	37	39	28	26
Madsen: Conversational Sign Language II	1	1	2	4
O'Rourke: A Basic Course in Manual Communication	25	28	33	36
Riekehof: Talk to the Deaf	7	8	9	11
Stokoe, Casterline, Croneberg: A Dictionary of American Sign Language	1	1	1	2
Watson: Talk with your Hands	11	13	13	16

those preschool and elementary programs reporting changes to Total Communication are using a new form of manual English.

Finally, programs were asked whether they had made any attempt to standardize the signs they used within their programs. Of the 565 programs which had reported the use of Total Communication at some level, 340 responded yes, they had attempted standardization. Sixty-seven responded that such an attempt had not been considered, and 87 responded that while they had not made such an attempt, it was possible that they would do so in the future.

DISCUSSION

The data reported here made clear that communication modes in education of the deaf is a dynamic area. Three hundred forty-three programs, 43% of the 796 programs which responded, reported a recent change in the mode of communication used in the classroom. Of those 343, 302 changed from the Oral/Aural method and 333 changed to Total Communication. Conversely, 5 programs changed to the Oral/Aural method and 8 changed from Total Communication. Clearly there is a large change taking place in the direction of Total Communication.

A look at the number of classes using the various communication modes (Table 2) lends strong support to the conclusion that a majority of programs now use some form of Total Communication. Across school levels, the number of classes for each method is as follows: Cued Speech = 37, Oral/Aural =

2,370, Rochester = 155, and Total Communication = 4,619. Total Communication is thus the method of communication used in some 64% of all those classes included in the responses.

Another very interesting finding is the large number of formal classes teaching fingerspelling and signs. According to the responses received, there were 318 programs offering or participating in classes teaching signs to parents, and 308 teaching signs to hearing impaired students. There are many questions which could be asked concerning these classes, such as how frequently they meet, the qualifications of the teachers, whether or not credit is given, what text is used, and so on. This is a fertile area in need of further research.

Much more could be learned, too, about the standardization of signs within programs. It would be interesting to know on what criteria standardization decisions are made, by whom, how these decisions are disseminated, how permanent and useful the changes prove to be, and how they are received by the general deaf community.

Finally, it must be noted again that these are summary data from the entire country. Data for individual states or cities are on hand, and a directory of programs, arranged by state, is in the planning stage. It should also be noted that while the rapidity of change reported here indicates that such information will be very quickly outdated, these data can nevertheless be of significant value to professionals and parents in that they point to large and increasing changes in the area of communication in education of the deaf.

---

*Since this survey was done, the Conference of Executives of American Schools for the Deaf has agreed upon a definition of Total Communication: Total Communication is a philosophy requiring the incorporation of appropriate aural, manual, and oral modes communication in order to ensure effective communication with and among hearing impaired persons. (Annals, April 1976, p. 358)

AN UPDATE ON COMMUNICATION TRENDS AT PROGRAMS FOR THE DEAF

I.K. Jordan, Gerilee Gustason and Roslyn Rosen
Gallaudet University

This study was a followup of an earlier survey reported in the December 1976 *Annals* on communication trends in schools and programs for the hearing impaired in the United States. Although a lower response rate makes direct comparison of numbers impossible, the percentage of classes using the various communication modes is consistent with the earlier study, despite responses from only 25% of the state residential schools for the deaf. A modification in the question on recent mode changes points to an even more dramatic rate of change in the early 1970's and a continuation of the trend towards Total Communication. A shift towards the use of manual English sign texts is noted. Questions were added concerning the enrollment of hearing-impaired students in classes for nonhandicapped children (mainstreaming) and the provision of interpreters for such classes.

INTRODUCTION

The December 1976 *Annals* carried a report on a nationwide survey indicating that there was a large and growing trend towards the use of Total Communication in schools and classes for the hearing impaired in the United States. This survey included responses from 82% of all programs in the country listed by the Office of Demographic Studies at Gallaudet College, which included even more programs than the April directory issue of the *Annals*. Changes in the primary communication mode used in the classroom were reported by 343 programs, or 43% of those responding. Some 302 programs had reported discontinuing the exclusive use of Oral/Aural communication as the primary mode in at least some classes, and 333 programs reported the adoption of Total Communication usage in some of all classes. Roughly two-thirds of all classes were reported to be using Total Communication, and one-third the Oral/Aural mode, with very small percentages reporting the use of Cued Speech or the Rochester Method.

A year-by-year graph of the 1976 responses indicated that the rate of change was dramatic and most marked at the preschool and elementary school levels. In addition, program reports of sign language texts checked as primary references indicated that at the lower school levels 45-50% of the books reported were Manual English texts. Books reported which were not on the list were usually local texts with a strong Manual English orientation, which added another 7-11% to these percentages. These trends towards the use of Total Communication, with an emphasis on Manual English, suggested that the Manual English texts might have been a factor in influencing such change.

One problem with the previous study, however, was a lack of clarity in the question concerning **change**, which asked for a reporting of RECENT changes. This created some confusion as to what was meant by **recent**. In an attempt to obtain a clearer picture of changes over the past decade and to determine whether the trend towards Total Communication and Manual English was continuing, had levelled off, or had reversed, a followup study was done in the spring of 1978. The 1978 survey also sought information on the number of children enrolled with nonhandicapped students for one or more classes at each school level (i.e., the number of children mainstreamed) and whether or not interpreters were provided for these mainstreamed children.

METHOD

The 1978 survey used the same definitions of communica-

tion modes as the 1976 study: Oral/Aural -- the use of amplification and speechreading without manual cues; Rochester -- the use of fingerspelling in conjunction with speechreading and amplification; Total Communication -- the use of manual signs, fingerspelling, speechreading, and amplification; Cued Speech -- the system of hand cues utilized with speech for speechreading developed by Dr. Orin Cornett of Gallaudet College. A questionnaire, similar to the one utilized in the 1976 survey, was developed, asking (a) the total number of students, classes, and schools involved in the reporting program, (b) the primary communication mode used in the classroom at preschool, elementary, junior high, and high school levels with the numbers of classes for each, (c) an explanation if none of the four modes described seemed appropriate as a description of that utilized in a program, (d) what, if any, supplementary mode of communication was used for any purpose, and (e) whether or not a change had taken place in a primary mode during the last 10 years and, if so, the number of classes affected at each level, the previous mode, present mode, and year of change. A simplified list of books based those most often reported in 1976 was included with the quest that a program check the one primary reference book each school level. Provision was made, as in 1976, for the ification of books other than those listed to guard again ights. A question concerning the standardization of si ithin the program was again included. New questions w added on the number of children mainstreamed or enrolled with nonhandicapped children in one or more classes at each level and whether interpreters were provided for all, some, or none of these mainstreamed classes.

This questionnaire was sent in the spring of 1978 to the 1,051 programs on the Office of Demographic Studies mailing list, with a followup letter and second questionnaire sent later to nonresponding programs. By midsummer responses had been received from 642, or 61%. In addition, 67 programs had returned the questionnaire as inappropriate for their populations (i.e., programs for hearing mentally retarded students, audiological service centers, and the like) or because the programs had closed. If these programs are omitted from the total, the 642 programs responding in the study represent 65% of the programs surveyed.

RESULTS

The responses were coded and entered on a computer for analysis. The first analysis was a simple count of the number of students, classes, and schools reported by the 642 programs (Table 1). It will be noted that the effect of mainstreaming has

Reprinted with permission from *American Annals of the Deaf*, June 1979.

Table 1. Total number of students, classes and schools included on the response at different school levels.

	Students	Classes		Schools
Preschool	1,424	851	(59)	582
Elementary	16,324	2,369	(101)	1,163
Junior High School	6,399	894	(84)	557
High School	7,138	988	(93)	479
Total	31,285	5,102		1,795

*Students reported as being individually scheduled for classes are shown in parentheses.

Table 2. Total number of classes reporting primary use of the four modes of communication at different school levels.

(Percentages are presented in parentheses)										
	Preschool		Elementary		Junior High		High School		Total	
					1975-1976					
Cued Speech	10	(0.8)	14	(0.4)	6	(0.6)	7	(0.6)	37	(0.5)
Oral/Aural	522	(41.5)	1,240	(35.2)	359	(33.1)	249	(19.0)	2,370	(33.0)
Rochester Method	38	(3.0)	72	(2.0)	33	(3.0)	12	(1.0)	155	(2.2)
Total Communication	689	(54.7)	2,196	(62.4)	688	(63.4)	1,046	(79.6)	4,619	(64.3)
Total	1,259		3,522		1,086		1,314		7,181	
					1977-1978					
Cued Speech	0	(0.0)	9	(0.4)	0	(0.0)	3	(0.3)	12	(0.2)
Oral/Aural	341	(37.6)	946	(37.5)	273	(31.7)	247	(26.3)	1,807	(34.6)
Rochester	3	(0.3)	19	(0.7)	3	(0.4)	0	(0.0)	25	(0.5)
Total Communication	563	(62.1)	1,546	(61.4)	585	(67.9)	691	(73.4)	3,385	(64.7)
Total	907		2,520		861		941		5,229	

created some problems in counting the number of classes, with 337 "classes" reported as individually scheduled. This should be kept in mind when comparing these numbers with the number of classes in 1976 and the number reporting the use of various modes. It should be noted that the total of 31,285 students reported here compares to the total enrollment of 47,3__ students reported in the April 1978 issue of the *Annals*.

Primary mode of communication

The second analysis was the number of classes reported using each mode as the primary communication mode in the classroom and the total number of classes. Table 2 presents this information for both the 1976 and 1978 surveys. Since the different number of programs and classes which responded to the two surveys makes comparing data difficult, percentages are also presented. The widely different number of classes reported (7,181 in 1976 vs. 5,229 in 1978) make any interpretation difficult. It may be noted that in 1976, the mean number of classes per program was nine, and in 1978, eight. A direct comparison of the numbers of programs and classes reveals a difference of 154 programs and 1,952 classes with the mean number of classes 12.7, suggesting that programs not responding in 1978 tended to be the larger programs. A check of returned questionnaires bears out this as-sumption, revealing that 41 of 55 state residential schools for the deaf chose not to participate in the 1978 survey. The difference between 1976 and 1978 in the total number of programs and classes reporting has not greatly affected the percentages of classes reporting the use of the various communication modes, which are basically the same.

Supplementary mode of communication

The use of a supplementary mode for a specific purpose, such as the use of Cued Speech to aid in teaching a foreign language, is summarized in Table 3 for both 1976 and 1978. Given the fewer number of programs responding to the 1978 survey, the larger number reporting the use of a supplementary mode suggests that programs are moving more towards the use of such supplements. The percentage of programs reporting such supplementary use is still relatively low (18% in 1978).

Table 3. Number of programs reporting use of a *supplementary* mode of communication.

	Number of Programs	
Mode	1975-1976	1977-1978
Cued Speech	09	13
Oral/Aural	33	57
Rochester Method	10	12
Total Communication	24	31
Other	14	20
Total	90	113

Changes in communication modes

In 1976, changes in the major communication mode used in the classroom were reported by 343 programs, or 43% of those responding, when the question was phrased to ask about **recent** changes. This question was clarified in 1978 to ask about changes that took place within the past 10 years and the number of responses increased sharply to 495 or 77% of those

Table 4. The number of programs reporting changes from (previous) and to (present) the different communication modes.

	Preschool		Elementary		Junior High		High School		Total	
	Prev.	Pres.	Prev.	Pres.	Prev.	Pres.	Prev.	Pres.	Prev.	Pres.
					1975-1976					
Cued Speech	2	0	3	0	1	0	1	0	7	0
Oral/Aural	90	3	131	1	44	1	37	0	302	5
Rochester	1	1	1	0	1	0	0	0	3	1
Total Communication	5	97	2	138	1	52	0	46	8	333
Other	4	3	2	1	4	0	6	0	16	7
					1977-1978					
Cued Speech	2	0	4	3	3	0	2	0	11	3
Oral/Aural	140	2	200	3	84	0	57	1	481	6
Rochester	2	2	2	1	1	2	1	0	6	5
Total Communication	2	149	4	212	0	100	2	76	8	537
Other	4	0	5	0	5	0	7	0	21	0

responding. It should be noted that when programs report a change, not all classes in a program are necessarily affected. The number of programs changing to and from the various communication modes is presented in Table 4 for 1976 and 1978.

While some of the differences between 1976 and 1978 reflect changes in the past two years, the larger number of reported changes for 1978 also includes previously unreported changes uncovered by the more specific wording of the question. This should be remembered when considering the greater number of changes reported and the stability of the percent of classes reporting primary use of the various communication modes.

The year-by-year number of programs reporting changes is shown graphically in Figure 1. Numbers of programs at the preschool and elementary school levels have been combined, as have junior high school and high school levels. Compared with 1976 figures, the changes in the early 1970's are much more pronounced. Far more changes have taken place on the preschool and elementary levels than at the higher levels, in keeping with the larger number of programs in existence at the lower levels. The drop in the number of changes reported in 1976 and 1977, coupled with the similar percentages of modes

Figure 1. Total number of program changes each year (not cumulative)

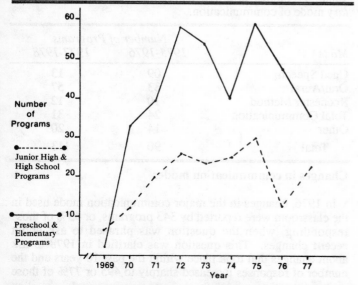

used at each level in the two surveys, may indicate a levelling off of the trend towards change, despite the larger number and percent of programs reporting such changes in 1978. Changes, however, are still taking place, and in the direction of Total Communication.

Primary reference books

Within the programs that utilize Total Communication, there appears to be a growing use of a Manual English sign system in the classroom, as indicated by the number and percent of Total Communication programs checking each sign language text as a primary reference. As in 1976, a question as to which sign language book the program considered its primary reference source at each level was included. This was an attempt to determine what type of manual communication was used while avoiding the confusion of terminology variations. Table 5 summarizes the number of programs checking each book at each level in 1978, with the number for 1976 given in parentheses. Table 6 reports the percentage of all books checked. It will be noted that if the category "other," which includes local texts for the most part, is not included, only one text which is not Manual English has increased in use at any level. The growing trend in Total Communication programs towards some form of Manual English, especially at the preschool and elementary school level, can be seen when the percentages of Anthony, Bornstein, and Gustason books are combined. If books from the category "other" are included, the picture is even more striking. These books now comprise a majority at the junior high level also and use at the high school level is increasing. Table 7 summarizes the Manual English books checked as percent of all books checked at each level in 1976 and 1978, with the "other" category percentages in parentheses.

Standardization attempts

The number of programs checking more than one book and the number reporting the use of a local text brings us to the question whether programs have made any attempt to standardize the signs within their programs. Of the 473 programs responding to this question on attempts to establish within-program consistency, 209 reported they had reached some agreement and 156 were working on such a project. Only nine programs had attempted, but discontinued, such efforts; 50 felt they might make an attempt in the future; and only 49 reported

Table 5. Number of programs reporting books as a primary reference source at each level, 1978 (1976).

Book	Preschool		Elementary		Junior High		High School	
Anthony: Seeing Essential English	33	(44)	53	(54)	25	(22)	19	(17)
Bornstein: Gallaudet Preschool Signed English Storybooks/Dictionary	94	(45)	82	(36)	25	(9)	13	(8)
Fant: Ameslan	5	(9)	11	(22)	9	(10)	18	(13)
Fant: Say It with Hands	12	(27)	17	(39)	11	(23)	14	(17)
Gustason, Pfetzing, Zawolkow: Signing Exact English	116	(119)	183	(159)	110	(59)	71	(49)
O'Rourke: A Basic Course in Manual Communication	42	(80)	71	(116)	62	(69)	58	(69)
Reikehof: Talk to the Deaf	13	(22)	27	(33)	17	(19)	15	(22)
Watson: Talk with your Hands	11	(37)	27	(54)	21	(28)	18	(30)
Other	39	(36)	44	(38)	31	(26)	25	(28)
Total number of programs at each level (using TC)	275	(324)	374	(411)	221	(216)	175	(192)
Total books checked	365	(419)	515	(551)	311	(265)	251	(253)

Table 6. Percentage of all books checked for each book, within levels, 1978 (1976).

	Preschool		Elementary		Junior High		High School	
Anthony: Seeing Essential English	9	(11)	10	(10)	8	(8)	8	(7)
Bornstein: Gallaudet Preschool Signed English Storybooks/Dictionary	26	(11)	16	(7)	8	(3)	5	(3)
Fant: Ameslan	1	(2)	2	(4)	3	(4)	7	(5)
Fant: Say It with Hands	3	(6)	3	(7)	4	(9)	6	(7)
Gustason, Pfetzing, Zawolkow: Signing Exact English	32	(28)	36	(29)	35	(22)	28	(19)
O'Rourke: A Basic Course in Manual Communication	12	(19)	14	(21)	20	(26)	23	(27)
Reikehof: Talk to the Deaf	4	(5)	5	(6)	5	(7)	6	(9)
Watson: Talk with your Hands	3	(9)	5	(10)	7	(11)	7	(12)
Other:	11	(9)	9	(7)	10	(10)	10	(11)

Table 7. Manual English books checked as percent of all books checked at each level. Percent of "other" books are presented in parentheses.

	1975-1976		1977-1978	
Preschool	50	(9%)	67	(11%)
Elementary	46	(7%)	62	(9%)
Junior High	33	(10%)	51	(10%)
High School	29	(11%)	41	(10%)

that attempts had not been considered. In sum, 77% of the programs responding to this question in 1978 reported either actively working on this question or having reached agreement, compared to 69% in 1976. The problem of within-program consistency is apparently receiving an increasing amount of attention.

Mainstreaming of hearing-impaired students

In regard to the question of mainstreaming, programs were asked to list the number of children at each level enrolled in one or more classes with nonhandicapped children. At the preschool level, 178 programs reported such mainstreaming for 728 children out of a total number of 1,424 students reported by all programs at this level. Table 8 presents the number

of hearing-impaired students reported mainstreamed and the percent that this number represent of all hearing-impaired children in the survey.

No attempt was made to determine the number or type of classes in which hearing-impaired children were mainstreamed, e.g., academic, recreational, or vocational. These figures include, therefore, both students who may attend classes for the nonhandicapped the entire day and students who attend only one such class, spending the remainder of their day in special classes for the hearing-impaired.

Interpreters in mainstreaming classrooms

A related question was whether interpreters were provided for all, some, or none of these mainstreamed classes. The number and percent for each response are shown in Table 9.

DISCUSSION

The difference in response rates to the 1976 and 1978 surveys makes direct comparison difficult. However, the data indicate a continuing trend toward Total Communication in terms of program changes (Tables 2 and 4), an increased use of supplementary modes (Table 3), and a shift towards the use of Manual English texts at all levels (Table 6). The amount of change during the early 1970's is greater than was at first

Table 8. Number of children reported mainstreamed, and total number of children in survey.

	No. of children mainstreamed		Total children in survey
Preschool	728	(51%)	1,424
Elementary	5,518	(34%)	16,324
Junior High	2,736	(43%)	6,399
High School	2,583	(36%)	7,138
TOTAL	11,565	(37%)	31,285

supposed, although the proportions of the various communication modes have not changed significantly during the past two years.

New issues, such as individualized programming and mainstreaming, increase the complexity of summarizing data concerning number of classes. A similar difficulty in class counting exists for programs with rotating classes: Should one divide the number of students by a fixed number, such as eight, to arrive at the number of classes, or count the number of teachers of the hearing-impaired, or dispense with class-counts altogether and consider numbers of individual students? Such a problem must be addressed in future surveys.

It is obvious, however, that the area of communication in education of the deaf remains dynamic. The influence of legislative developments, expanded public information on deafness and communication, and the like, change the picture from year to year.

More information is needed on the large number of children reported mainstreamed for one or more classes, especially in view of the fact that the majority of these classes are without the services of an interpreter. It must be remembered that questions were not asked concerning other possible resource personnel. The marked shift towards Total Communication usage in special classes, as shown in this study, reinforces the assumption that there is an increasing acceptance of the merits of Total Communication. It seems puzzling that this acceptance is not evident in situations where hearing-impaired children are mainstreamed without the benefit of either Total Communication or appropriate interpreter services. The large number of students reported mainstreamed and the small number of interpreters provided makes this area invite further research, especially in relation to the provisions of Public Law 94-142 and an "appropriate" education.

It is obvious that the seventies has been a decade of change in education of deaf students and that many questions can and should now be researched concerning the effectiveness of these changes.

Table 9. Provision of interpreters in mainstreamed classes by programs reporting mainstreaming.

Level	No. of Programs	None		Some Classes		All Classes	
		No.	%	No.	%	No.	%
Preschool	178	135	(76)	16	(9)	27	(15)
Elementary	438	295	(67)	74	(17)	44	(10)
Junior High	305	180	(59)	68	(22)	39	(13)
High School	270	159	(59)	71	(26)	40	(15)

INFLUENCE OF CERTAIN LANGUAGE AND COMMUNICATION ENVIRONMENTS IN EARLY CHILDHOOD ON THE DEVELOPMENT OF LANGUAGE IN DEAF INDIVIDUALS

Kenneth E. Brasel and Stephen P. Quigley
University of Illinois, Champaign

Four groups of deaf subjects between the ages of 10-0 and 18-11 years were tested, employing the Test of Syntactic Ability, and the language subtests of the Stanford Achievement Test, in a study of the influence of early language and communication environment on later syntactic language ability. The groups, 18 subjects in each, were dichotomized by whether the parents were hearing or deaf and further subgrouped by the language ability of the parents if the parents were deaf, and by the amount and intensity of oral preschool training provided by the parents if the parents were hearing. The groups were labeled by the type of language used with them in infancy and early childhood: manual English, average manual, intensive oral, and average oral. Results showed significant superiority of the manual English group over the two oral groups on five of the six major test structures of the Test of Syntactic Ability. On the Stanford Achievement Test, the manual English group performed significantly better than the other three groups on all four subtests. The two manual groups performed significantly better than the two oral groups on every test measure employed.

From what is known about the development of language in the normal child, there appears to be an optimum period for such development. The critical years, or language formative years, appear to be those between birth and age five, when the most rapid development of verbal language takes place (Furth, 1964, 1966; McNeill, 1966). It has been estimated that the normal child enters school at age six with a speaking vocabulary of some 2,500 words and a recognition vocabulary two to 20 times that size (Smith, 1926, 1941, as described in Hilgard, 1962). The verbal language acquired in the early childhood years provides the foundation for all later language development and other learning in the normal-hearing child, and anything that interferes with the development of that foundation will likely interfere also with all subsequent learning. This early verbal language development is apparently strongly influenced by the quality of the language input the child receives from his parents and others he is exposed to in the first few years of life. The better the language model provided by the parents the better will be the language developed by the child -- provided there is no impedance to communication between the child and the parent.

In the case of deaf children, little impedance probably exists if the parents are themselves deaf and use manual communication with the deaf child. However, even when this is the case, the language input to the child will depend on the language level of the deaf parents, which in most cases will deviate considerably from Standard English. The problem between most deaf parents and their deaf children, then, in the development of early childhood language, is largely a matter of the language level of the parents rather than a problem of means of communication. Between hearing parents and deaf children, the quality of the language model is equally as important, but so, too, is the matter of impedance, since the hearing parent is likely to use the less visible means of oral communication. These two factors, type of communication and level of parental language, could be critical factors in the development of language in deaf children. The present investigation was designed to study their effects on such language development.

Most studies in this area to date have involved only one of these two factors--the factor of method of communication. These studies have attempted to determine the relative effectiveness of oral and manual methods of communication by examining the educational achievement, social adjustment, and language development of deaf children raised by deaf parents who used manual communication with them as compared to the progress on those variables made by deaf children raised by hearing parents who used oral communication methods (Quigley and Frisina, 1961; Stuckless and Birch, 1966; Meadow, 1968; Vernon and Koh, 1970; Schlesinger and Meadow, 1971). All of these studies have reported significant differences in favor of the groups receiving exposure to some form of manual communication in early childhood.

The basic hypothesis tested in the present study was that the language competence of parent models would interact with the method of communication used with the child in infancy and early childhood to influence the development of language in prelingually and profoundly hearing-impaired (that is, deaf) children. With the amount and type of exposure to communication and language controlled, it was expected that differences in parental language competence would be reflected in corresponding differences in language ability in the deaf children of those parents.

Table 1. Study Design (n=72).

| Chronological Age | Manual Groups | | Oral Groups | | |
	Manual English	Average Manual	Intensive Oral	Average Oral	Total
10-00 to 12-11	3m, 3f	3m, 3f	3m, 3f	3m, 3f	12m, 12f
13-00 to 15-11	3m, 3f	3m, 3f	3m, 3f	3m, 3f	12m, 12f
16-00 to 18-11	3m, 3f	3m, 3f	3m, 3f	3m, 3f	12m, 12f
Total	9m, 9f	9m, 9f	9m, 9f	9m, 9f	36m, 36f
	(N = 18)	(N = 18)	(N = 18)	(N = 18)	

METHOD

Study Design

As can be seen from Table 1, the study design included four groups of deaf subjects selected from three age categories: CA 10-00 through 12-11, 13-00 through 15-11, and 16-00 through 18-11.

Instruments

A questionnaire sent to the target population parents was used to help select the subjects of the study, and two measuring instruments were employed to compare the four study groups: (1) the Test of Syntactic Ability (TSA) and (2) the reading and language subtests of the Stanford Achievement Test.

Questionnaire. The questionnaire was a 21-item survey-type instrument to be completed by the parent with primary responsibility for the prospective subjects' care and training during the early childhood years. It was designed to screen the target population for suitable candidates for inclusion as subjects in the study by identifying the type of language and communication environment the child was exposed to in infancy and early childhood.

Test of Syntactic Ability (TSA). The instrument used for measuring syntactic language ability was the TSA, which was developed by Quigley and Power (1971) to study the development of syntax in the language of deaf children. The instrument was developed for use in a large-scale investigation which has been extensively reported in the research literature (Power and Quigley, 1973; Quigley, Smith, and Wilbur, 1974; Quigley, Wilbur, and Montanelli, 1974; Wilbur, Quigley, and Montanelli, 1975). The major reason for selecting the TSA for the present investigation was that syntax was hypothesized to be the variable most likely to be sensitive to the different types of language input to which the four groups of subjects were exposed in early childhood.

Stanford Achievement Test (SAT). With three exceptions, all of the study subjects were administered the Stanford Achievement Test batteries appropriate to their ages and grade levels in April or May 1972 by the schools in which they were enrolled. The three exceptions were administered the test by one of the investigators since the school in which all three were enrolled did not use the SAT. These three subjects were also tested in April or May 1972. Only the reading and language-related subtest scores of the SAT (paragragh meaning, word meaning, language, and spelling) were used in comparing the groups.

Subjects

General Criteria for Selection. Initial selection of the subjects for the study target population was based on the following criteria: (1) CA 10-00 to 18-11 years; (2) age at onset of deafness, 24 months or younger; (3) hearing-threshold level, greater than 90 dB (ANSI, 1969) in the better ear without amplification, averaged in the octave frequency range of 500 to 2,000 Hz; (4) minimum Performance IQ (PIQ) of 90 on the WISC, WAIS, or comparable measures of IQ; and (5) no educationally significant handicaps other than deafness, except for minor disabilities such as corrected visual defects.

Location of Subjects. After consulting the Office of Demo-graphic Studies (ODS) at Gallaudet College, 29 educational programs were contacted with a request for permission for the ODS to release pertinent demographic data on potential subjects. Names and addresses were obtained from schools which, according to the ODS, showed five or more students whose parents were deaf and who met previously outlined criteria for subjects. From the ODS, and from other sources, a target population of 470 names was obtained, 64 of which were eliminated for various reasons. Four-hundred and six questionnaires were then mailed, 266 to deaf parents of prospective subjects and 140 to hearing parents. Responses were subsequently received from 246 parents. Of the returned questionnaires, 32 were subsequently rejected for a number of reasons (too young, too old, one parent hearing and the other deaf, too much residual hearing, incomplete information, and so forth), leaving a population of 214 from which the study sample was drawn.

Manual English (ME) Group. The ME group had a mean Performance IQ (PIQ) of 121. They were discovered to be deaf at a mean age of approximately six months, were enrolled in a formal educational program for deaf children at a mean age of approximately four and one-half years, and had deaf parents who had good command of English and who used manual communication (MC) in the form of Manual English (ME) with them from infancy. Thirteen in the group had deaf siblings. Average income of the subjects' families was $15,972. Socioeconomic status (SES) factor was 1.14.

Intensive Oral (IO) Group. IO group subjects had a mean PIQ of 119, were discovered to be deaf at a mean age of 1.2 years, were enrolled in a formal oral educational program for deaf children at a mean age of just under two years, had parents who received formal training in using oral methods with their children, and used these exclusively and intensively in the home to supplement school training. Subjects had been enrolled continuously in educational programs since initial enrollment. Only oral methods of communication were still being used in the home for the majority of subjects, and in no case had any form of manual communication been introduced in the remainder before the subjects had reached nine years of age. One in this group had a deaf sibling. Mean income for the subjects' families was $17,569. SES factor was 2.62.

Average Manual (AM) Group. The AM group had a mean PIQ of 114. They were discovered to be deaf at a mean age of four and one-half months, were enrolled in a formal educational program for deaf children at just over four years of age, had deaf parents whose written language showed gross deviations from Standard English, and who used American Sign Language (Ameslan) with the subjects from infancy. Fourteen in the AM group had deaf siblings. Average income of the subjects' families was $9,306. SES factor was -2.02.

Average Oral (AO) Group. Subjects in the AO group had a mean PIQ of 107, were discovered to be deaf at a mean age of 1.2 years, were enrolled in a formal oral educational program for deaf children at a mean age of just over four years, had parents who received no formal training in oral methodology, and did not attempt any special training of their children before enrolling them in school. Only oral methods of communication were still being used in the home with the majority of the subjects, and in no case had any form of manual communication been introduced in the remainder before the subjects had attained eight years of age. None in this group had deaf siblings. Average income for the families was $10,000. SES factor was -1.61.

Table 2. Descriptive data, subjects, and parents, by group ($N = 72$, 36 male and 36 female subjects).

Descriptive Item	Manual English N = 18	Average Manual N = 18	Intensive Oral N = 18	Average Oral N = 18
Mean CA	14.8	14.8	14.8	14.8
PIQ°	121	114	119	107
Age deafness confirmed	0.6 yr.	0.4 yr.	1.2 yr.	1.2 yr.
Age began schooling†	55.8 mo.	50.7 mo.	23.9 mo.	50.5 mo.
SES factor of parents‡	1.14	-2.02	2.62	-1.61

° Difference in PIQ was significant ($p>0.05$) only between the ME and the AO groups.

† Difference between the two oral groups is the result of the selection process. (No control was exerted over the two manual groups in age began schooling.)

‡ Intensive oral group was significantly higher in SES than the other three groups ($p>0.001$).

Table 3. Parent and child preschool training: by group.

	Parents Received Training			Child Received Training from (Number of Types)			
Group	Both	Mother Only	Total	4 or More	3	2	1
Manual English	0	1	1	0	0	0	7
Average Manual	0	0	0	0	0	0	9
Intensive oral		14	22	8	6	4	0
Average oral		2	8	0	0	0	9

Table 4. Mean age subjects began schooling; number of hours per week of preschool training; and hearing aid usage.

	Preschool Training			Mean Age Began Continuous Schooling in Years
Group	Mean Age Began in Mos.	Mean Hrs. per Week	Mean Mos. in Attend Prior to Age 6	
Manual English	55.8	11	18.5	4.5
Intensive oral	23.9	18	47.2	2.8
Average manual	50.7	-	28.0	4.3
Average oral	50.5	11.2	21.7	4.2
Mean	45.2	15.1	28.9	4.0

	Hearing Aid Usage				
			Still Wearing Aid		
Group	No. Fitted w/ Aid	Mean Age When Fitted (yrs.)	All Or Most Of Time	Only When Req'd	No Longer Wearing Aid
Manual English	14	5.1	2	2	10
Intensive oral	18	3.2	8	7	3
Average manual	8	4.9	0	5	3
Average oral	13	5.1	3	7	3
Total	53	-	13	21	19
Mean	-	4.6	-	-	-

Procedures

The procedures used for administration of the TSA were those outlined in the TSA test manual. The SAT, as mentioned earlier, was routinely administered to all but three subjects in the study. One of the investigators administered the test to those three.

Statistical Analyses. Selected data obtained from the questionnaire were examined for differences among the groups in SES and PIQ. The rest were tabulated and are presented in table form in the "Questionnaire Results" section. The TSA and SAT were subjected to multivariate analyses of variance (MANOVAs) with three covariates (SES, PIQ, and CA) to three-way analyses of variance (ANOVAs), and to compare the combined manual groups with the combined oral groups, t tests of pooled means and pooled variances were used (Guenther, 1964).

The groups were also tested for homogeneity and independence using the chi-square test, and for equality of variance using Cochran's test (1941) (to check for possible differences in variance which would have precluded using the method of Scheffe for contrasts).

Descriptive Data

As can be seen from Table 2, the mean CA of each group was identical (14.8 years), and for three out of the four groups no significant difference was found in PIQ. The only difference in PIQ was between the ME group and the AO group (p > 0.05). Note that parents of the two manual groups determined that their children were deaf at around six months of age, while the oral group parents did not make this confirmation until their children were a little more than one year of age. It is likely this was due to the high degree of awareness of congenitally deaf persons that their child might be deaf. The socioeconomic status score (SES), an index composed of income, occupational level, and educational level, was highest for the IO group; next came the ME group, then the AO group, and finally the AM group.

Tables 3 and 4 show that the parents of the IO group, as contrasted with the other groups, sought out parent-infant and preschool training when the subjects were very young (mean

age 23.9 months). They also reported the subjects were in school an average of 18 hours per week during the preschool years, and the respondents reported intensive follow-up of school training in the home.

Four of the ME and 10 of the AM subjects were never fitted with hearing aids (Table 4). Among those in the two groups who were fitted with aids (at a mean age of about five years), only two ME subjects were still wearing their aids when not required to do so. The others in both groups had either discontinued wearing them entirely, or wore them only when required to do so at school.

All of the IO subjects had been fitted with the aids, at an average age of about two and one-half years, and eight still continued to wear them even when not specifically required to do so. Among the remainder, three had discarded their aids entirely and seven wore them only in school. The AO group included 13 who had been fitted for aids, three who still chose to wear them all or most of the time, seven who wore them only in school, and three who had discontinued wearing them at all.

RESULTS

Stanford Achievement Test

Only the scores obtained on the four language-related subtests of the SAT were analyzed. Because of the range of SAT batteries employed in the schools (from Primary I through Advanced I), it was not possible to obtain scores on the same four subtests for all subjects. Therefore, only those subjects were used for whom scores were obtained on the language, paragraph meaning, word meaning, and spelling subtests. One-way ANOVAs for unequal Ns and Scheffs's contrasts were used in the initial analysis of the data.

To take advantage of the more liberal Tukey (t method) contrasts, which requires equal Ns in the groups, the groups were balanced by either eliminating the scores of the subject of the most deviant age within a cell or by filling a gap with a cell by adding a hypothetical subject for whose scores the cell mean was employed. Effort was made to ensure that each cell was balanced on the number of subjects at each age level in such manner as to avoid skewing the data by eliminating subjects whose scores would raise or lower the group means unduly.

Table 5. Stanford Achievement Test means, all language subtests, and unbalanced and balanced cell *Ns*.

Subtests	Unequal Ns				Equals Ns			
	ME	AM	IO	AO				
Language No. Subjects	14	17	17	17	17	17	17	17
Mean CA	14.9	14.8	15.1	14.9	15.0	15.0	15.1	14.9
Mean Grade	8.1	5.6	5.6	4.4	8.0	5.6	5.6	4.4
SD	2.1	1.8	1.9	1.7	1.9	1.8	1.9	1.7
Paragraph Meaning No. Subjects	18	18	17	17	17	17	17	17
Mean CA	14.8	14.8	15.1	14.9	15.0	15.0	15.1	14.9
Mean Grade	7.0	4.9	5.3	3.9	7.2	5.1	5.3	3.9
SD	2.4	1.9	2.1	1.5	2.2	1.8	2.1	1.5
Word Meaning No. Subjects	11	14	9	11	9	9	9	9
Mean CA	13.7	14.0	13.8	13.6	13.7	14.0	13.8	14.0
Mean Grade	5.3	4.3	3.6	3.0	5.7	4.9	3.6	3.2
SD	1.6	1.7	0.9	0.2	1.4	1.7	0.9	1.0
Spelling No. Subjects	16	14	13	12	12	12	12	12
Mean CA	15.0	15.8	15.9	16.3	15.4	15.4	15.7	16.3
Mean Grade	9.4	7.9	7.8	6.8	10.9	8.2	7.5	6.8

Table 5 gives a composite picture of the four groups on all language subtests as analyzed by both types of ANOVAs. The ME group performed significantly better than the other three groups on all dimensions when the ANOVA for equal Ns was employed.

Test of Syntactic Ability

Multivarite analyses of variance (MANOVAs) were performed and showed highly significant differences among the groups on all 22 subtests of the TSA as well as on the six major syntactic structures tested, even after removing the effects of SES, PIQ, and CA singly and in combination. The results of removing the effects of SES, PIQ, and CA were as follows:

1. For multivariate test of equality of mean vectors, effects of SES eliminated: $F=2.19$; df 18,176; $p > 0.0051$.
2. For multivariate test of equality of mean vectors, effects of SES and PIQ eliminated: $F=1.87$; df 18, 173; $p > 0.0209$.
3. For multivariate test of equality of mean vectors, effects of SES, PIQ, and CA eliminated: $F=2.40$; df 18,170; $p > 0.0020$.

Due to limitations in the University of Illinois MANOVA program it was not possible to make paired comparisons of the groups on the six test variables to identify the source of the differences found. Accordingly, balanced design, three-factor analyses of variance (BALANOVAs) were used, with CA, sex, and group as three covariates.

CA and Sex. The BALANOVA showed significant differences in performance among the age groups on all test structures, with test performance improving significantly with age. Table 6 shows the mean percentage scores for male and female subjects in each age group on each of the six categories of tests. As can be seen, the females generally did better than the males but only on the negation subtests was this difference significant, and then only in the youngest age group (age 10 to 13).

Differences Among the Groups. As can be seen from Table 7, the ME group consistently outperformed the other three groups; the AM group outperformed the IO and AO groups; the IO group outperformed the AO group; and the two manual groups outscored the two oral groups. The significance of the differences can be seen in Table 8, which summarizes the results of Scheffe contrasts performed to pinpoint the source of the differences among the groups found by the BALANOVAs.

In analyzing the results of the six groups of tests of the TSA, it was found that the relativization structures were apparently the most difficult for the groups to master. Next most difficult were the verb usage structures, followed by pronominalization, conjunction, question formation, and negation.

When the two groups having deaf parents were contrasted with the two groups having hearing parents, significant differences were found in favor of the deaf-parent groups on every one of the six general structures as well as on overall TSA performance ($p > 0.005$). This supports previous findings which reported statistically significant better performance of deaf children who have deaf parents, over deaf children of hearing parents on various language tasks. It is when the groups are contrasted individually, however, that the reason for this better performance becomes clear. The ME group

performed significantly better than the IO group on four of the six major test structures; significantly better than the AO group on all test structures; but significantly better than the AM group on only one test structure (the most difficult relativization test) -- whereas the AM group was significantly better than the AO group on only one test structure (question formation); and not significantly better than the IO group on any of the six major test structures despite higher mean scores. Thus, the differences between the two groups having deaf parents and the two groups having hearing parents were contributed largely by the ME group.

DISCUSSION

Every effort was made in the present study to select four distinctly different groups of subjects. The ME group was composed of subjects whose parents were language-competent deaf persons who used MC from the time the subjects were discovered to be deaf. In 13 of the 18 families, there were deaf siblings who also used MC. This would mean that most or all of the daily conversations the subjects were exposed to were carried on in MC, with the language competence of the parents reflected in the grammatical structure of the form of MC used--Manual English.

The AM group was composed of subjects whose deaf parents' written language was grossly deviant from Standard English. The parents, therefore, would be unable (and possible would deny any need) to correct their children's communications to conform to Standard English, so the child would continue to use ASL. However, since the parents (and in 14 of the families the siblings) were MC users, the child would at least be able to communicate freely both receptively and expressively, and to observe and benefit from a great deal of communication going on around him, whether or not he was directly involved.

The IO group was composed of subjects whose parents reported they expended every effort toward obtaining the most intensive oral training they could find for their children; all mothers, and some of the fathers as well, sought and received training in oral methodology and used this training to implement and augment school training in the home--sometimes to the extent where the home became, in effect, an extension of the school and the parents become surrogate teachers. From the reports, it was clear that the parents of the IO subjects lost no opportunity to bombard the subjects with language through oral and written means, labeling the furniture, taking pictures and pasting them in scrapbooks with labels underneath, cutting out different colored objects and requiring subjects to match them with the spoken descriptions, and so on. Fixing up a special learning area in the corner of one of the rooms in the family home was a frequent tactic employed by parents who worked daily with their children.

The parents of the subjects in the AO group more or less left to the schools the educating and training of their children in language. Interestingly, the parents of this group often reported that the siblings were better able to communicate with the deaf child than were the parents or anyone else. It is possible that the siblings used gestures or pantomime to get their messages across to the deaf child. At any rate, language input was most likely severely restricted until the child entered a formal training program.

The major conclusion to be drawn from the present study is that language input made possible by early employment of MC permits parental language competence to influence the

Table 6. Test Of Syntactic Ability, mean percentages, all groups combined, by CA and sex (N = 72).

Total	Relativization	Question Formation	Negotiation	Conjunction	Verb Usage	Pronominal- ization
CA 10-00 to 12-11						
Male	60.7	59.8	71.5	61.5	64.9	57.6
Female	61.4	70.0	82.0	71.7	68.3	68.2
Total	61.1	64.9	76.7	66.6	66.6	62.9
CA 13-00 to 15-11						
Male	71.4	79.4	89.2	76.5	78.3	76.6
Female	67.6	79.4	89.7	78.3	72.3	78.5
Total	69.8	79.4	89.4	77.4	75.3	77.5
CA 16-00 to 18-11						
Male	70.3	85.4	87.8	80.1	74.9	85.0
Female	76.0	92.4	94.1	89.2	80.6	90.7
Total	73.2	89.9	91.0	84.6	77.7	87.9
All ages						
Male	67.4	74.9	82.8	72.7	72.7	73.1
Female	68.3	80.0	88.6	79.7	72.7	79.1
Total	67.9	77.8	85.7	76.2	73.7	76.1

Table 7. Test of Syntactic Ability, mean percentage scores, ranges and standard deviations by group and structure (N = 72).

Total	Relativization	Question Formation	Negotiation	Conjunction	Verb Usage	Pronominal- ization
ME						
Mean %	80.9	89.8	91.9	87.5	82.2	89.9
Range %	40.8-95.2	59.2-99.3	82.9-100.0	36.3-98.8	65.8-94.7	66.7-99.3
SD %	11.9	11.4	4.9	15.8	8.9	9.5
IO						
Mean %	66.3	76.0	84.9	73.1	69.4	71.2
Range %	47.6-92.4	34.5-99.3	53.4-97.3	26.3-100.0	42.1-89.5	23.3-98.0
SD %	13.3	19.7	12.3	21.2	14.3	23.1
AM						
Mean %	66.4	81.3	86.7	76.5	74.5	78.7
Range %	47.6-90.3	52.1-94.4	47.3-97.3	37.5-96.3	50.0-90.8	40.7-96.0
SD %	13.6	15.3	12.4	16.8	11.4	19.1
AO						
Mean %	58.1	64.0	79.4	67.6	66.8	64.6
Range %	43.6-75.8	28.2-94.4	43.8-95.2	30.0-93.8	51.3-85.5	32.7-97.3
SD %	8.5	18.6	15.3	15.8	10.7	19.3
Total						
Mean %	67.89	77.78	85.72	76.20	73.20	76.08
Range %	43.6-95.2	28.2-99.3	43.8-100.0	26.3-100.0	42.1-94.7	23.3-99.3
SD %	11.1	13.6	10.3	16.6	10.8	15.4

Table 8. Summary of Scheffe contrast results.*

Contrast	Rel.	Q- Form.	Neg.	Conj.	Verb.	Pron.
ME-IO	$p<0.01$	$p<0.05$	$p<0.10$	$p<0.007$	$p<0.025$	$p<0.01$
ME-AM	$p<0.01$	NS	NS	NS	NS	NS
ME-AO	$p<0.001$	$p<0.0001$	$p<0.005$	$p<0.01$	$p<0.005$	$p<0.0001$
IO-AM	NS	NS	NS	NS	NS	NS
IO-AO	NS	$p<0.10$	NS	NS	NS	NS
AM-AO	NS	$p<0.01$	NS	NS	NS	$P<0.10$
(ME + AM)- (IO + AO)	$p<0.003$	$p<0.001$	$p<0.03$	$p<0.03$	$p<0.005$	$p<0.002$

*No significant differences found in Cochran's test of equality of variance and chi-square test of independence.

child's developing language ability. MC provides the child with a ready means of communication that he can use to test his developing language ability with his parents, siblings, and other MC-using persons in his environment, and that he can modify according to the feedback he receives. If the manual language input is in grammatically correct ME, the child has greater opportunity to generate grammatical rules consistent with Standard English than if the language input is in Ameslan where the child's tendency to develop grammatical rules different from those of Standard English is heightened. By the same token, when communication is limited and labored, as in the case of only oral input, then language input is limited to the words he is able to learn to recognize on the lips, and language output is restricted to the words the child has learned to pronounce intelligibly. Generation of syntactic rules of grammar, therefore, would be dependent upon the quantitative and qualitative rate at which the child's speech and speechreading skills develop. Few children develop speechreading skills rapidly enough to be able to follow the verbal communication taking place among the adults and any hearing siblings in the child's environment; thus, the child is deprived of important language input during the first few years of his life.

The dozen or so studies of deaf children of deaf parents that have been conducted during the past 15 or 20 years have provided useful information on factors affecting the development of language in deaf children. Until recently, however, those studies have followed the same simple design of comparing just two groups of deaf children--those with deaf parents and those with hearing parents. The differences usually found in favor of the children with deaf parents have been ascribed to the use of manual communication by those parents. But this might be only one of several language-related factors on which the two sets of parents differ. Even though comparison of mean scores on a variety of variables generally produces results favorable to children with deaf parents, distributions of individual scores for the two groups usually reveal great overlap, indicating that hearing status of the parents accounts for only part of the variance. This should not be surprising. Since a whole complex of factors influences development of language in hearing children, it is reasonable to expect at least similar complexity with deaf children.

The present study has introduced a new factor into the basic design of previous studies--the quality of the English language used by the parents--and has shown this to be a significant variable, along with manual communication, in language development. A recent study by Corson (1973) introduced another variable--parental acceptance of a child's deafness--by studying deaf children of oral and manual deaf parents as well as deaf children of hearing parents. Corson concluded that parental acceptance was as important as the early use of manual communication in the development of deaf children. Additional studies are needed to further specify important variables. Among others, the following studies would add significantly to our knowledge.

1. Comparison of deaf children of oral deaf parents with the four groups of the present study would more clearly isolate the factor of manual communication and allow more controlled study of its effects. This would also control for the factor of parental acceptance of deafness.
2. The ability of hearing parents, or of others working with deaf infants and very young children, to acquire and use manual communication effectively requires investigation.

The results in language obtained by the deaf ME parents in the present study are impressive, but their ability to use Manual English as a native language might not be easily duplicated by hearing parents.
3. There is need for study of the use of sign systems designed to represent English. (See Bornstein, 1974 for discussion of various systems.) The Manual English used by the ME group parents in the present study was the combination of signs and fingerspelling typically used for that purpose by deaf people, few of whom use the recently developed systems such as Seeing Essential English (SEE). Those systems, which use only signs, might have some advantages over the Manual English of the present study, especially with very young children.

ACKNOWLEDGEMENT

Requests for reprints should be sent to Stephen P. Quigley, Institute for Child Behavior and Development, University of Illinois, 39 ICBD Building, 51 Gerty Drive, Champaign, Illinois 61820.

REFERENCES

American National Standards Institute (1969). *Specification for Audiometers.* ANSI S.36-1969. New York: American National Standards Institute.

Bornstein, H. (1974). Signed English: A manual approach to English language development. *Journal of Speech and Hearing Disorders*, *39*, 330-343.

Cochran, W. G. (1941). The distribution of the largest of a set of estimated variances as a fraction of their total. *Ann. Eugen., 11*, 47-52.

Corson, H. J. (1973). Comparing deaf children of oral deaf parents and deaf parents using manual communication with deaf children of hearing parents on academic, social, and communications functioning. Doctoral dissertation. Univ. of Cincinnati.

Furth, H. G. (1964). Research with the deaf: Implications for language and cognition. *Psychological Bulletin, 62*, 145-164 (1964).

Furth, H. G. (1966). *Thinking without Language.* New York: Free Press.

Guenther, W. C. (1964). *Analysis of Variance.* Englewood Cliffs, N.J.: Prentice-Hall.

Hilgard, E. R. (1962). *Introduction to Psychology.* (3rd ed.) New York: Harcourt, Brace, and World.

McNeill, D. (1966). The capacity for language acquisition. *Volta Review, 68*, 17-33.

Meadow, K. P. (1968). Early manual communication in relation to the deaf child's intellectual, social and communicative functioning. *American Annals of the Deaf, 113*, 29-41.

Power, D. J., and Quigley, S. P. (1973). Deaf children's acquisition of the passive voice. *Journal of Speech and Hearing Research, 16*, 5-11.

Quigley, S. P., and Frisina, D. R. (1961). *Institutionalization and Psycho-Educational Development of Deaf Children.* Washington, D.C.: Council for Exceptional Children.

Quigley, S. P., and Power, D. J. (1971). *Test of Syntactic Ability, Rationale, Test Logistics, and Instructions.* Urbana, Ill.: Institute for Research on Exceptional Children.

Quigley, S. P., Smith, N. L., and Wilbur, R. B. (1974). Comprehension of relativized sentences by deaf students. *Journal of Speech and Hearing Research,* 17, 325-341.

Quigley, S. P., Wilbur, R.B., and Montanelli, D.S. (1974). Development of question-formation in the language of deaf students. *Journal of Speech and Hearing Research, 17,* 699-713.

Schlesinger, H. S., and Meadow, K. P. (1971). *Deafness and Mental Health: A Developmental Approach.* SRA Project No. 14-P-55270/3-03 (RD-2835-S). San Francisco, Calif.: Langley Porter Neuropsychiatric Clinic.

Smith, M. E. (1926). *An Investigation of the Development of the Sentence and the Extent of Vocabulary in Young Children.* Iowa City: Univ. of Iowa Child Study Welfare, *3.*

Smith, M. K. (1941). Measurement of the size of general English vocabulary through the elementary grades and high school. *Genetic and Psychological Monographs, 24,* 331-345.

Stuckless, E. R., and Birch, J. W. (1966). The influence of early manual communication on the linguistic development of deaf children. *American Annals of the Deaf, 3,* 452-462.

Vernon, M., and Koh, S. D. (1970). Effects of early manual communication on achievement of deaf children. *American Annals of the Deaf, 115,* 527-536.

Wilbur, R. B., Quigley, S. P., and Montanelli, D. S. (1975). Conjoined structures in the written language of deaf students. *Journal of Speech and Hearing Research, 18,* 319-335.

INFLECTIONAL MORPHEMES IN THE MANUAL ENGLISH OF YOUNG HEARING-IMPAIRED CHILDREN AND THEIR MOTHERS

Kathleen E. Crandall
National Technical Institute for the Deaf
Rochester, New York

Spontaneous sign-language samples were collected in a controlled interactive situation from 20 young hearing-impaired children and their mothers. Inflectional morphemes in the samples were described by cher attributes and classified for syntactic function within utterances. Inflectional morpheme productivity did not increase significantly with age; mean manual English morphemes per utterance did increase with age. The first six inflectional morphemes used by the children studied were the same as those used by normal-hearing children. A good predictor of the child's use of inflectional morphemes was the mother's use of these morphemes.

Teachers of preschool hearing-impaired children use various forms of sign language that attempt to convey English. Parents of young hearing-impaired children are also being encouraged to use these forms of sign language with their children. One goal for the use of a highly visible manual form of the English language, along with aural-oral communication, is to accelerate the acquisition of English during early childhood years. Another goal is to increase the level of English proficiency achieved by the hearing-impaired population.

Recently, various sign systems directly related to English have been developed (Gustason, Pfetzing, and Zawolkow, 1972; Bornstein et al., 1973; Anthony, 1971). American Sign Language (ASL), the language used by many deaf adults in the United States, has a grammatical system that is not directly related to English (Stokoe, Casterline, and Croneberg, 1965; Bellugi, 1972; Bellugi and Fischer, 1972; Frishberg and Gough, 1973; Battison, 1974). However, many of the signs used in ASL are also used in these new sign systems. All sign-language systems have a means for carrying syntactic and semantic information that differs from that of spoken languages. The means in sign language is manual gesture, while the means in spoken language is articulated sound. When we attempt to convey English through sign language, we use the means--manual gestures (chers)--of ASL and the form--syntax and semantics--of English.

This situation raises the immediate question of whether the structure of one language can be conveyed to the language learner through a mode not native to that language. This study investigated one aspect of this basic question. It focuses on the acquisition of English inflectional morphology in an environment that includes manual English.

Research on the acquisition of spoken English has helped to clarify the process whereby normal-hearing children learn the bound morphological structure of their language. Brown (1973) reported that normal-hearing children learn the commonly used functor morphemes of English during their preschool years and that there is a consistent pattern to the order of acquisition of these common morphemes of English. Among the 14 most commonly occurring functor morphemes specified by Brown are seven inflectional morphemes. Brown rank orders these seven morphemes from most to least frequently observed as follows: present progressive, plural, past irregular, possessive, past regular, third-person regular, and third-person irregular. Brown reported three conclusions on the use of functor morphemes: (1) developmental order is relatively constant, (2) rate of development varies widely, and (3) mean morphemes per utterance is a good indicator of level of development of grammatical morphemes.

When English inflectional morphemes are represented in manual English they consist of chers, while the corresponding spoken morpheme is made up of phones. The chers used in ASL have been described by Stokoe et al. (1965). They proposed three distinct aspects for the lexical description of signs. According to Stokoe et al., a sign is composed of a tab (the location of the sign in space or on the body), a dez (the configuration of articulating hand or hands), and a sig (the movement pattern of the hand or hands). A fourth aspect, orientation, also seems necessary to distinguish between pairs of signs (Battison, 1974). Orientation refers to how the hands spatially relate to one another or to other body parts. In the Stokoe et al. notational system a sign is transcribed in the format $TD_o{}^s$, where T is a tab cher, D a dez cher, o an orientation cher, and s a sig cher. The tab feature is the aspect that distinguishes THINK, [1] $\cap G_T{}^x$, from ME, $[\,]G_T{}^x$. These signs are different only because of their placement; THINK is made at the forehead and ME at the trunk. A dez feature distinguishes THINK from KNOW, $\cap B_T{}^x$. Only the hand configuration differs in these two signs; THINK is made with 'G' handshape and KNOW with a 'B' handshape. THINK is distinguished from DREAM, $\cap G_{,}{}^{\check{\wedge}}$, by a sig feature. The motion for THINK is contractual and for DREAM is an upward repetitive wiggling of the index finger. TRAIN, $\bar{H}_o{}^{\ddagger}H_o{}^x$, contrasts with SHORT, $\bar{H}_>{}^{\ddagger}H_{\angle}{}^{\check{\imath}}$, because of its orientation. The palms of the hands face downward in the sign TRAIN and toward each other in the sign SHORT. These four distinct classes of chers constitute the cheretic component of ASL. This system can be considered as the level of ASL analogous to the phonological level of speech. In manual English, cheretic features

---

[1]Following convention, English glosses of signs are indicated by capitalization.

Reprinted with permission from the Journal of Speech and Hearing Research, 21:372-386 (1978). Copyright the American Speech-Language-Hearing Association, Rockville, MD.

are used to form the morphemes in spoken English. Currently, we do not know whether the hearing-impaired language learner will process this information and master the English language.

There are more differences between spoken English and manual English that may pose obstacles to acquisition. Phones occur sequentially to form syllables, while chers occur simultaneously to form signs. There is no sign level analogous to that of the syllable in speech (Bellugi and Fischer, 1972). A sign is a simultaneous combination of a tab, dez, sig, and orientation element. There are specific limits on the possible combinations of chers that are allowable in sign languages (Battison, 1974), just as there are specific limits on the possible combinations of phones allowable in spoken languages. However, there is no direct correspondence between a cher of manual English and a phone of spoken English.

In addition to chers occurring simultaneously, morphemes also occur simultaneously in sign languages. An ASL morphological element is not necessarily an independently occurring visible segment, but may be an aspect of a simultaneously occurring set of visual units (Battison, 1974; Bellugi and Fischer, 1972). For example, many verb signs in ASL include a spatial layout of people or objects in relation to the speaker to indicate semantic agent or object, or both. This information is conveyed by varying the direction of the movement of the sign while using the remaining chers of the sign to indicate the verb meaning. In manual English as in spoken English, morphemes are produced sequentially, and simultaneous morphological features of ASL may be dropped or may supply the receiver with redundancies.

In ASL, these features work to conserve time. Because of the simultaneous occurrence of morphemes, more information can be conveyed in a sign of ASL than in a spoken word and fewer signs than words are necessary to convey an equivalent message. This phenomenon has been substantiated by Bellugi and Fischer (1972), who report that a sign usually takes twice as long to produce as a word. Thus, they hypothesize that there may be a relation between the means of production of a language and the form that the language takes.

For the young hearing-impaired child to become proficient in English through a manual language, the information presented to the visual channels must stimulate language-learning mechanisms with usable English linguistic information, as does information presented to the auditory channels for the typical normal-hearing child. Existing information on ASL provides evidence suggesting that human visual neurological systems may dictate a different form of language when manual gestures are used. Manual English, a word- or morpheme-for-sign translation of spoken English, necessitates the use of more signs to convey a message than ASL. This rate change may make it more difficult for the receiver to perceive, discriminate, process, and recall the critical attributes of the language.

Table 1. Characteristics of subject group.

Age Group	ID	Age in Months	Age in Mos. at Initial Use of Sign in Home	Hearing Status of Parents	Hearing Level of Child (db ANSI, 1969)	Hiskey IQ
1	a	42	28	Normal	103	114
	b	43	00	Impaired	93	138
	c	44	00	Impaired	90	120
	d	49	24	Normal	87	110
	e	50	34	Normal	103	141
Mean		45.6	17.2		95.2	124.6
SD		3.7	16.1		7.4	14.1
2	f	58	24	Normal	109	102
	g	58	00	Impaired	107	143
	h	65	00	Impaired	100	100
	i	66	48	Normal	107	116
	j	68	36	Normal	96	114
	k	69	00	Impaired	104	130
	l	69	36	Normal	104	103
Mean		64.7	20.6		103.9	115.4
SD		4.8	20.5		4.5	16.1
3	m	71	47	Normal	110	93
	n	72	44	Normal	107	125
	o	76	36	Normal	106	167
	p	76	24	Normal	109	103
	q	78	24	Normal	105	115
	r	81	18	Normal	105	148
	s	83	00	Impaired	107	109
	t	83	48	Normal	99	107
Mean		77.5	33.5		106.0	120.9
SD		4.6	18.0		3.3	24.9

Research in the area of English acquisition by hearing-impaired children has indicated that problems are encountered in word ordering, semantic word choice, recursive formations, and bound morphology (Charrow, 1974; Quigley et al., 1976). Hearing-impaired adults often continue to have severe difficulties with the inflectional morphemes of English after they have mastered word order and semantic word-choice rules of English (Crandall, 1976). In manual English, distinctive use of English inflectional morphemes in a sequential fashion is advocated. However, we do not know whether a visual language input system that presents morphemes sequentially will allow the learner to form the correct hypotheses about the sequential morphemes of English. This study investigates the acquisition of the common inflectional morphemes of English by hearing-impaired children exposed to manual English. The specific questions raised were:

1. Is age related to development of manual English morphemes?
2. Do hearing-impaired children acquire manual English inflectional morphemes in the same developmental order as normal-hearing children?
3. Is there a relation between the child's use of these morphological structures and the mother's use?

METHOD

Subjects

The group studied included 20 pairs of mothers and children. The children were selected on the basis of the following criteria: (1) average hearing loss for the octave frequencies 250 through 4000 Hz greater than 85 dB (ANSI, 1969) in the better ear, (2) onset of hearing impairment before the age of two years, (3) parental use of manual English with the child by the age of four years, (4) IQ of 90 or higher on the Hiskey-Nebraska Test of Learning Aptitude (Hiskey, 1966), (5) 20/30 vision or better with or without corrective lenses, (6) absence of apparent motor disability, and (7) no indication of emotional disturbance.

Children were grouped by chronological age into three age ranges. Group 1 consisted of five children ranging in age from 42 to 50 months, Group 2 of seven children ranging in age from 58 to 69 months, and Group 3 of eight children ranging in age from 71 to 83 months. Table 1 shows some pertinent characteristics of the group studied. Hearing status of parents was not a subject selection criterion. Six of the children had hearing-impaired parents. All parents reported that they attempted to use manual English when communicating with their children, and all children had teachers attempting to use manual English in their classrooms. No effort was made to assess English proficiency of any of the parents. It was assumed that only the hearing-impaired parents had any knowledge of the grammar of ASL.

The manual English used by parents and teachers of the children in the study was a form in which contentives and free functors were borrowed from ASL whenever possible. The English derivational morphemes, inflectional morphemes,

demonstratives, and articles used by the group in the study were a selection of those described by Gustason, Pfetzing, and Zawolkow (1972) and O'Rourke (1973).

Language Samples

Each child-mother pair was observed for several 1-hr. periods within a 2-wk. span. Language productions were recorded on a videotape system. Recordings were played back for transcription using equipment with the capability for both normal and slow-motion display. Pictures, not objects, were used whenever possible to elicit language samples so that the child's hands would not be involved with a directly competing activity. To obtain representative samples of both the mother's language as used with the child nd the child's language, age-appropriate materials, free from direct interlinguistic reinforcement (printed reading matter), were chosen. The language stimuli consisted of mounted picture-sequence stories selected from a reading readiness program (Robinson et al., 1965). If the child had a favorite picture storybook, this was used if necessary. The mother was asked to tell the child a story from one of the pictures and respond to any of the child's comments or questions. They, she asked the child to tell her what he or she saw and, if possible, a story from another set of pictures. This interactive, rotating storytelling procedure continued for approximately 20 min. during each of several recording sessions. A sample of typical spontaneous two-way conversations that took place between the mother and the child was the desired outcome. Caution was taken not to elicit only one-word answers to specific questions such as "What's he doing?" or "What's that?" All language samples were collected in the home to increase the likelihood of obtaining a representative sample of the child's and mother's language. Parents were informed that this was an investigation of language acquisition and were asked to use the most comfortable form of communication for them when interacting with their child. Parents were not specifically asked to use manual English--it was felt this might bias their communication efforts. However, the investigator used manual English in the children's homes. This alone may have influenced some parents' use of that variety of sign language.

One hundred consecutive signed utterances were analyzed for each mother-child pair. Brown (1973) and Lee and Canter (1971) have reported that for spoken English a representative sample can be obtained from this corpus size. Language samples for all mother-child pairs were transcribed using the cheretic notational system developed by Stokoe et al. (1965) and using English glosses. Rules established by Lee and Canter (1971) for determining sentence boundaries and utterance count were followed. Additional rules for this study were established as follows: Utterances that had portions including doubtful English gloss transcription were counted, utterances that had portions for which the production of chers was not visibly intelligible were not counted.

Rules for establishing manual English morphological boundaries were developed (Crandall, 1974). The rules used conformed closely to Brown's (1973) guidelines for spoken English and included the following:

1. A morphological boundary (shown in transcriptions as | |) was noted when consecutive signs, TD_O^S units, differed in at least one cheretic parameter--a different tag (placement), dez (hand shape), sig (movement pattern), or orientation cher; for example, SAW, $\smallsmile V_T^{\perp}||$ ø $\sqrt{}B_{TT}^{0}$; BOYS, $\frown 5_D$ $_{\bot}^{\#[o]}$ || ø$S_{\bot}^{\cdot}$; DON'T KNOW, $\frown B_{\bot}^{\cdot}||_{D}^{\vee}$ The last example contains two distinct sig chers, x and $_P$. (Those signs notated with the pattern TD_O^{ss} contained two distinct sig chers, while signs following the pattern TD_O^{s} contained one sig cher for which two symbols were needed for an accurate description.)

2. All exact repetitions were counted as distinct morphemes, but repeated efforts at a single sign were counted once in their most complete form. When signs were repeated to indicate emphasis, for example, NO NO, ø3#ø3#, each occurrence was counted as a separate morpheme. Repetitions of signs to indicate noun plural would have been counted if contrasts indicating singular form had been present in the same transcription, for example, GIRL, $\lambda A_{<}^{\perp}$, GIRLS, $\lambda A_{<}^{\perp}||$; or CHILD, ø$B_D^{\vee}$, CHILDREN, ø$B_D^{\vee}||$. There was no indication in any subject's sample that such a distinction was being made.

3. Compound signs, for example, TODAY, ø$Y_D Y_D$ $^\vee||$ $\sqrt{}B_D G_D^{\vee}$; MAN, $\frown 5_D{}_{\bot}^{\#[o]}||$ ø $\sqrt{}B_D^{\Lambda}$, were counted as two morphemes; their two sign units differ in at least one cheretic parameter, and children seem to use the individual morphemes generatively. For example, the sign MAN shown her consists of two separate components that, when used individually, would be glossed BOY and TALL, respectively.

4. Signs for which the English gloss consisted of two morphemes but that did not contain at least one distinct cheretic change during production were counted as one morpheme, for example, CLOSE DOOR, $B_{\bot}^{\cdot}{}' B_T^{D}$. (This particular example is contrasted in ASL with OPEN DOOR, $B_{\bot}^{\cdot}{}' B_{\bot}^{D}$. In a morphemic analysis of ASL, these signs could be considered to consist of two morphemes, the sig and orientation chers denoting the action--open or close--and the tab and dez chers denoting the object.)

5. All verb auxiliaries were counted as one morpheme, for example, IS, $\smallsmile I_{<}^{\perp}$, WAS, $\lambda W^{T[s]}$ because there was no indication in the samples that children related these to a base form.

6. Negatives such as CAN'T, $\overline{G}_D{}^{\ddagger}G_D^{\vee}$, and DON'T, ø$B_D{}^{\ddagger}B_D$ were counted as one morpheme because the children did not seem to relate these to the positive form.

7. Proper names such as John Smith are counted as one morpheme by Brown. No occurrences of the combined use of

Table 2. Language datas for mother-child pairs.

Age Group	ID	Hearing Status of Parents	% Inflec. Morphs in Sample*		No. Dif Inflec. Morphs in Sample		MEMU	
			Child	Mother	Child	Mother	Child	Mother
1	a	Normal	0	0	0	0	1.28	1.23
	b	Impaired	0	0	0	0	1.44	3.11
	c	Impaired	0.4	0	1	0	2.49	3.80
	d	Normal	0.5	2.2	1	1	2.00	3.63
	e	Normal	0.5	3.9	1	3	1.87	3.27
Mean			0.3	1.2	0.6	0.8	1.82	3.01
SD			0.3	1.8	0.6	1.3	0.48	1.03
2	f	Normal	0	4.3	0	4	1.75	2.20
	g	Impaired	1.2	0.3	2	1	2.74	3.73
	h	Impaired	1.3	0.2	3	1	3.59	4.64
	i	Normal	0	3.3	0	2	2.33	2.48
	j	Normal	2.2	5.2	3	4	2.89	4.76
	k	Impaired	0	0	0	0	2.57	3.37
	l	Normal	3.7	5.2	5	7	4.64	6.17
Mean			1.2	2.7	1.9	2.7	2.93	3.91
SD			1.4	2.4	2.0	2.4	0.94	1.39
3	m	Normal	0.8	0.7	1	1	2.70	2.83
	n	Normal	1.5	9.0	3	4	3.34	4.36
	o	Normal	10.4	8.2	6	9	5.18	6.34
	p	Normal	9.2	7.4	5	7	3.79	5.38
	q	Normal	2.2	3.8	4	3	2.72	2.38
	r	Normal	2.2	1.0	1	2	4.54	3.92
	s	Impaired	0.8	0	1	0	2.57	2.45
	t	Normal	0.4	0	1	0	2.41	3.51
Mean			3.4	3.8	2.8	3.2	3.41	3.90
SD			4.0	3.9	2.0	3.3	1.02	1.42

*Number of inflectional morphemes per 100 morphemes in sample.

first and last names were observed in the samples studied. Ritualized reduplications, for example, **choo-choo** and **quack-quack** are also counted as one morpheme by Brown. In this study such reduplications were observed in the language sample of only one child who used the sign

WOOF-WOOF, $\eta\bar{\bar{B}}_\cup\ddot{B}_\cap{}^\perp$. This was counted as one morpheme. Diminutives such as **doggie** and **kitty** were not observed, neither were catenatives such as **gonna** and **wanna**.

8. Fingerspelled words were counted according to Brown's rules for spoken English.

The above rules apply to an analysis of the use of English morphemes in a manual mode and are not acceptable for an analysis of the morphemes of ASL. Because this study investigated the use of frequently occurring English inflectional morphemes in a manual English mode, morphemes that may have been used unique to ASL were not assessed.

Data Analysis

The language data obtained for each mother-child pair were (1) total number of sign morphemes used in the 100-utterance sample, (2) average number of manual English morphemes per utterance (MEMU), (3) total number of inflectional manual English morphemes used in the same sample, and (4) number of different inflectional manual English morphemes used in the sample.

A frequency ratio of inflectional sign morphemes to total sign morphemes used by each mother-child pair was determined and the percentage of inflectional sign morphemes was calculated (number inflectional morphemes/total number sign morphemes X 100). Analysis of variance and Newman-Keuls procedures (Winer, 1971) were used to compare percentages of inflectional sign morphemes, variety of inflectional morphemes, and MEMU at the three age levels. Those inflectional morphemes that occurred more than once in the language samples of the children were rank-ordered and contrasted with the rank order reported by Brown (1973) for these same morphemes in normal-hearing children's speech.

Regression analysis was used to study relations between the use of inflectional manual English morphemes by the child and language productions of the mother. Two backwards stepwise regression programs (Mate and Walsh, 1975) were run-- the first using percentage of inflectional morphemes, numbers of different inflectional morphemes, MEMU, and interactions between these variables in the mothers' samples as independent variables and the percentage of inflectional morphemes in the children's samples as the dependent variable; the second using the same independent variables and the observed number of different inflectional morphemes in the children's samples as the dependent variable.

RESULTS

Development of Inflectional Morphology

As shown in Table 2, older children as a group produced more English inflectional morphemes than younger children.

Table 3. Frequency of occurrence for bound morphemes by age group.

Morphemes	Number of Occurrences		
	Group 1	Group 2	Group 3
Past° ($\emptyset\,\sqrt{B_t}$) or ($[\,]\,\sqrt{B_t^\top}$)	2	9	40
Present progressive ($\emptyset I^>$)	1	10	39
plural ($\emptyset A_s^\perp$) or ($\emptyset A_s^>$)	1	5	6
Past† ($\emptyset D^\perp$) or ($\emptyset D^>$)	-	2	11
Possessive ($\emptyset A_s^a$)	-	1	3
Third person ($\emptyset A_s^\perp$) or ($\emptyset A_s^>$)	-	-	-

° Irregular form (occurred with English strong verbs).
† Regular form (occurred with English weak verbs).

Table 4. Comparison of order of acquisition of inflectional morphemes in hearing-impaired children's signs and normal-hearing children's speech.

Morpheme	Rank Normal-Hearing Children°	Rank Hearing-Impaired Children
Present progressive	1	1.5
Plural	2	3.5
Past irregular	3	1.5
Possessive	4	5.5
Past regular	5	3.5
Third person regular	6	5.5

°Brown (1973).

The mean percentage of inflectional morphemes used was 0.3% at 42 to 50 months, 1.2% at 58 to 69 months, and 3.4% at 71 and 83 months. Analysis of variance for percentage of inflectional morphemes by age level indicated age was not a significant factor ($F = 2.44$; $df = 2,17$; $p > 0.05$).

The number of different inflectional morphemes produced also changed with age (Table 2). The mean number of different inflectional morphemes used by children at 42 to 50 months was 0.6, at 58 to 69 months, 1.9; ande at 71 to 83 months, 2.8. Analysis of variance indicated age was not a significant factor for number of different inflectional morphemes produced by children ($F = 2.26$; $df = 2.17$; $p > 0.05$).

The children's MEMU for each of the three age groups increased by age (Table 2). The mean MEMU for those children at 42 to 50 months was 1.82; at 58 to 69 months, 2.93; and at 71 to 83 months, 3.41. Analysis of variance for MEMU by age level indicated age to be a significant factor ($F = 4.97$; $df = 2,17$; $p < 0.05$). Newman-Keuls tests indicated significant differences between the MEMU of the youngest group and the two older groups ($r_{1-2} = 1.11$, $p < 0.05$, $r_{1-3} = 1.59$, $p < 0.05$). The difference in MEMU between the two older groups was not significant ($r_{2-3} = 0.48$, $p > 0.05$).

Children in the study used from zero to six different inflectional morphemes in their sign-language samples. Mothers in the study used zero to nine different inflectional morphemes in their samples. When only those inflectional morphemes occurring more than once in a child's sample were considered, from greatest to least occurrence in the children's samples were the past irregular, present progressive, plural regular, past regular, possessive, and third person morphemes. The term past irregular is used here because it contained chers different from the past regular morpheme and occurred on those words glossed as strong verbs.

Table 3 shows the six most commonly used inflectional morphemes by age group and frequency of occurrence. Table 4 presents a comparison of the order of acquisition of these six inflectional morphemes by normal-hearing children studied by Brown and hearing-impaired children studied here.

Allomorphic variations consisting of two placement patterns were noted in the children's productions of the past irregular morpheme. The sign was placed either at a neutral location directly in front of the signer's body or at the right shoulder area of the signer's trunk. The placement of this morpheme may be a result of the placement of the previous sign. For example, the verb THOUGHT might be signed ⌢G₇ˣ||[] √B⁰₇ (the past morpheme contains the shoulder tab). Verbs that contained a head or trunk placement cher were followed by right-shoulder allomorphic variation. However, verbs consisting of other placement chers were followed by either variation. It seemed that these allomorphs occurred in free variation unless the preceding verb contained a head or trunk placement cher. There were insufficient data to reach a definitive conclusion on this observation.

Allomorphic variations consisting of two movement patterns were noted in the children's productions of the plural, past reg-

ular, and third person morphemes. The movement of the sign was either away from the signer's body or rightward. No consistent patterns for this variation were observed.

Relationships Between Mothers' and Children's Productions

One of the purposes of this study was to investigate the relationships between the child's use of inflectional morphemes and that of the mother. A backwards stepwise regression analysis was run using percentage of inflectional morphemes ($X1$), number of different inflectional morphems ($X2$), MEMU ($X3$), and interactions between these variable ($X1X2$, $X1X3$, $X2X3$) in the mothers' samples as the independent variables, and percentage of inflectional morphemes in the children's samples ($Y1$) as the dependent variable. The equation that yielded the best combination of low standard error of the residual, high F-value, and high multiple R was selected as the best model. The equation that met this criterion included the percentage of inflectional morphemes used by the mother and the interaction between percentage and number of different morphemes used by the mother ($F = 60.08$; $df = 2,17$; $p < 0.001$)[1]. The coefficient of determination indicated that this equation accounted for 88% of the total variation observed in the children's samples. $X1X2$ alone produced an equation whose coefficient of determination accounted for 79% of the variation. Inclusion of $X1$ in the equation accounted for an additional 9% of the variation. Inclusion of all remaining variables would have only accounted for an additional 2%.

A backward stepwise regression analysis was next run using the same independent variables to predict the number of different inflectional morphemes used by a child ($Y2$). The best equation was selected according to the above-mentioned principle. This equation included the number of different inflectional morphemes used by the mother and the mother's MEMU ($F = 27.75$; $df = 2,17$; $p < 0.001$)[2]. The coefficient of determination indicated that this regression equation accounted for 77% of the total variation observed in the number of different inflectional morphemes in the children's samples. $X2$ alone produced an equation whose coefficient of determination accounted for 67% of the variation. The insertion of $X3$ accounted for an additional 10% of the variation. Inclusion of all the remaining variables would have only accounted for an additional 0.4%.

DISCUSSION

Development of Inflectional Morphology

Data collected in this study showed no significant effect of age on percentage of inflectional morphemes or number of different inflectional morphemes in samples of hearing-impaired children's manual English. This finding does not mean that there was no change in morphological structure with age. The large variance observed within each age group suggests that factors other than age are at work, or that individual differ-

---

[1] $Y' = 0.78 - 0.63 (X1) + 0.21 (X1X2)$

[2] $Y' = -0.13 + 0.36 (X2) + 0.63 (X3)$

ences and age trends are being confounded. A longitudinal study is needed to understand better the function of age. This finding with respect to age is in agreement with Brown's (1973) conclusion that rate of development varies widely.

Investigation of order of development of inflectional morphemes revealed parallelisms between the hearing-impaired children in this study and the normal-hearing children studied by Brown (1973). As was previously discussed, Brown described the 14 most commonly occurring functor morphemes in young normal-hearing children's speech. Included among theses 14 morphemes are seven inflectional morphemes. The first six inflectional morphemes acquired by three normal-hearing children studied by Brown were the same six used by hearing-impaired children here. This observation supports Brown's conclusion that order of development of English grammatical morphemes is relatively consistent across children. Of these six morphemes, the past irregular and the present progressive were the only ones used with any great degree of consistency even by the oldest group of children. Brown (1973) reported that by the end of Stage IV, the language samples of three children he studied contained the present progressive, plural, past irregular, and possessive morphemes at least 90% of the time in obligatory contexts. None of the hearing-impaired children studied here had attained this proficiency level even though several of them had a MEMU exceeding the Stage V mean morpheme per utterance count (4.0) of the normal-hearing children studied by Brown. This finding suggests that for children in this study, Brown's stages cannot be used to reach the same conclusions as they can for normal-hearing children with respect to knowledge of English grammatical morphemes.

Four out of the six hearing-impaired mothers did not use English inflectional in their samples, while only two of the 14 normal-hearing mothers did not. Hearing-impaired mothers may either not be as fluent in the English language as normal-hearing mothers or they may have found it more linguistically convenient to avoid the use of these morphemes in their manual English forms. The hearing-impaired mothers also may have been conveying the semantic information contained in these English inflectional morphemes through facial expressions, differential use of space, or other ASL devices. As previously mentioned, such usages were not accounted for in this investigation, and thus would have been overlooked. The two normal-hearing mothers who used no inflectional morphemes in their signed samples consistently produced correct English inflectional morphemes in the speech that accompanied their sign, and there was no reason to suspect that they were ASL users. When these two normal-hearing mothers were compared with other mothers, including hearing-impaired mothers, these two mothers used a smaller variety of contentive morphemes than the other mothers. This suggests that these mothers were not as proficient in overall knowledge of lexical items as were the other mothers, and that the lack of English inflectional morphemes in their sign productions was caused by an overall manual-language disfluency.

In this study, age had a significant effect on MEMU of children. Children 42 to 50 months had significantly lower MEMUs than children 58 to 69 months and children 71 to 83 months. MEMU is potentially sensitive to increases in production of content words and free functor words as well as inflectional morphemes. For the hearing-impaired children in this study, increase in MEMUs were primarily caused by increases in the use of content and free functor words rather than by increases in the use of inflectional morphemes.

The following tentative conclusions regarding the development of English inflectional morphology in a manual English environment can be made from this study: (1) children do use English inflectional morphemes, (2) the order of development of these morphemes is consistent with that of normal-hearing children learning spoken English, (3) acquisition of manual English inflectional morphemes by hearing-impaired children occurs at a slower rate than acquisition of spoken English inflectional morphemes by normal-hearing children, (4) age is not a good index of level of development of inflectional morphemes, and (5) MEMU does not carry the same implications on the development of inflectional morphemes by hearing-impaired children as mean morphemes per utterance does for normal-hearing children.

Relationships Between Mothers' and Children's Productions

Analyses conducted in this study indicated that significant relationships exist between the language productions of children and their mothers. The percentage of inflectional morphemes used by a child was related to the percentage of inflectional morphemes and the interaction between percentage and number of different inflectional morphemes used by the mother. This finding is interpreted to mean that consistency of usage as well as variety of usage are important components in the child's linguistic environment, and that for a child to make the correct hypotheses about English inflectional morphemes, an environment that supplies him or her with consistent and contrastive use of these morphemes is needed.

The number of different inflectional morphemes used by a child was related to the number of different inflectional morphemes used by the mother and the mother's MEMU. This finding suggests that it is important for mothers to use a variety of inflectional morphemes in a rich environment of contentive morphemes when communicating with their children.

The mothers' use of manual English accounted for 88% of the variance observed in the percentage of inflectional morphemes used by the children and for 77% of the variance observed in the number of different inflectional morphemes used by the children. These results indicate that 12% and 23% of the respective variances could not be accounted for by mothers' language behaviors measured in the study, and that the remaining variance might be accounted for by the language behaviors of teachers and peers in the school environment. Several of the children in this study were in the same classes at school. However, children from the same classes often had large differences in the language behaviors assessed in this study. This observation suggests that the teachers' and peers' use of manual English is of limited value in predicting the child's use of inflectional morphemes and that the mother probably plays the primary role in the language acquisition process.

Investigators of normal-hearing children's acquisition of English morphology have not found significant relationships between the frequency of specific morpheme usage of the mother and that of the child (Brown, 1973). However, Brown reported that mothers of normal-hearing children consistently used these morphemes and only rarely were omissions observed. This was not the case with the mothers of hearing-impaired children. From the data presented in Table 2, it is clear that mothers showed a tendency to use more inflectional morphemes than their children at all age levels. However, the mothers in this study did not use these morphemes at the same frequency with which they were used in their corresponding spoken utterances.

The above results are interpreted to mean that the child's development of English inflectional morphology through sign language is related to his mother's use of manual English. This conclusion is not surprising as it is well known that children acquire the language of their surroundings. The above results also suggest that the basic inflectional morphology of English can be conveyed to the language learner through manual gestures. As the mother's form of sign language more closely resembles that of spoken English, so does the form of sign language used by the child.

Even though the children in the study were able to use English grammar in their sign language, it was not used with a high degree of consistency by either the children or their mothers. If parents and teachers are to be encouraged to use a form of sign language that closely resembles spoken English, they must be given instruction focusing on the use of a form of sign language that resembles English. Additionally, parents must be made aware of their critical role in the language-acquisition process. Without such instruction, the use of manual English will serve minimally in its goal to raise the English competency level of the hearing-impaired population.

ACKNOWLEDGMENT

The author expresses sincere gratitude to the West Suburban Association for the Hearing Impaired, Lombard, Illinois; the Lake-McHenry Regional Program for the Hearing Impaired, Gurnee, Illinois; and the North Suburban Special Education District, Highland Park, Illinois for their assistance in recruiting children and parents to participate in this study. Special thanks is extended to the children and mothers who so willingly and enthusiastically shared their language. This article is based on the author's doctoral dissertation directed by Patricia A. Scherer at Northwestern University, Evanston, Illinois.

REFERENCES

American National Standards Institute (1969). *Specifications for Audiometers*. ANSI S3.6-1969. New York: American National Standards Institute.

Anthony, D. A. (Ed.) 1971. *Seeing Essential English*. (2 Vols.) Anaheim, California: Educational Services Division, Anaheim Union High School District.

Battison, R. (1974). Phonological deletion in American Sign Language. *Sign Language Studies, 5*, 1-19.

Bellugi, U. (1972). Studies in sign language. In Terrance J. O'Rourke (Ed.), *Psycholinguistics and Total Communication: The State of the Art*. Washington, D.C.: American Annals of the Deaf, 68-84.

Bellugi, U., and Fischer, S.A. (1972). A comparison of sign and spoken language. *Cognition, 1*, 173-200.

Bornstein, H., Kannapell, B. M., Saulnier, K. L., Hamilton, L. B., and Roy, H.O. (1973). *Signed English Pre-School Dictionary*. Washington, D.C.: Gallaudet College Press.

Brown, R. (1973). *A First Language: The Early Stages*. Cambridge, Massachusetts: Harvard Univ. Press.

Charrow, V. R. (1974). *Deaf English--An Investigation of the Written English Competence of Deaf Adolescents*. Psychology and Education Series Tech. Report No. 236. Palo Alto: Stanford Institute for Mathematical Studies in the Social Sciences.

Crandall, K. E. (1974). A study of the production of chers and related sign language aspects by deaf children between the ages of three and seven years. Doctoral dissertation, Northwestern University.

Crandall, K. E. (1976). The NTID written language test: Procedures and reliability. Paper presented at the Annual Convention of the American Speech and Hearing Association, Houston.

Frishberg, N., and Gough, B. (1973). *Morphology of American Sign Language*. Working paper, La Jolla, California: Salk Institute for Biological Sciences.

Gustason, G., Pfetzing, D., and Zawolkow, E. (1972). *Signing Exact English*. Silver Spring, Maryland: Modern Signs.

Hiskey, Marshall S. (1966). *Hiskey-Nebraska Test of Learning Aptitude*. Lincoln, Nebraska: Union College Press.

Lee, L. L., and Canter, S. M. (1971). Developmental sentence scoring: A clinical procedure for estimating syntax development in children's spontaneous speech. *Journal of Speech & Hearing Disorders, 36*, 315-340.

Mate, K., and Walsh, M. (1975). *Getting Acquainted with IDA*. Rochester, New York: University of Rochester.

O'Rourke, T. J. (1973). *A Basic Course in Manual Communication*. Silver Spring, Maryland: National Association of the Deaf.

Quigley, S. P., Wilbur, R. B., Power, D. J., Montanelli, D. S., and Steinkamp, M. W. (1976). *The Development of Syntactic Structure in the Language of Deaf Children*. Urbana, Illinois: Institute for Research on Exceptional Children.

Robinson, H. M., Monroe, M., Artley, A., Hack, C., Jenkins, W., Aaron, A., Weintraub, S., and Greet, W. (1965). *Basic Reading Program*. Glenview, Illinois: Scott, Foresman.

Stokoe, W. C., Jr., Casterline, D. C., and Croneberg, C. G. (1965). *A Dictionary of American Sign Language on Linguistic Principles*. Washington, D. C.: Gallaudet College Press.

Winer, B. J. (1971). *Statistical Principles in Experimental Design*. New York: McGraw-Hill.

A VIABLE CLASSROOM MODEL FOR USING VARIOUS COMMUNICATION MODES

Becky L. Reimer, M.Ed.

The author in this article defines manual communication as consisting of fingerspelling, meaning-based sign systems, and morphemic-based systems. An eclectic approach towards utilization of all these systems is elaborated with special emphasis placed upon one morphemic-based system; that of Signing Exact English (SEE[2]). The author describes the English-related aspects of this system and its necessity of use for speech as well as English language development of hearing-impaired children.

The education of deaf children has been plagued with heated controversies ever since its institution in the United States. We have been more concerned with pedagogical beliefs than what is good and right for the individual child. This seems to be as true today when discussing manual communication and what should be the current system of preference and use within the schools.

Within this article the author will briefly describe various modes of manual communication, elaborate upon an eclectic utilization of such modes, and explain the **modus operandi** of one manual English system and how it can work to complement the speech and language development of hearing-impaired students.

MANUAL COMMUNICATION

For purposes of discussion, we can safely divide manual communication into three areas: (a) meaning-based systems, (b) morphemic-based systems, and (c) fingerspelling. Table 1 groups some of the more popular systems according to this categorization scheme.

Meaning-based systems in general are signed according to the meaning of the statement being communicated. For instance, the word **pipe** in the two examples following would each have a different respective sign since each means something different:

1. The **pipe** is full of tobacco.
2. The drain **pipe** was clogged so it flooded the street.

Within the group of meaning-based systems are two subcategories. One subcategory is American Sign Language (ASL), a language unto itself with its own syntax, idiomatic expressions, and unique ordering of concepts apart from the word order of English (Bellugi & Klima, 1976; Fant, 1972). All other systems listed under the meaning-based category are those that are combinations of English and ASL.

Morphemic-based systems are so named because signs cor-respond to morphemic units of words. The basic point of disagreement among the morphemic-based systems listed in Table 1 is their definition of what the morphemic roots are of syntax. These systems abide by the following rule structure (Anthony, 1971; Bornstein & Schreiber, 1976; Gustason, 1975; Gustason & Woodward, 1973):

1. One sign represents one English word/morpheme.
2. Signs must be used for morphemic endings and beginnings of English words.
3. The decision as to which sign is used for the English word is based upon the sound, spelling, and meaning of the English word. If the word has two of those three the same in various contexts, then one and only one sign is used in all contexts.

In the two example sentences given before, the word **pipe** would have one sign since it is spelled the same and sounds the same in the two uses of the word.

Along with the various sign language modes, fingerspelling can also be used -- an alphabetic system whereby one hand configuration represents one letter of the alphabet. Communication is done via spelling out words or parts of words and abbreviating.

Thus it is demonstrated that a system of manual communication encompasses meaning-based systems, and morphemic-based systems, as well as fingerspelling.

ECLECTIC UTILIZATION OF MANUAL COMMUNICATION

Within the classroom setting, all the various modes of manual communication are employed. Meaning-based systems are used along with morphemic-based systems as well as fingerspelling, but in a systematic fashion. The type and amount of a particular system used with an individual child depends upon

Table 1. Manual Communication Modes.

Meaning-based systems	Morphemic-based systems	Fingerspelling
[1] American Sign Language ASL Ameslan	[1] Seeing Essential English (SEE [1]) [1] Signing Exact English (SEE [2]) [1] Manual English (ME) Washington State	Rochester Method [1]Fingerspelling Alphabet Manual Alphabet Visible English
Amelish	[1] Linguistics of Visual English (LOVE, LVE)	
[1] Signed English Siglish		

[1] Published forms of these systems exist.

Reprinted with permission from *American Annals of the Deaf*, December, 1979.

(a) the child's language development level, (b) level of material presented, (c) setting, and (d) purpose of material or activity.

Child's Language Development

The general rule of thumb is the higher the level of language, the more a morphemic-based system becomes utilized. With young hearing-impaired children or hearing-impaired children in very early stages of language development, meaning is the all important factor for establishing communication. Meaning-based signs are used to establish communication, but morphemic-based signs are introduced very quickly and used as well. Justification for this appears later under the discussion of a manual English system. Fingerspelling is used also due to the fact that its frequency of use increases as the student acquires more language.

Level of Material Presented

If the material is extremely complex, a meaning-based system is used to transmit information to the student. If the material is a little above the child's linguistic capabilities, generally a morphemic-based language is used, thus constantly challenging the student linguistically and supplanting English language growth.

Setting

Special guest speakers, school assemblies, and other types of rapid presentation activities all generally require the use of meaning-based systems. The rapidity of presentation as well as distance from interpreter necessitates using a meaning-based system. Within the classroom settings, a morphemic-based system is emphasized but complemented by the other manual communication modes (see discussion under Language Development as a Receptive Process).

Purpose of Material of Activity

This is closely connected to setting. If the purpose is for pure transmittal of meaning, then meaning-based is usually used.

One student, when reading "The mother deer **called** to her baby deer" signed:

1. call (phone)
2. call (yell) + ed
3. call (name)

and then said and signed "call (phone), call (yell) and call (name) all the same; I like call (phone)." This demonstrates the ability of the students to become flexible within their manual communication system. Flexibility in language is an all encompassing goal for future language and cognitive growth as well as adaptability to society (Brown, 1973; Hewitt, 1974; Dale, 1976).

SIGNING EXACT ENGLISH (SEE[2])

The morphemic-based system this author implements within the classroom is SEE[2] (Gustason, 1975). This system was chosen for priority of usage because (a) it is a published system, (b) the text is easily read as it is in alphabetic form and uses picture representation, and (c) its definition of morphemic bases of words is more attuned to the author's concept of the same.

The author is presenting an indepth look at SEE[2] and how it can be used to complement speech and language development for the hearing-impaired student. The length of this section is necessary so that positive effects of this system utilization can be demonstrated which will hopefully be used in conjunction with the other manual communication modes. SEE[2] will be discussed according to some of its English-related components of homographs, affixes, contractions, and pronouns. Justification for its usage follows.

Homographs

Table 2 contrasts homographs with homonyms, heteronyms, and their respective representation in the two sign language modes of meaning-based and morphemic-based. Homographs, like the example of **right** in Table 2, are signed according to sound and spelling rather than meaning; thus allowing the hearing-impaired child to assimilate meaning from context as does a hearing child. A hearing child upon first hearing the use of **lock in a lock of hair** will think of lock as something that a key is put into, but will discount this definition because it would be nonmeaningful in that context. He/she will either ask what it means, figure out the meaning from context, or forget about it until the word comes up again. More discussion on this follows under idiomatic expressions.

Table 2. Representation of Homonyms, Homographs, and Heteronyms in the Sign Language Modes.

	Meaning-based	*Morphemic-based*
HONONYMS I *sent* you a letter. This penny is worth 1 *cent*.	2 different signs	2 different signs
HOMOGRAPHS Take a *right* turn. It is my *right* to be free. You are *right*.	3 different signs for each of the different contexts	1 sign—the word *right* sounds the same, spelled the same; thus meets 2 of the 3 criteria.
HETERONYMS The *wind* is blowing. *Wind* up the watch.	2 different signs	2 different signs

Table 3. Questions Forms Dependent upon Affixes in Response.

Question Form [1]	Affix Required [1]	Example
How?	-ly	How did he hop? quick*ly*
When?	-ed	When did you walk there? I walk*ed* there...
What kind of?	un-, -ing, -s	What kind of doll do you want? A walk*ing*...
How many?	-s, dis-	How many dogs were there?
Who?	-er	Who is she? My teach*er*
Whose?	-'s	Whose is that? Joe*'s*
What?	-ness	What is deaf*ness*?

[1] Simmons-Martin, A., 1977.

Affixes

Affixes in English are morphemes added to roots. SEE[2] has an elaborate system of 70 "sign markers" or affixes added to a base sign or root word. Some of the more familiar ones are: -ness in deafness, -ly in really, -ed in walked, and un- in unlike. These particular sign morphemes come into play in question/response situations as outlined in Table 3. Affixes also play a part in developing complex syntax, e.g.,

The critic nega*tively* critic*ized* the play but didn't just*ify* why. Not everyone was in agree*ment*.

This example is easy to sign in a meaning-based system or ASL but what happens to the linguistic input -- it is processed as a form without English affixes and functors.[1] Need we wonder why then the written expressive language of the hearing-impaired sometimes lacks functors as well as affixes when ASL is used alone?

Affixes are important in the following excerpt from "Frozen Victory" in *Images* (Houghton Mifflin, 1974), a fifth-grade basal reader.

Bret glanced back over his shoulder. There was a frightened look on his face. He seemed to realize that Jimmy had enough power left to overtake him before the lap was finished.

Then, at a time when he should have been putting every thought into passing Bret, Jimmy's eyes jerked sideways as though pulled by some unseen power. Off across the lake he saw Spot struggling. But more slowly. No one seemed to have seen or heard the dog. Everyone was so intent upon the race, and there was so much yelling, that no one was paying any attention to what was taking place across the lake.

In these two short paragraphs, affixes are required 26 times and are important meaning carriers for the reader as well as the writer. The affix "-ize" on realize certainly carries a meaning change for that word; the meaning gathered from usage and context by hearing language users.

Noun markers, a specific group of affixes, have been established in not only the morphemic-based systems but in Signed English as well. The more common of these markers are s, 's, -ist, and -er for dogs, dog's, pianist, and teacher, respectively. One student was drawing a picture of both his behind-the-ear aid and his friend's body aid. Underneath each he wrote: Garys aid, Brens aid. His friend, Gary came along and said, "Not many Garys, me, only one" and Bren said, "No, yours, Gary" and Gary signed back, "Gary's" to show Bren that it needed an apostrophe.

Another specific type of affix is the group of verb markers: -ing, -s, -ed, -en to represent present progressive, third person singular present, past, and past participle, respectively.

Other affixes are used for adverbs and adjectives. For a complete listing of these, refer to Gustason book *Signing Exact English* (1976, p. 2).

Pronouns

As is proper with ASL and like systems of signing, either a pointing system (Fant, 1972) is used for pronouns or they are fingerspelled. With SEE[2] a sign has been given for each identifiable pronoun (e.g., he, his, him, etc.). The author feels that changing from a pointing system to an identifiable sign has been very desirable. This helps to make sign language a less "active" process and requires the user as well as the receiver to process pronouns in much the same way hearing children do. This also helps the hearing-impaired child bridge the gap into the "vicarious" process of reading. Pronouns could be fingerspelled to do the same but with young children who constantly reverse he/she and him/her -- the SEE[2] signs give automatic and quick clarification along with gender identification. This does not mean the pointing system should be eliminated; when used simultaneously with SEE[2], it can complement and clarify as well.

Contractions

SEE[2] incorporates a unique sign for each of the following contractions: (n't), ('re), ('d), ('ll), ('ve), ('s), ('m). Observing hearing-impaired students acquire such contractions and then implement them in their daily language appears to follow the rule: They will first sign and say do + not for don't. Later they will say and sign do + n't in negation sentences (I don't like . . .); but in a command sentence (Don't do that!) they seem to sign do + not.

Language Development as a Receptive Process

Vocabulary development is one essential component to the receptive portion of language development. As a result of using initialized signs and requiring one to one correspondence between sign and word, SEE[2] has an enormous sign vocabulary.

It is common knowledge that the language of the hearing impaired is plagued with problems in English language development. Simmons-Martin (1977) has summarized research findings in terms of language problem areas and gives suggestions for what we need to do to increase English linguistic competency of the hearing-impaired. The author cites three such summaries along with suggestions and SEE[2] interactions in Table 4.

Along with English vocabulary problems, the hearing-impaired generally have difficulties with passive voice in both receptive and expressive processes (Russell, Quigley, & Power, 1976). ASL is signed always in the active case (Fant, 1972). In the passive situation, "The dog was hit by the car," it would be signed "car dog hit." SEE[2] helps this situation because signing straight word order is required. Passive voice development can be encouraged as it is in the following example:

Student (orally) . . . I --ut my hair.
Teacher (orally) . . . I hurt my hair.
(modeling)
Student (orally) . . . I hurt my hair.
Teacher (signs, SEE[2]) . . . How did you hurt your hair?
Student (signs) . . . No, I cut my hair.
Teacher (signs, SEE[2]) . . . You had your hair cut.
Student (signs) . . . Uh huh, I had my hair cut.

Another major problem area in language is idiomatic expressions. This relates back to the multiple meanings homographs carry. Young hearing children learn the multiple meanings of words through their experiences of hearing that word used in various contexts. The word generally sounds the same to the child even though it may be emphasized or de-emphasized. The following are sentences taken from a picture-sentence matching worksheet in *Rainbows* (Houghton Mifflin, 1974), a first-grade reader:

1. Here is the candy **store.**
2. They **store** things in trees.
1. There's no more **room.**
2. This is my **room.**
1. I want a **lot** of fish.
2. We can play ball on this **lot.**
1. Get me the **saw.**
2. We just **saw** the picture.

In all but one case (saw), SEE[2] would use the same sign for both words. Hearing children very early and easily sort out the multiple meanings of words even though they sound and are spelled the same.

As stated earlier, this is the area most disliked about the morphemic-based systems. Gustason (1975), in her introduction, says that the aim is not to replace the old systems with new but rather to make hearing-impaired children bilingual. To foster this type of growth in children, SEE[2] can be used in simultaneous combination with meaning-based systems like the following example:

Teacher: The car ran over the box. (SEE[2])
Student: Run over? (demonstrates literal interpretation)
Teacher: The car **ran over** the box. (meaning-based)
Student: Oh!
Teacher: The car ran over the box. (SEE[2])
Student: The car ran over the box. (SEE[2])

Teacher signs in SEE[2]: If student doesn't understand, teacher signs in meaning-base system and then goes back to SEE[2]. It is important that the student not only be exposed to meaning-base but also be exposed to SEE[2] so that "bilingualism" may be fostered.

Another example follows where a student used meaning-base and teacher went back to SEE[2]. The teacher signed and said to the student, "We will go to lunch when the long hand is between the 8 and 9." The child gestured by using one hand/arm to represent a line to 8 and one hand/arm to represent 9 and then pointed to the space in between the two arms and said, "tween?" Teacher then signed in SEE[2] as well as spoke, "Yes, when the big hand in **be+tween** the 8 and 9; at 23 minutes until 12."

Mothers and hearing children interact in much the same way as the above two examples. Mom says, "Get your buns in gear." Child says, "buns? . . ." Mom (most Moms, that is) proceeds to explain what it means and will generally go back and repeat, "Get your buns in gear."

Boatner and Gates (1969) have estimated that approximately two-thirds of our language contain idioms. Along with this, Simmons-Martin's (1977) summaries on research state that the hearing-impaired find metaphors difficult to grasp, e.g., I see, I hear you, I smell a rat. If these were signed in SEE[2] as well as a meaning-based system, intonation used, and were used in meaningful contexts, the students would begin to grasp the metaphoric uses. Simmons-Martin (1977) goes on to say that "teachers need to make a point of bringing metaphors and idioms in early; hearing children don't comprehend them at first either, but no one checks to see except 'candid camera' or Paul McKee." (Paul McKee is one of the authors of the Houghton Mifflin Reading Series to which I have referred.)

The author will briefly describe the development of the understanding of "You're pulling my leg" with her kindergarteners. She used it in a situation where students were telling some fib. The students responded with literal meaning comprehension, "I'm not pulling your leg (pointing to the teacher's leg). See, I'm not." The teacher responded with "No, you're teasing me. You're pulling my leg." This expression was used in SEE[2] for several days. During this time the students went from literal meaning and denial of action to interpreting it in their own words (teasing you), to using the expression (I'm pulling your leg). Other idiomatic expressions have developed faster than the first, such as "That's the breaks," "too bad."

The story in Table 5 is taken from *Lions,* a primer-level reader from the Houghton-Mifflin series (1974). Look at the following words and their idiomatic uses: **go, come, get, after, see, away, have.** Even at the primer level, students must be able to translate meaning from context; one way to expedite this procedure is to use SEE[2] or a morphemic-based sign system with students.

Title: **Fun With a Lion**
Come with me, Bob, I'm going to the jungle. I'm going to hunt a lion.
Where is this jungle?
Come on, I'll take you there.
I'm not going to hunt for a real lion. Real lions scare me.
It's not a real lion. You'll see.
There's the jungle, Bob. Do you see that lion? That's the lion we'll hunt.
This isn't a real jungle. And that lion can't run. We can't hunt lions here.
We can play that it's a real jungle. We can play that the lion can run
We'll run after it.
Lion, we're going to get you! Oh, oh! Here comes a dog! Look at its big teeth.
This lion is scared of big dogs. Run, lion, run! That big dog is after you.
Run, lion, run! You have to get away! That big dog will get you!
What's going on out here?
A big dog is after the lion.
That is a nice dog. A lion isn't scared of dogs, is it?
That lion is scared!
We have books here. We can look at pictures of lions. We can look at pictures of dogs. You'll see that dogs do not scare lions.
Here are the picture books.

Table 4. Research Summaries of Simmons-Martin and SEE[2] Relationship.

Research[1]	Suggestions[1]	SEE[2] Relationship
Inadequate use of synonyms.	If a child is using a given word in spontaneous speech, the teacher should be using *synonyms*.	S: He likes to show us new games. T: Yes, he dose *demonstrate a lot of new games*. *Show* and *demonstrate* are differentiated in SEE[2] by initializing.
Use fewer shades of meaning.	Be specific in the appropriate word. "Make a fetish about using the correct word for communication."	S: I see a group of cows. T: I see a herd of cows, not a group. Again, initializing distinguishes words for this purpose.
When they don't have appropriate vocabulary, they go the long way around. Instead of "lightning rod," they use "pole on the barn which draws lightning."	Use appropriate vocabulary, if given definition, make sure that you show it can be replaced by one word.	SEE[2] overcomes this by having one sign to word correspondence. ASL sometimes goes the long way around when depicting a concept; it is important to use SEE[2] in conjunction with ASL.

[1]Taken from *Optimal Learning by the Deaf Children*, developed for CEC's Early Childhood Education Institute Series: Institute Coordinator — Audrey Simmons-Martin, 1977.

Look at this big dog, Jim. Look at its big teeth.
Here is a big lion. Look at its big teeth! No dog can scare this lion!
Can we take the books to school?

Note: Story taken from Houghton Mifflin Reading Series, 1974.

Functors

The class of functors was discussed briefly before and is discussed in more depth here. There are about 160-175 of these little words in our English language that occur one-third of the time as researched by Roberts and Fries (Simmons-Martin, 1976). These little words have been commonly deleted from ASL as well as other meaning-based systems:

Dress pretty me have, instead of **I have a pretty dress.**

Most of these functors carry meaning but are typically unstressed in sentences and usually do not carry a strong auditory signal for hearing-impaired students, thus demonstrating the necessity for signing them. Say the following sentences aloud to yourself and notice the similarities in audition:

I have **a** pencil.
I have **the** pencil.

Each carries a different meaning and would be used as a different response, depending on the question asked.

In the Carrow Test for Auditory Comprehension of Language/TACL (1973), the test item for **front** has three pictures.

A dog in front of the car.
A dog in the front of the car.
A dog beside the car.

The stimulus sentence is "Point to the dog in front of the car." Another demonstration of the necessity of understanding functors.

The development of functors in hearing children's language is very interesting to follow. At the beginning stages (Brown, 1973) children speak in a telegraphic-like form. They use only those words most important for conveyance of message and delete the lessor important functors. As children mature, the functors are developed but only slowly and during quite a long time span even though they constantly are hearing these high occurring words. Those functors first to appear are those with high frequency, high perceptual saliency, and an important semantic role (Brown, 1973). This gives us all the more reason to be constantly signing or fingerspelling the functors for the hearing-impaired student.

Speech Production

The author finds SEE[2] to be a great help to speech production and intelligibility. Initialized signs help students with initial sound production. For syllable reproductions, SEE[2] helps carry the syllables across to hearing-impaired students. As an example, a student was saying **side down** for **upside down.** When signed in SEE[2] as up + side + down, the student was able to say all three syllables. One student consistently said the word **noise** for **noisy.** With SEE[2] this was clarified very easily by signing **noise** + **y** and the child could then reproduce **noisy.** Much the same could be accomplished via writing but it is cumbersome, interrupts the flow, and is not serviceable for the young child.

SEE[2] also helps make the auditory-vocal match for students. This is an example given to me by another teacher where only meaning-based signs were being used. In a verse from a song, the words are **I'm so glad.** Glad is signed as happy (meaning-based), and students mouthed happy or some other two-syllable counterpart. With SEE[2], a distinct sign is used for glad, thus allowing vocal, auditory, and meaning match.

Language Development as an Expressive Process

Language modeling as well as expansion are two techniques found to exist in the language interaction of a mother to her hearing child. The child says, "Mommy, flower dirt." Mother says, "Yes, I'm planting the flowers in the dirt (expansion).

These are pretty white flowers called daisies (modeling)." Simmons-Martin says that this phenomenon occurs 30% of the time with hearing students and should thus be the same or more with hearing-impaired students (1977). SEE[2] aids modeling and expansion through its one-to-one sign-written word correspondence, enlarged sign vocabulary, and system of affixes.

The morphemic-based systems have been under attack by experts within the field of deaf education (Bornstein & Schreiber, 1976; Stokoe, 1975). Stokoe (1975) says these new systems defy the psycholinguistic development of children from whole to part as they learn language. Some disagreement can be voiced on this point. Hearing children's initial responses are very gross or global, but gradually they become differentiated and structured (Brown, 1973). Simmons-Martin (1977) states that children learn coarse contrast first and move gradually to greater refinement following the pattern described by Jakobsen and Halle (Simmons-Martin, 1977) even though these hearing children are exposed to the refined English pattern constantly. SEE[2]/English output should not be expected for a long time for much the same reason hearing children do not become masters of English until many years after they start processing it. Young deaf children should not be forced to speak/sign in complete sentences when young hearing children do not. We should keep our language demands of hearing-impaired children more attuned to normal hearing children's language development.

SUMMARY

An eclectic approach to using various manual communication modes was presented within this article. This method of implementation, particularly of the SEE[2] system, has not been substantially justified by research at this date. Little research exists, that this author is aware of, on the effectiveness of morphemic-based systems even though their popularity in usage increases. Research is desperately needed; possibly research addressed to the acquisition of English as a second language (SEE[2]) would be of most benefit. Research methods, such as performance analysis (Hakufa & Cancino, 1977), could be used now by researchers of second language acquisition.

REFERENCES

Anthony, D. & Associates. (1971). *Seeing Essential English*. Anaheim, California: Educational Services Division, Anaheim Union High School District.

Bellugi, U., & Klima, E. (1976). The roots of language in the sign talk of the deaf. *Psychology Today*, 6, 61-64.

Boatner, M.T., & Gates, J. (1969). *A dictionary of idioms for the deaf*. Washington, D.C.: National Association of the Deaf.

Bornstein, H., & Schreiber, F. (1976). New signs...the pros and cons. *Deaf American*, 53, 4-6.

Brown, R. (1973). *A first language*. Boston: Harvard University Press.

Carrow, E. (1973). *Test for auditory comprehension of language*. Austin, Texas: Learning Concepts.

Dale, P. (1976). *Language development: Structure and function*. Winston, New York: Holt, Rinehart & Winston.

Fant, L. J. Jr. (1972). Ameslan: *An introduction to the American Sign Language*. Silver Spring, Maryland: National Association for the Deaf.

Gleason, H. A. Jr. (1961). *An introduction to descriptive linguistics* (rev. ed.). New York: Holt, Rinehart, and Winston.

Gustason, G. (1975). *Signing Exact English*. Silver Spring, Maryland: National Association of the Deaf.

Gustason, G., & Woodward, J. (1973). *Recent developments in manual English*. Washington, D.C.: Gallaudet College Press.

Hakuta, K., & Cancino, H. (1977). Trends in second language acquisition research. Harvard Educational Review, 47, 294-313.

Hewitt, F., & Forness, S. (1974). *Education of exceptional learners*. Boston: Allyn & Bacon.

Russell, W. K., Quigley, S. P., & Power, D. J. (1976). *Linguistics and deaf children*. Washington, D.C.: A. G. Bell Association for the Deaf.

Simmons-Martin, A. (1977). Optimal learning by deaf children. Reston, Virginia: Council for Exceptional Children.

Stokoe, W. C. (1975). The use of sign language in teaching English. *American Annals of the Deaf*, 120, 417-421.

BIBLIOGRAPHY

Bornstein, H. (1973). A description of some current sign systems designed to represent English. *American Annals of the Deaf*, 118, 454-463.

Bornstein, H., Kannapell, B., Saunept, K., & Hamilton, C. (1972). *Signed English basic pre-school dictionary*. Washington, D.C.: Gallaudet College Press.

Bragg, B. (1973). Amelish -- our American heritage. *American Annals of the Deaf*, 118, 672-674.

Conley, J. (1976). The role of idiomatic expressions in the reading of deaf children. *American Annals of the Deaf*, 121, 381-385.

Gilman, L., & Raffin, M. (1975). *Acquisition of common morphemes by hearing impaired children exposed to the Seeing Essential English sign system*. Paper presented at the annual convention of the American Speech and Hearing Association, Washington, D.C.

Madsen, W. (1967). *Conversational sign language: An intermediate manual*. Washington, D.C.: Gallaudet College Press.

Moores, D. (1970). An investigation of the psycholinguistic functioning of deaf adolescents. Exceptional Children, 34, 645-651.

Power, D., & Quigley, D. (1973). Deaf children's acquisition of the passive voice. *Journal of Speech and Hearing Research*, 16, 5-11.

COMPREHENSION OF INFLECTIONAL MORPHEMES BY DEAF CHILDREN EXPOSED TO A VISUAL ENGLISH SIGN SYSTEM

Michael J. M. Raffin
Northwestern University, Evanston, Illinois

Julia M. Davos
University of Iowa, Iowa City

Leslea A. Gilman
Keystone Area Education Agency, Dubuque, Iowa

A test of morpheme-based concepts was administered to 67 deaf children who were exposed to Seeing Essential English (SEE). Results indicated that these children show the following order of acquisition for the inflectional morphemes tested: plural -s, past tense -ed, present progressive -ing, possessive -'s, third person present indicative -s, comparative -er, superlative -est, and present perfect -en. There were no effects of sex, age, or school from which the subjects were selected. The main contribution to the subjects' performances were their lengths of exposure to SEE.

Within the past 10 years, education of the deaf in the United States has undergone significant changes. One of these has been the increasing use of manual communication systems as an adjunct to other teaching techniques for teaching English to hearing-impaired children. Several systems have been developed to represent the English language, including the suffix morphemes that carry information regarding tense, plurality, possession, and other meanings. Some controversy exists among educators of the deaf on the use of these systems with young children, particularly with regard to which of the manual communication systems is likely to enhance the learning of English most efficiently.

Recent research in the acquisition of English by deaf children has indicated that prelingually deaf children have not yet acquired the rules for many grammatical structures (Quigley, Wilbur, and Montanelli, 1974; Power and Quigley, 1973; Quigley, Smith, and Wilbur, 1974; Wilbur, Quigley, and Montanelli, 1975; Wilbur, Montanelli, and Quigley, 1976). The teaching methods to which the children in these studies were exposed were not specified.

A review of published research regarding development of morpheme usage by the deaf revealed only two studies directly pertinent to the problem. It is understood that the presence of given morphemes in certain grammatical constructions and the way morphemes are combined into words are determined by a verbally based language's morphological rules. All children, including the deaf, must follow the specific language's system if they are to produce meaningful and grammatically correct sentences in that language. Cooper (1967) proposed to evaluate the English language receptive and expressive abilities of 140 deaf children with second-grade reading ability, 176 older deaf children, and some normal-hearing children. He administered a 48-item test adapted from Berko (1958). The deaf subjects were selected from a school in which an oral-only approach to language learning was used. He found that the older deaf subjects performed at a level that was similar to seven-year-old normal-hearing children: 19-year-old deaf subjects were unable to attain the level of normal-hearing nine-year-olds. On the receptive test, he found that the order of acquisition of selected morphemes was the same for the deaf group as for the normal-hearing group.

Gilman and Raffin (1975) evaluated the expressive acquisition of some common inflectional morphemes in hearing-impaired children using Seeing Essential English (SEE). They administered a 40-sentence, four-item multiple-choice, sentence-completion test to 20 hearing-impaired subjects. These subjects were selected from various schools in Iowa and were eight to 12 years old. Each sentence was presented in association with a picture. The result demonstrated a definite order of acquisition for the morphemes tested. It was also found that the children's performances were highly dependent on whether the classroom teacher was consistent in her use of signs with the children. It was difficult to attribute the performance of the children to their exposure to a morpheme-based sign code, because the reading levels of the children were highly correlated with the number of years the subject had been exposed to SEE. It also could not be determined whether the results of the study were generated by the children's reading ability or by their exposure to a sign system that differentiated between the various inflectional morphemes because of (1) the small number of subjects who were tested, and (2) the nature of the task required of the children. Our 1975 results indicate that hearing-impaired children are likely to have considerable difficulty in the use of English morphology and syntax. The difficulties that the deaf exhibit with morphology may be, in part, a product of the communication systems to which they are exposed.

Because the consistent signing of morpheme-based codes is not a simple task, educators need to have empirical data on which to base decisions related to the use of such systems. The morpheme-based sign system of signed English, *Seeing Essential English* (Anthony, 1972) (SEE), *Signing Exact English* (Gustason, Pfetsing, and Zawolkow, 1972) (SEE2), and Wampler's 1971 *Linguistics of Visual English* [1] (LOVE) assume that deaf children are able to make sense of and to use the various signs for inflectional morphemes. This study was designed to acquire data either to support or contradict this basic assumption.

METHOD

Test Materials

The test materials consisted of sentences, spoken and signed simultaneously, which represented both correct and incorrect

---

[1] No longer available

use of eight commonly used morphemes. The sentences were signed in Seeing Essential English using the version available in 1971. The morphemes tested were past tense **-ed**, third person singular present indicative **-s**, present progressive **-ing**, present perfect **-en**, plural **-s** on nouns, possessive **-'s**, comparative **-er**, and superlative **-est**. Each morpheme was represented by six sentences (two in which they were used correctly and four in which they were used incorrectly) ranging in length from four to seven words. Forty-eight sentences were presented.

The sentences had the same structure and the same number of words. Basic sentence structure throughout the test was noun-phrase, verb-phrase, and noun or verb-phrase. For the comparative **-er** and the superlative **-est**, however, it was necessary to modify this basic structure. Sentences in which a comparative was being tested contained **than the** and sentences in which the superlative was being tested contained **of all**. Vocabulary in the test was chosen to be within the vocabulary knowledge of the subjects used. The sentences used are presented in Raffin, 1976.

Delineation of Artifacts in Test Materials

The test materials were administered to a group of normal-hearing children to delineate any artifacts that might affect the results. The purpose was to determine whether young children could understand the task required of them and whether young normal-hearing children's performances on the test were comparable to those reported in the literature.

Procedures. The test was administered to 12 normal-hearing children ranging in age from four years and nine months to six years and two months. The sentences were tape-recorded by a female speaker and presented to each subject individually in a room free of distractions. The speaker spoke each sentence distinctly and with normal inflections and failed to exhibit any regional accent. The following instructions were given:

> On this tape you will hear some sentences. You will hear each sentence two times. If you think the sentence is right, circle the smiling face in front of you. If you think the sentence is wrong, circle the unhappy face on your answer sheet. Do you understand?

Subjects were given as long as necessary to respond to each sentence, and no sentence was given until a response had been obtained for the previous sentence. Eight practice sentences were presented with immediate feedback, followed by the 48 test sentences, without feedback.

Results. None of the normal-hearing subjects required a clarification of the instructions. The scores of these subjects ranged from 33 to 45 correct out of a possible 48. The frequency distribution of these scores is as follows:

Score	Frequency
33	1
36	1
37	1
38	2
39	2
40	3
42	1
45	1

No sentence was missed by all subjects, nor was any sentence missed substantially more often than any other sentence,

except for those testing **-en** and **-est**. The distribution of errors for normal-hearing subjects, according to the morphemes tested, was:

Morpheme	Numbers of Errors
Present perfect *-en*	31
Supurlative *-est*	19
Comparative *-er*	14
Third person singular present indicative *-s*	13
Possessive *-'s*	10
Present progressive *-ing*	8
Plural *-s*	7
Past tense *-ed*	7

Discussion. Normal-hearing subjects between four and six years of age performed beyond the 0.01 level above chance, and 11 of the 12 subjects performed beyond the 0.001 level above chance. These results are in agreement with the data published in the literature that indicate that children in this age group can accurately use the morphemes tested. The poorer performance of the subjects on sentences testing the present perfect **-en** suffix is also in agreement with Brown's data, which suggest that normal-hearing children often do not use this inflectional morpheme accurately, even in eighth grade. The relative order of acquisition demonstrated by the subjects in the present experiment also agrees with the order found by Brown (1973). These results were interpreted as evidence that no serious artifacts existed in the stimuli that would cause skewed performance in the experimental population.

Recording of Test Materials

A native American female, proficient in the signing of Seeing Essential English (SEE), spoke and simultaneously signed the sentences. Her spoken and signed sentences were recorded on a black-and-white videotape recorder. The instructions for the task and practice sentences were recorded, followed by the 48 sentences, each of which was signed and spoken twice. A 1000-Hz pulse also was recorded immediately following each sentence.

Testing Paradigm

Each subject was tested individually in a room free from distractions. The instructions to the subjects were repeated until subjects indicated they understood. A two-button system was employed. Subjects pressed one button if they thought the sentence presented was right, and the other button if they thought the sentence presented was wrong. To facilitate the subjects' understanding of this procedure, the buttons were labeled and color-coded in black and white. Although the subjects were instructed to proceed as quickly as possible, a sentence was not presented until a response had been obtained for the preceding sentence.

The experimental test tape was played back on a videotape recorder. The transport system and record and playback heads of the recorder fed the signals to a videotape monitor (12 in. [30 cm] diagonal, black and white). The soundtrack output of the recorder also was fed to a Universal EPUT and timer. The pulse at the end of each sentence served to trigger this timer. When a subject pressed either button the timer would stop. To obtain a graphic copy of the reading on the timer, a printer was connected to the timer. One of the buttons being pressed caused the printout from the printer to be in red, the other button caused it to be in black. Thus, it was possible to obtain a

Table 1. Frequency distribution of scores obtained from deaf subjects.

Score	Frequency	Percentage of Subjects
26	1	1.5
28	1	1.5
29	2	2.9
30	4	6.0
31	6	9.0
32	5	7.5
33	9	13.4
34	8	11.9
35	5	7.5
36	7	10.4
37	6	9.0
38	6	9.0
39	4	6.0
40	1	1.5
41	1	1.5
44	1	1.5

permanent copy of the reaction times of each subject, as well as an indication of the correctness of each subject's responses.

Reaction times were measured in an attempt to obtain some information about the relative confidence the subjects had in their answers. It was believed that if the subjects were confident of their answers, reaction times would be faster, and if the subjects were not so confident in their answers there would be some hesitation reflected in slower reaction times.

The sound track output was adjusted so that the sound level was at a comfortable loudness for a normal-hearing listener (approximately 60-dB SPL overall).

Instructions. Instructions were as follows.

On this tape, you will see some sentences. You will see each sentence two times. If you think the sentence is right, press the white button in front of you (this was demonstrated on the videotape). If you think the sentence is wrong, press the black button in front of you (this also was demonstrated). Wait until you see the sentence both times before you press a button. Answer as fast as you can after you see the sentence two times.

Practice sentences were then administered, followed by the test sentences.

Subjects

Subjects were selected from three different school districts whose educational procedures included simultaneous signing and speaking by teachers using SEE. Seventeen schools were contacted in an attempt to obtain subjects exposed to various communication systems; however, because of the unwillingness of school administrators to participate, it was not possible to have such subjects for use as controls.

The record files of more than 200 subjects were examined. Only 69 of these met preselection criteria. The subject with the least loss of auditory sensitivity yielded thresholds (for the better ear) of 70-dB HL at 250 Hz, 75-dB HL at 500 Hz, 85-dB HL at 1000 Hz, 95-dB HL at 2000 Hz, 105-dB HL at 4000 Hz, and no responses for higher frequencies. Except for this subject, all other subjects yielded pure-tone averages exceeding 90-dB HL (for 500, 1000, and 2000 Hz). All hearing losses were noticed in the prelingual stages of development, and were of a bilateral, sensorineural nature. The oldest audiogram was dated nine and a half months before the present

study. None of the 69 subjects showed any evidence of multiple handicaps. IQ scores derived from test results obtained with the Weschler Intelligence Scale for Children (WISC) were available for only 28 subjects, and the lowest recorded performance score was 84, the highest was 122. School teachers and psychologists for the remaining 41 subjects stated that none of these children seemed to have other than normal intelligence. All of the subjects wore hearing aids that were working normally at the time of testing. The youngest subject was five years and six months old, and the oldest was just over 11 years and six months of age. The mean age for the subjects was eight years and two months.

RESULTS

Measurements of reaction time and of performance were obtained on 67 deaf children. All statistical analyses were computed, by the Statistical Analysis System (Service, 1972) on a computer, on raw scores.

Performance of Deaf Subjects on Test

Two of the 69 subjects were unable to understand the directions clearly, and were eliminated from the study. Each sentence was missed at least once, and no sentence was missed by all the subjects. Furthermore, there were no consistent differences in errors for sentences within each morpheme tested.

The distribution of scores obtained from deaf subjects on the test is given in Table 1.

In Table 1, only four of the 67 subjects failed to perform beyond the 0.05 level above chance or better, although all the subjects' scores were higher than the mean chance score of 24. Fifty-three of the subjects performed beyond the 0.01 level above chance, of which 31 performed beyond the 0.001 level above chance.

If the subjects' responses were the result of chance alone, the distribution of the scores would best be described by a binomial distribution with a mean score of 24 (50%). The standard deviation of this chance-score distribution may be calculated from the formula

$$SD = [\ (n) \ (p) \ (1 - p) \ ]^{0.5}$$

where **SD** is the standard deviation, **n** is the number of test items (48) on the test, and **p** is the probability of a correct response by chance alone (0.5 for two alternatives).[2] The standard deviation of a distribution of scores obtained by chance on the test used in the present study was calculated to be 3.46. Critical scores may be calculated using a Z-score table. Critical scores of 30, 32, and 35 or greater will not occur by chance alone at the 0.05, 0.01, and 0.001 level of confidence, respectively.

Redundancy Cues. The performances of the subjects were categorized according to the type of redundancy cues in any given sentence. These cues are either semantic or grammatical, depending on the nature of the information that cues the correct sentence form. Sentences that were correct were not used in this analysis. Sentences testing the semantic cues are contained in past tense **-ed** sentences (because of the word **last**), plural **-s** (because of the words **many, few, three,** and so forth), possessives (can Noun 1 possess Noun 2?), and some **-ing** sentences. The mean performance score for sentences containing semantic redundancy cues was 77%, and the mean performance score for sentences containing grammatical cues was 66%. An analysis of variance was computed to determine whether the performance of the subjects differed as a function of redundancy cues. The performances of the subjects on sentences containing semantic cues were significantly greater than performances on sentences containing grammatical cues ($F = 40.87$; **df** = 1, 66; **p** < 0.0001).

Strategy Determination. When guessing on a test involving a true-false paradigm, young children have a tendency to respond with "true," especially when the test is administered by an adult.[3] If this is the case with subjects used in the present study, the conclusions based on a comparison of the subjects' performance scores with scores expected by chance alone may be invalid. In an attempt to compensate for this potential effect, twice as many incorrect sentences as correct sentences were built into the test. If the subjects in the present study consistently guessed by identifying a sentence as "correct," then the percentage of errors on the built-in incorrect sentences should exceed the percentage of errors obtained on the built-in correct sentences. A strategy-by-subject analysis of variance was computed to determine whether such a strategy was used by the subjects. The mean percentage score for the correct sentences was 73.4, and for the incorrect sentences was 70.8. There were no significant differences in perfor-mance as a function of the correctness of the sentence presented (**F** = 1.81; **df** = 1, 66; **p** = 0.1802).

Performance as a Function of Sex. The mean performance score of males (**n** = 38) was 34.39, and the mean performance score of females (**n** = 29) was 34.31. These results, although not formally analyzed, do not appear to be significantly different.

Performance as a Function of School District. Because the administrators of the various school districts from which the subject pool was drawn requested data that would show whether there were differences in performances according to the subjects' school districts, an appropriate analysis of variance was computed. The mean performance score for subjects in District 1 (**n** = 8) was 35.8, for subjects in District 2 (**n** = 20), 35.3 and for subjects in District 3 (**n** = 39), 33.6. The analysis of variance showed no significant differences in performance between subjects as a function of the school district to which they belonged ($F = 2.57$; **df** = 2, 64; **p** = 0.08). The nominal differences may reflect variance in performance caused by differences in years of experience with SEE. Subjects from District 1 had an average of 5.4 yr of experience with SEE in the classroom, while subjects from District 2 and District 3 had an average of 4.8 and 4.0 yr of experience with SEE in the classroom, respectively.

Order of Acquisition

Performance. If the inflectional morphemes tested are acquired in a specific order, the subjects should exhibit differences in performance as a function of which morpheme is being tested. This was analyzed by means of a treatments-by-subjects analysis of variance (Lindquist, 1953; Myers, 1972). The performances of the subjects were significantly different as a function of the morpheme tested ($F = 24.50$; **df** = 7, 462; **p** = 0.0001). The mean performance scores (in percentage) for each morpheme tested were:

Inflectional Morpheme	% Score
Present perfect -en	58
Superlative -est	61
Comparative -er	67
Third person singular, present indicative -s	70
Possessive -'s	76
Present progressive -ing	79
Past tense -ed	79
Plural -s	84

A Tukey studentized range technique (Tukey, 1949) was applied to these data to determine which of these morphemes

Table 2. Summary of differences in performance between morphemes tested using the Turkey studentized range technique

Morpheme	-est	-er	Present	Possess.	-ing	-ed	Plural
-en	2.98	8.71°	11.44°°	17.66°°	20.65°°	20.90°°	25.37°°
-est		5.72	8.46°	14.68°°	17.66°°	17.91°°	22.39°°
-er			2.74°	8.96°	11.94°	12.20°°	16.67°°
Present				6.22	9.20°	9.45°°	13.98°°
Possess.					2.99	3.23	7.71
-ing						0.24	4.72
-ed							4.47

° Differences in performance exceeding the critical difference of 8.05 at the 0.05 level of confidence.
°° Differences in performance exceeding the critical difference of 9.44 at the 0.01 level of confidence.

---

[2] L.S. Feldt, personal communication (1976).
[3] D.R. Whitney, personal communication (1975).

Table 3. Number of subjcets for each interval of age (in years) as a function of years of experience with SEE.

| Age | Years of Experience with SEE | | | | |
	3	4	5	6	Total
6	8	2	-	-	10
7	10	5	2	-	17
8	-	6	4	-	10
9	-	4	2	1	7
10	-	1	7	3	11
11	-	1	3	8	12
Total	18	19	18	12	67

represent significant differences in performance. The results of this procedure are provided in Table 2.

Effects of Age and of Experience with SEE. For these analyses, subjects were divided into groups of yearly intervals for both their experience with SEE in the classroom and their chronological age. Frequency distributions of the number of subjects in each yearly interval are shown in Table 3. To determine whether the subjects differed in their performance on the test as a function of their chronological age and of their experience with SEE, appropriate analyses of variance were computed. The results of these analyses showed that there were significant differences in performance as a function of the subjects' chronological age ($F = 3.5$; $df = 5, 61$; $p = 0.0077$) as well as of the subjects' length of experience with SEE in the classroom ($F = 8.7$; $df = 3, 63$; $p = 0.0002$).

Relative Effects of Age and of Experience with SEE on Performance. The performances of the subjects on the test are somewhat related to both age (Pearson product-moment correlation coefficient (r) = 0.43) and to experience with SEE in the classroom ($r = 0.53$). To determine whether the subjects' performances were more closely related to age or to experience with SEE, partial correlations were computed. It was found that the correlation between performance score and age when the effects of experience with SEE are removed was -0.04. This correlation was not statistically significant at the 0.05 level. When the effects of age were first removed, the correlation between performance and experience with SEE was 0.35. This correlation is statistically significant at the 0.05 level.

Because the variables of chronological age and years of experience with SEE in the classroom were closely related ($r = 0.85$), a multiple regression analysis (Harris, 1975; Overall and Klett, 1972) was employed to determine whether the significant differences as a function of experience with SEE were reflecting differences in performance as a function of chronological age. This analysis was computed using both a linear model and a quadratic model for acquisition by chronological age. It was necessary to consider both models because there were some reversals in performance when the subjects were grouped according to the chronological age in yearly intervals. In addition, the mean performance of the subjects, when grouped according to age, indicated a possible curvilinear relationship (see Table 4). The multiple regression analyses indicate that when the effects of age (using both the linear model and the quadratic model) are subtracted, there are significant differences in performance between subjects as a function of experience with SEE in the classroom ($p = 0.0053$). However, when the effects of experience with SEE are first removed, there are no significant differences in performance between subjects as a function of age for either the linear acquisition model ($p = 0.500$) or the quadratic acquisition model ($p = 0.500$). The mean performance of the subjects as a function of chronological age is shown in Table 4. In general, with increasing age, the subjects tended to yield higher performance scores. However, between age 10 and 11, there is a reversal.

Mean scores for the subjects as a function of years of experience with SEE in the classroom are listed in Table 5. The data

Table 4. Mean performance scores of subjects as a function of chronological age (yearly intervals).

Chronological Age	n	Mean Score
6	10	31.90
7	17	33.41
8	10	34.30
9	7	34.29
10	11	36.82
11	12	35.83

Table 5. Mean performances of subjects as a function of experience with SEE in the classroom (yearly intervals).

Years of Experience	n	Mean Score
3	18	32.11
4	19	33.88
5	18	35.00
6	12	37.50

presented in Table 5 indicate that when the subjects were grouped into yearly intervals according to their experience with SEE in the classroom, they exhibited differences in performance that were significant beyond the 0.01 level. The overall mean score on the test for all the deaf subjects was 34.4, a score that is significantly greater than chance at the 0.01 level of confidence. There is a consistent increase in performance as a function of years of experience with SEE in which no reversals were observed. There is no evidence to suggest an asymptotic effect in performance scores as a function of years of experience with SEE.

DISCUSSION

The performance of the children in this study is in agreement with the findings of Gilman and Raffin (1975), who suggest that young hearing-impaired children are able to use common inflectional morphemes correctly when they are exposed to a morpheme-based sign system consistently. The children in this study were able to recognize syntactically correct sentences from those that were incorrect at a level well above chance. Systematic exposure to a morpheme-based sign system seems to result in effective learning of the significance of common inflectional morphemes to the meaning of sentences, a linguistic ability necessary to the competent use of the English language. Children who had been exposed to a visual English sign system exhibited knowledge of morphemes similar to that of Berko's subjects aged four to seven years, although the experimental tasks cannot be compared directly. Nevertheless, deaf children who are exposed consistently to a morpheme-based sign system may lag behind normal-hearing children by as much as two to six years. This represents much less delay in the use of morphemes than that reported for Cooper's subjects.

When the test items were divided according to the type of redundancy cues they contained, the subjects obtained higher scores on those items that contained semantic cues than on those items that contained grammatical cues. Bloom (1970) found that young normal-hearing children use correct semantic form before they use correct syntactic form. The results of the present study support this contention. Other researchers (Moulton and Beasley, 1975) have indicated that semantic development may play a bigger role than syntactic development in the language acquisition of the deaf.

The results of the present study demonstrate a definite hierarchy of knowledge of the morphemes tested, as evidenced by the increase in the scores on the test as a function of the number of years of experience with SEE. In addition, those subjects with less experience with SEE made more errors on the more "difficult" inflectional morphemes than on the "easy" morphemes (those learned first). Most of the errors made by the subjects with the most experience with SEE occurred on sentences testing -en and -est. Thus, relative error pattern for the morphemes tested was the same across subject groups based on years of experience with SEE.

Considerable differences exist between the results of the present study and those reported by Brown (1973) for young hearing children. There is a reversal in the order of acquisition for -ing and plural -s between these two sets of data. In addition, Brown's subjects acquired the past tense -ed at a later time relative to the development of other morphemes than that demonstrated by the subjects used in the present study. It should be noted that Brown's data, based on the performance of three normal-hearing young children, were highly

variable, and that the order of acquisition for the morphemes was different for each of his three subjects.

It seems possible that the differences observed between the results of the present study and those obtained with normal-hearing subjects (Berko, 1958; Brown, 1973) may be the result of differences in the educational experiences of the children. Specifically, the order of acquisition reflected by the performance of the subjects used in this study may be related to the order in which the various morphemes are introduced or practiced in the classroom. For the normal-hearing children, the data may reflect the results of acquiring language orally. The primary mode of input for the subjects used in the present study was visual, and such an input may not be equated with an auditory input. Differences between the results obtained with normal-hearing children and deaf children also may reflect some subtle differences caused by changes in speaking habits people exhibit when communicating with the deaf.

The fact that the subjects' performances on sentences testing the present tense -s were significantly poorer than their performances for plural -s (even though the signs for plural -s and present tense -s are indistinguishable in SEE) suggests that the deaf children used in the present study were not learning the inflectional morphemes by memorization of the sign representing them. It therefore seems likely that their behavior relative to these morphemes is rule-generated and that they acquired an understanding of the rules for plural -s before understanding the rules related to the present tense -s. If this is the case, then the results of the present study support one of the underlying premises of the visual English sign systems, which is that such rules will be learned and internalized naturally on sufficient exposure to a sign system that is faithful to the English language.

Of those variables examined in the present study, exposure to a morpheme-based sign system seems the most responsible for the results obtained. In any case, since the performances of the subjects in this study were much better than those reported by Cooper (1967), and since present results indicate that the subjects have obtained an understanding of the correct usage of selected inflectional morphemes, it does not seem that a visual English sign system impedes deaf children's ability to learn the proper usage of inflectional morphemes.

Because of the lack of any evidence to suggest an asymptotic effect in performance by subjects as a function of years of experience with SEE, it might be possible that deaf children exposed to a visual English sign system could demonstrate, eventually, a mastery of the correct usage of common inflectional morphemes.

Anthony (1972) hypothesized that children exposed consistently to a morpheme-based sign system that accurately represents English syntax (such as SEE) might show an improvement in their ability to read English. Several teachers of the deaf, from whose classes subjects for the present study were selected, indicated that this was the case. The results of Gilman and Raffin (1975) indicated that the performances of hearing-impaired children are related to reading ability, and the test used in their study did require some reading. However, the testing paradigm used in the present experiment did not require reading ability of the subjects. It seems probable therefore that the reading ability of deaf children may be enhanced when they learn the English language through a sign system that accurately represents English syntax, although there are no published data to support this hypothesis. It was not possible to perform such an analysis for the subjects used in the present study because reading scores were not available.

In addition, it is possible that the results obtained in the present study on subjects exposed to Seeing Essential English could be obtainable from subjects exposed to any of the signed English systems that include the systematic use of sign for various inflectional morphemes.

ACKNOWLEDGMENT

This study was supported, in part, by Public Health Service Training Grant 5 TO1 NS05425 from the National Institute of Neurological and Communicative Disorders and Stroke. This research was initiated as part of the doctoral dissertation of Michael J. M. Raffin, University of Iowa, Iowa City, Iowa, 1976. Portions of these findings were reported at the Canadian Speech and Hearing Association Annual Convention, Halifax, Nova Scotia, 1976, and at the Annual Convention of the American Speech and Hearing Association, Houston, Texas, 1976. Requests for reprints should be sent to Michael J. M. Raffin, Audiology Clinics, 2299 Sheridan Road, Evanston, Illinois 60201.

REFERENCES

American National Standards Institute (1969). *Specifications for Audiometers.* S3.6-1969. New York: American National Standards Institute.

Anthony, D.A. (Ed.) (1972). *Seeing Essential English.* (2 Vols.) Anaheim, Calif.: Educational Services Division, Anaheim Union High School District.

Berko, J. (1958). The child's learning of English morphology, *Word. 14*, 150-177.

Bloom, L. (1970). *Language Development.* Cambridge, Mass.: MIT Press.

Brown, R. (1973). *A First Language: The Early Stages.* Cambridge, Mass.: Harvard University Press.

Cooper, R. L. (1967). The ability of deaf and hearing children to apply morphological rules, *Journal of Speech and Hearing Research 10*, 77-86.

Gilman, L. A., and Raffin, M. J. M. (1975). Acquisition of common morphemes by hearing-impaired children exposed to the Seeing Essential English sign system. Paper presented at the Annual Meeting of the American Speech and Hearing Association, Washington, D.C.

Gustason, G., Pfetsing, D., and Zawolkow, E. (1972). *Signing Exact English.* Rossmoor, Calif.: Modern Signs.

Harris, R. J. (1975). *A Primer of Multivariate Statistics.* New York: Academic.

Lindquist, E. F. (1953). *Design and Analysis of Experiments in Psychology and Education.* Boston: Houghton Mifflin.

Moulton, R. D., and Beasley, D. S. (1975). Verbal coding strategies used by hearing-impaired individuals, *Journal of Speech and Hearing Research 18*, 559-570.

Myers, J. L. (1972). *Fundamentals of Experimental Design.* Boston: Allyn and Bacon.

Overall, J. E., and Klett, C. J. (1972). *Applied Multivariate Analysis.* New York: McGraw-Hill.

Power, D. J., and Quigley, S. P. (1973). Deaf children's acquisition of the passive voice, *Journal of Speech and Hearing Research 16*, 5-11.

Quigley, S. P., Wilbur, R. B., and Montanelli, D. S. (1974). Question formation in the language of deaf students, *Journal of Speech and Hearing Research 17*, 699-713.

Raffin, M. J. M. (1976). The acquisition of inflectional morphemes by deaf children using Seeing Essential English. Doctoral dissertation, University of Iowa.

Service, J. (1972). *A User's Guide to the Statistical Analysis System.* Raleigh, N. C.: Student Supplies Store, North Carolina State University.

Tukey, J. W. (1977). Comparing individual means in the analysis of variance, *Biometrics. 5*, 99-114.

Wilbur, R. B., Montanelli, D. S., and Quigley, S. P. (1976). Pronominalization in the language of deaf students, *Journal of Speech and Hearing Research 19*, 120-140.

Wilbur, R. B. Quigley, S. P., and Montanelli, D. S. (1975). Conjoined structures in the written language of deaf students, *Journal of Speech and Hearing Research 18*, 319-335.

USE OF COMMON MORPHEMES BY HEARING-IMPAIRED CHILDREN EXPOSED TO A SYSTEM OF MANUAL ENGLISH

Leslea A. Gilman, Julia M. Davis, and Michael J. M. Raffin

Department of Speech Pathology and Audiology
University of Iowa, Iowa City, Iowa 52242

INTRODUCTION

Studies of language comprehension and usage by hearing-impaired children reveal consistently poor performance on tasks requiring knowledge of English grammar and syntax (Quigley et al., 1974a, b; Pressnell, 1973; Davis and Blasdell, 1975; Moores, 1971; Wilcox and Tobin, 1974). Understanding of the rules governing the use of common inflectional morphemes is an important aspect of English syntax. These morphemes include markers that signal verb tense, plurality, possession, adverbiality, and adjectival meaning. Developmental studies of language acquisition in normal children have revealed that young children master knowledge of inflectional morphemes by the age of 7 yrs. and in the following approximate order: /ing/, plural /s/, possessive /s/, and /ed/ (Berko, 1958; Brown, 1973; Miller and Ervin, 1964).

Investigation of hearing-impaired children's usage of inflectional morphemes has been minimal. Cooper (1967) utilized Berko's nonsense materials with deaf children and reported that 19-yr-old deaf Ss performed at a level of knowledge below that of 9-yr-old hearing children. Although the performance of the deaf Ss was drastically lower than that of hearing children, the pattern of their responses indicated that deaf persons may develop usage of common morphemes in the same sequence as do hearing children.

The poor performance of deaf children on language tasks is reflected in their low academic achievement (Wrightstone et al., 1962; Boatner, 1965; Babbidge, 1965). The Babbidge report cited the underlying cause of poor academic achievement as the failure of educational programs to launch an aggressive assault on basic problems of language learning by the deaf. Recent changes in education of the deaf in this country include the growing use of manual communication systems designed to provide visual representations of English vocabulary and structure (Bornstein, 1974). The use of these systems is controversial, with their proponents declaring that knowledge of English syntax and grammar will be significantly increased by exposure to Manual English (Anthony, 1971), and their opponents stating that the complexity and artificiality of the new systems will serve to confuse deaf children (Stokoe, 1974). In spite of the importance of the possible effects of the use of signed English systems with young deaf children and the need to evaluate widely-used procedures in an effort to improve basic language learning by them, little experimental evidence exists to substantiate or deny the claims made for manual English systems. Schlesinger and Meadow (1971) reported advanced language development in young children exposed to signed English. Raffin et al. (1978) reported a significant relationship between the number of years exposure to Seeing Essential English (SEE) and deaf children's comprehension of common inflectional morphemes. That study also indicated that the deaf children tested did perform well above chance on the comprehension of inflectional markers for verb tense, plurality, and possession. Expression of common inflectional morphemes by young deaf children has not been investigated.

The purpose of this study was to investigate the use of common inflectional morphemes by young deaf children whose educational procedures included daily exposure to SEE, a sign system in which the morphemes are presented in visual form. Because so little is known about the contribution of many factors that may affect language acquisition in deaf children, the effects of sex, age, severity of hearing loss, reading level, years of exposure to the teaching strategy employed, and consistency of the teachers' use of the stated teaching strategy were analyzed.

METHOD

Subjects

Severely hearing-impaired children (11 boys, 9 girls) served, aged 8-12 yrs. All children had been exposed to SEE in the classroom for 2-4 yrs. Each S had a pure-tone hearing loss > 80 db averaged over .5, 1, and 2 kc/s. All used amplification consistently. In the classrooms, FM auditory trainers were used, and individual hearing aids were worn outside the classroom. All Ss were judged by school psychologists to be within the normal range of intelligence. Judgments were based on formal testing using a variety of performance scales for assessing intellectual status.

To be included in the study, each S had to exhibit a first grade reading ability as measured by standardized instruments including the Metropolitan Reading Inventory and the Stanford Reading Inventory.

Teachers

Prior to testing, the children were observed in their classrooms by two impartial observers, who rated the teacher of the class at this time with regard to the consistency in the use of SEE. A teacher was judged "consistent" only if every word spoken was accompanied by the appropriate sign or signs. For example, in SEE, the word "running" requires the use of 2 signs: one for "run" and one for "ing". If "run" alone was signed, the teacher was not rated as consistent. This stringent criterion was felt to be necessary in a preliminary study of this type, because of the need to establish the relationship between the stated educational procedures and the actual procedures employed.

Table I provides a description of each S, including the overall score on the experimental task described in the following sections.

Reprinted with permission from the Journal of Auditory Research, 1980, 20, 57-69.

Table 1. Description of subjects.

Subj. No.	Sex	C.A.	Teacher	Hearing Loss (PTA) in Db HTL	Years Expos. to SEE	Approx. Reading Level	Score on Task
1	F	10.7	1	95	4	3.2	31
2	F	10.3	1	90	4	3.1	30
3	M	8.4	1	90	4	2.1	18
4	M	10.4	1	85	4	4.1	37
5	M	11.4	2	100	3	2.5	14
6	M	11.5	2	80	3	2.5	20
7	M	10.1	2	95	3	2.6	35
8	M	10.4	2	80	3	2.9	33
9	M	10.6	2	100	3	3.1	36
10	M	10.4	2	80	3	2.5	33
11	F	10.5	2	110	3	2.1	9
12	F	9.7	3	95	3	2.0	14
13	F	10.4	3	90	3	2.1	14
14	F	10.4	3	90	3	2.1	15
15	F	11.4	3	100	3	2.1	17
16	F	11.3	3	95	3	1.9	13
17	M	9.0	4	85	2	1.0	13
18	F	9.6	4	100	2	1.5	19
19	M	10.3	5	85	2	2.1	25
20	M	9.2	4	100	2	1.5	26

Figure 1. Example of answer sheet (Sentence No. 17)

The rabbit is _____ than the duck.

A. bigging   C. biggest

B. big   D. bigger

Materials

A 40-sentence written test (see Appendix A) involving a 4-item multiple-choice paradigm was administered individually to each child; 5 different sentences were used to test each of the following 8 inflectional morphemes: plural /s/, possessive /s/, present tense singular /s/, past tense /ed/, present progressive /ing/, adjectival and adverbial /ly/, comparative /er/, and superlative /est/. Ss were required to choose 1 of the 4 choices to fill in a blank in each sentence.

Pictures illustrating each of the 40 sentences were presented (see example in Fig. 1). Each sentence and its 4 possible answers were printed below a picture as well as on a separate answer sheet. Ss were required to circle the correct answer. Children as young as 6 yrs. of age have been shown to have no difficulty with this task procedure (Whitney, 1975).

All sentences were composed of vocabulary selected from Botel's Reading List of primer and first-grade-level words (Botel, 1966). Only 1 correct answer was available for each sentence. Sentences ranged in length from 4 to 9 words (mn = 6 words). Sentence length was dictated by the inflectional morpheme being tested, with each sentence utilizing the simplest grammatical structure possible. Sentences were randomized for presentation, but each S received the sentences in the same order.

Procedure

Testing was performed by a single examiner in an isolated room, free from visual and auditory distractions. The following instructions were spoken and signed simultaneously:

"Look at the picture. Then read the sentence on your paper and circle the best answer."

The examiner then demonstrated the procedure by reading an example sentence and its answers with each S and circling the correct answer. The child was then required to complete a second example sentence independently before testing began. Children were given as much time as necessary to complete each item before proceeding to the next and they were required to respond to each item. Although instructions were signed and spoken by the examiner, the test sentences were read by the children. The child's score was the number of correct responses on the 40-item task; sub-scores for each morpheme were also computed.

Group-Mean Performance

Table II shows the group-mean performance for each morpheme tested and its level of confidence. To determine whether a given score represented performance better than chance, critical scores for the confidence levels of .05, .01, and .001 were determined by use of a binomial distribution with a mean score of 10 (i.e., 25%-correct). The standard deviation of this distribution was computed by the formula $SD = (n \times P \cdot 1-P)^{1/2}$ (Feldt, 1976). Critical scores were found to be 15 (37.5%) for the .05 level, 17 (42.5%) for the .01 level, and 19 (48.5%) for the .001 level of confidence. An individual score falling below 15 represented performance at or below chance level. Of the 20 children, 5 exhibited scores 1-2 points below chance; 1 scored well below chance.

Table 2. Group Performance on the Concepts Tested.

Concept	Percent Correct	Level of Confidence	
'est'	36	--	
'ly'	39	0.05	37%=critical score for p<.05
'er'	43	0.01	42%=critical score for p<.01
present tense 's'	44	0.01	
possessive 's'	51	0.001	47%=critical score for p<.001
past 'ed'	61	0.001	
'ing'	84	0.001	
plural 's'	92	0.001	

Differences Among Morphemes

Group performance was above chance for all morphemes tested except for the superlative /est/. Differences among morphemes were tested by an ANOVA (Barr and Goodnight, 1972), yielding an F of 16.55; df = 7.133; p < .001. A Tukey technique (Tukey, 1949) was performed to determine which differences among morphemes were contributing to the significant F ratio. Table III shows that the morphemes /ed/, /ing/, and plural /s/ accounted for most of the differences. Plural /s/ and /ing/ were used correctly a significantly greater number of times than all other morphemes; /ed/ was used correctly significantly more than the morphemes /est/ and /ly/ which represent those used incorrectly most often by these Ss. There were no significant differences among usage of the morphemes /est/, /ly/, /er/, present tense /s/, and possessive /s/, except where noted above, although the data indicated increasing levels of performance on the morphemes as listed in Table III.

Table 3. Comparison of Differences Between Group Means by Concept

Group Mean	LY	ER	PRES(S)	POSS	ED	ING	PL(S)
.36 EST	.03	.07	.08	.15	.25*	.48**	.56**
.39 LY		.04	.05	.12	.22*	.45**	.53**
.43 ER			.01	.08	.18	.41**	.49**
.44 PRES(S)				.07	.17	.40**	.48**
.51 POSS					.10	.33**	.41**
.61 ED						.23*	.31**
.84 ING							.08
.92 PL(S)							

*Critical Difference (.05)=0.226   **Critical Difference (.01)=0.2661

Age

Children were grouped into (1) < 9 yr 6 mo, (2) between 9 yr 7 mo and 10 yr 6 mo, and (3) > 10 yr 7 mo. An ANOVA revealed no significant differences among scores yielded by the 3 age groups (F = .51, df = 2.17; p <.60).

Hearing Level

Children were grouped according to the PTAs at 5-db intervals from 80-110 db HL. An ANOVA on test scores for these groupings was not significant (F = .43, df = 5.14; p > .82). The data were reorganized into 2 groups, those with HLs > 90 and < 90 db HL (10 Ss in each group). An ANOVA yielded an F = .31, df = 1.18; p < .58. The degree of hearing loss did not appear to affect performance on this task.

Sex

An ANOVA indicated a significant difference between the performances of boys and girls (F = 5.11, df = 1.18;p < .03) (see Table IV).

Table 4. The Effect of Sex on Performance.

Sex	No.	Mean in Percent Correct	
M	11	65.9	(F=5.11;df=1.18;p<.03)
F	9	44.4	

The variable of sex is confounded in this study by the fact that 2 of the classrooms were single-sex classes. The variable of teacher consistency appears to be the confounding factor and will be discussed below.

Reading Level

Children were sorted according to their reading achievement scores (1) from 1.0-2.0, (2) 2.1-3.0, and (3) > 3.1 grade level. An ANOVA indicated a significant difference among the scores obtained by the 3 groups (F = 5.67, df = 2.17; p < .01) (see Table V).

Table 5. The Effect of Reading Level on Performance.

Approx. Reading Level	No.	Mean in Percent Correct	
1.0 - 2.0	5	42.5	
2.1 - 3.0	11	52.5	(F=5.67; df=2.17;p<.01)
>3.1	4	83.75	

Years of Experience with SEE

Children were grouped by exposure to SEE in the classroom for 2, 3, and 4 yrs. An ANOVA indicated no significant difference in the performance on the task among the 3 groups, even though the children with 4 yrs. of exposure exhibited a much higher mean performance (see Table VI). Failure to achieve significance is probably related to the small number of Ss coupled with variability on the task. An ANOVA yielded an F = 1.24, df = 2.17; p < .31. This factor is also confounded with teacher consistency since children were placed in classrooms based on their years of enrollment in the school system.

Table 6. The Effect of Experience with SEE on Performance.

Years Experience with SEE		N	Group Mean Percent Correct	
2	2	4	51.8	
3	3	12	52.2	(F=1.24; df=2.17; p<.31)
4	4	4	72.5	

Teacher Consistency

When children's scores were grouped according to their teacher's (1) consistency or (2) inconsistency in the use of SEE with spoken utterances, an ANOVA indicated a highly significant difference between groups ($F = 16.45$, $df = 1.16$; $p < .001$. Mean performances for both groups are shown in Table VII.

Table 7. The Effect of Teacher Consistency on Performance

Teacher Rating	Teacher Number	N	Subtotal	Mean in Percent Correct	
Consistent	1	4			
	2	6	10	71	(F = 16.45,
Inconsistent	3	3			df = 1.16;
	4	6			p < .001)
	5	1	10	40	

In addition to the ANOVAs reported above, Spearman correlation coefficients were computed for score, reading level, severity of hearing loss, chronological age, sex, exposure to SEE, and teacher consistency. The results are shown in Table VIII. Highest correlations were found between years of exposure to SEE and teacher; the consistency rating of the teacher is not taken into account here. Reading level and teacher are also highly correlated as are reading level and experience with SEE. Since children in self-contained classes are assigned to classrooms according to their years in school and their academic achievement, these correlations are not surprising. Of interest, however, is the significant correlation between reading level and score on the task, and sex and score, and the poor correlations between experience with SEE and score, and between age and reading. These will be discussed below.

Table 8. Spearman Correlation Coefficients for the Variables Studied

	Reading	Hearing	Age	Expos. to SEE	Sex	Teacher
Score	.58**	.13	.05	.28	.48*	.52**
Reading		.23	.32	.71***	.09	.74***
Hearing			.30	.16	.30	.18
Age				.33	.15	.32
Expos. to SEE					.16	.91***
Sex						.17

Note: *,**,*** = significant at .05, .01, and .001 level respectively.

DISCUSSION

Although the Ss in this study were few, the repeated measure of items in the task allowed for a total of 800 responses (100 per morpheme tested). The results cannot be considered a definitive description of the morpheme usage of children exposed to SEE, but they do provide preliminary information about a number of factors. The children were able to use 7 of the 8 morphemes in a written task, beyond the chance level. A rank-ordering of the morphemes according to the relative difficulty they presented reveals a developmental pattern similar to that exhibited by normal children (Brown, 1973). The exception appears to be the past tense /ed/. At the time the data were collected, regular and irregular past tense forms in SEE were all signed by the same inflectional marker, a flipping of the open hand over the shoulder. Children exposed to such a sign system are therefore exposed to the past tense marker used to indicate /ed/ relatively more often than their hearing counterparts, since the hearing child experiences /ed/ only on regular verbs. Learning of the appropriate use of /ed/ might be confused with other past tense markers, in that the normal child must learn several rules instead of one. An additional factor may be the difference in visual saliency between the two morphemes. The signed past tense marker /ed/ (hand flip over shoulder) is more visually salient than the possessive /s/ (twisting of s handshape). These factors may account for the correct use of /ed/ before possessive /s/, and reversal of the order of acquisition seen in normal children.

By far the best performance occurs on the plural /s/ and the present progressive /ing/. The plural /s/ finding is particularly interesting when compared to the poor performance on the present tense /s/. The morphemes marking present tense /s/ and plural /s/ are signed exactly the same in SEE and consist of the addition of a fingerspelled /s/ to the noun or verb involved. It is apparent from the data, however, that the two differ in meaningfulness to children who see them; performance by the group on these two items is significantly different at the .01 level (See Table III). This finding suggests that the children have internalized different rules for the addition of /s/ to plural nouns and singular verbs, and that memorization of the addition of /s/ to lexical items cannot account for their performance on these morphemes.

The /ing/ ending actually seems to be overused. This ending was substituted 68% of the time on errors involving the /er/ ending. Since /er/ words were always preceded by **is** (Example: the yellow wagon **is** (**longer**) than the red wagon), it is assumed that the children interpreted the **is** as a signal for the /ing/ ending.

Although children ranged in age from 8 yr 4 mo to 11 yr 5 mo, no effect of age on performance was found. Years of experience with SEE also failed to affect performance significantly, although the children with 4 yrs experience with SEE scored noticeably higher on the task. These results seem to indicate that the opportunity to be exposed to morphemes is not the major contributing factor to a child's success in using them. The degree of hearing loss, at least within the small range represented by these children, also does not appear to affect performance.

What factors, then, do seem to contribute to the differences in performance on the task? According to the data, sex is an important factor, along with reading level and teacher consistency in usage of the morphemes in communicating with the children in the classroom. Unfortunately, these 3 factors are confounded due to the criteria used for placement of students into classrooms. A total of 5 teachers were involved; 2 of them taught in single-sex classrooms with one of them having 6 boys and the other 6 girls in class. The teacher whose students were all boys was rated as "consistent", while the one with all girls was rated "inconsistent" in usage of SEE. The significant difference between scores obtained by boys and girls is more likely to have been influenced by teacher consistency than the reverse, in view of the fact that sex differences in deaf children's language usage have rarely been observed and that the differences observed in both deaf and normal childrens' acquisition of language are consistently in favor of girls. The opposite seems to be the case in this study. Furthermore, as in many small programs for deaf children, most of the children in this study had been taught by the same teacher for more than 2 years. Thus, the influence of the teacher in the child's educational progress is profound.

Included in that progress is reading achievement, a factor that contributed significantly to the children's performance. The association between reading level and performance on the task raises the question as to whether the morpheme usage exhibited by the children can be attributed to the sign system used. It is possible that the morpheme tested could have been learned through reading experiences with them. A similar study utilizing non-reading younger children would provide important information about the contribution of the sign system alone to morpheme comprehension. Although the Ss of Raffin et al. (1978) included some young non-readers who exhibited knowledge of these morphemes, further study is necessary. It is important to note that proponents of signed English systems suggest that reading achievement will increase as a result of experience with English in manual form. These data do not disconfirm that contention. The "which came first" problem cannot be solved without rigorous research utilizing children who have been taught by a variety of procedures. One problem in accomplishing such research is exemplified by these data. Half the children in the experiment were in classrooms in which their teachers were inconsistent in the use of the sign system they purported to use. The striking influence of teacher consistency on the use of morphemes suggests that **consistent** exposure to the morphemes via sign may be a major determiner of the ability to use them in a task of this nature. Children having fewer years of experience with SEE but with a teacher whose use of the sign system was consistent, scored higher on the task than those with longer exposure to an inconsistent signer. Many very important questions concerning language learning in the hearing impaired and the efficacy of the procedures currently employed with them will not be answered adequately until teachers and clinicians practice what they preach.

SUMMARY

Severely hearing-impaired children (11 boys, 9 girls), whose educational procedures included the use of Seeing Essential English (SEE) were given an experimental task designed to test their use of 8 common inflectional morphemes: plural /s/, possessive /s/, present tense singular /s/, past tense /ed/, present progressive /ing/, adjectival and adverbial /ly/, comparative /er/, and superlative /est/. Each child read 20 sentences composed of primer and first grade level words, and circled 1 of 4 word choices to fill in a missing word in each sentence. All 4 word choices had the same root. Responses were analyzed relative to chronological age, sex, degree of hearing loss, duration of exposure to SEE, reading level, and consistency of teacher usage of SEE. Performance appeared to be most dependent on sex, reading level, and teacher consistency. Although these factors were confounded, results indicate that teacher consistency in usage of SEE may be the major determiner of performance on the task.

REFERENCES

Anthony, C. (1971). *Seeing Essential English.* Greeley, CO: Univ. Northern Colorado.

Babbidge, H. (1965). *Education of the Deaf.* Report to U.S. Dept. HEW by Advisory Comm. on Education of the Deaf. U.S. Gov't. Printing Office, 0-765-119.

Berko, J. (1958). The child's learning of English morphology, *Word, 14*, 150-177.

Boatner, E. B. (1965). The need for new vocational-technical programs for the deaf, *Proc. 42nd mtg Conv. Amer. Instructors of the Deaf.* U.S. Gov't Printing Office, No. *71*, 201-206

Bornstein, H. (1974). Signed English: A manual approach to English language development, *Journal of Speech and Hearing Disorders. 39*, 330-343.

Botel, M. (1966). *Botel Predicting Readability Levels.* Follett Educ. Corp.

Brown, R. (1973). *A First Language/The Early Stages.* Pp. 260-280, Harvard Univ. Press.

Cooper, R. L. (1967). The ability of deaf and hearing children to apply morphological rules, *Journal of Speech and Hearing Research, 10*, 77-86.

Davis, J., and Blasdell, R. (1975). Perceptual strategies employed by normal-hearing and hearing-impaired children in the comprehension of sentences containing relative clauses, *Journal of Speech and Hearing Research. 18*, 281-295.

Feldt, L. S. (1976). Personal communication. University of Iowa Statistics Consulting Center.

Gustason, G., Pfetzing, D., and Zawolkow, E. (1972). *Signing Exact English.* Rossmoor, Calif.: Modern Signs Press.

Kannapell, B., et al. (1969). *Signs for Instructional Purposes.* Wash., D.C.: Gallaudet College Press.

Miller, W. and Ervin, S. (1964). The development of grammar in child language. In: Bellegi, U. and Brown, R. (Eds.) *The Acquisition of Language.* Monogr. Soc. Res. Child Development. 29, 9-34.

Moores, D. (1971). Recent research on manual communication. Research, Development and Demonstration Center in Education of Handicapped Children, University of Minnesota, Minneapolis.

Northern, J. and Downs, M. (1974). *Hearing In Children.* Baltimore: Williams & Wilkins, p. 274.

Pressnell, L. (1973). Hearing-impaired children's comprehension and production of syntax in oral language, *Journal of Speech and Hearing Research. 16*, 12-21.

Quigley, S., Smith, N. and Wilbur, R. (1974a). Comprehension of relativized sentences by deaf students, *Journal of Speech and Hearing Research. 17*, 325-341.

Quigley, S., Wilbur, R., and Montanelli, D. (1974b). Question formation in the language of deaf students, *Journal of Speech and Hearing Research. 17*, 699-713.

Raffin, M. J. M., Davis, J. M. and Gilman, L. A. (1978). Comprehension of inflectional morphemes by deaf children exposed to a visual English sign system, *Journal of Speech and Hearing Research. 21*, 387-400.

Schmitt, P. (1968). Deaf children's comprehension and production of sentence transformation. Unpublished doctoral dissertation, Univ. Illinois.

Schlesinger, H. S. and Meadow, K. P. (1972). *Sound And Sign*. Berkeley: Univ Calif. Press.

Stokoe, W. C. (Oct 1974). Seeing and signing language, *Speech and Hearing News*, pp. 32-37.

Templin, M. (1964). Vocabulary knowledge and usage among deaf and hearing children, *Proceedings, 41st mtg Conv. Am. Instructors of the Deaf*, 977-980.

Tukey, J. W. (1949). Comparing individual means in the analysis of variance, *Biometr., 5*, 99-114.

Wampler, D. (1971). *Linguistics of Visual English*. 2322 Maher Dr. No. 35, Santa Rosa, Calif.

Whitney, R. (1975). Personal communication. Examination and Evaluation Center, University of Iowa.

Wilcox, J., and Tobin, H. (1974). Linguistic performance of hard of hearing and normal children, *Journal of Speech and Hearing Research. 17*, 286-293.

Wrightstone, J., Aronow, M. and Moskowitz, S. (1962). Developing reading test norms for deaf children, *Test Service Bull. 98*, N.Y.: Harcourt Brace.

APPENDIX

Sentences Used As Stimuli

1. The green book is the
   A. new   B. newer
   C. newest   D. newing

2. The yellow ball is _____ than the red ball.
   A. new   B. newer
   C. newing   D. newest

3. The dog is
   A. plays   B. playing
   C. play   D. played

4. The house looks
   A. lovely   B. love
   C. loving   D. loves

5. The boy _____ sad.
   A. look   B. looking
   C. looks   D. looker

6. It is the _____ toy.
   A. boying   B. boys
   C. boy's   D. boy

7. The dog _____ the apples.
   A. liker   B. like
   C. liked   D. liking

8. I see many
   A. bird   B. birder
   C. birded   D. birds

9. There are four
   A. trees   B. treer
   C. treed   D. tree

10. The box is
    A. mothering B. mother
    C. mother's   D. mothers

11. The cat looks
    A. lives   B. liver
    C. lively   D. live

12. The man is _____ the house.
    A. painting   B. paint
    C. painted   D. painter

13. The green wagon is _____ than the red wagon.
    A. long   B. longest
    C. longing   D. longer

14. The boy is _____ than the girl.
    A. taller   B. talling
    C. tallest   D. tall

15. The cow
    A. sleeper   B. sleeps
    C. sleeping   D. sleep

16. The girl _____ a kitten.
    A. wanted   B. want
    C. wanting   D. wanter

17. The rabbit is _____ than the duck.
    A. bigging   B. big
    C. biggest   D. bigger

18. The bear _____ the jar.
    A. opener   B. open
    C. opens   D. opening

19. The red ball is the
    A. big   B. bigger
    C. bigs   D. biggest

20. It is the _____ doll.
    A. girl   B. girling
    C. girls   D. girl's

21. It is the _____ bone.
A. dogs   B. dog's
C. dog   D. dogging

22. The girl is _____
A. sleeped   B. sleeping
C. sleeps   D. sleep

23. The cat is the _____
A. happiest   B. happy
C. happys   D. happier

24. I see two _____
A. apples   B. apple
C. appled   D. appler

25. The boy cries _____
A. sad   B. sadly
C. sader   D. sads

26. The boy _____ happy.
A. looking   B. look
C. looker   D. looked

27. The children play _____
A. happy   B. happily
C. happier   D. happys

28. The rabbit _____ fast.
A. runner   B. running
C. run   D. runs

29. The man is _____
A. laughing   B. laugh
C. laughs   D. laughed

30. The woman _____ the dog.
A. call   B. called
C. calling   D. caller

31. The girl _____ the car.
A. paints   B. painter
C. paint   D. painting

32. The book is _____
A. Sally   B. Sally's
C. Sallys   D. Sallying

33. The rabbit is _____
A. jump   B. jumped
C. jumping   D. jumps

34. The boy has three _____
A. toyed   B. toys
C. toy   D. toyer

35. The girl looks _____
A. friend   B. friendly
C. friends   D. friender

36. The boy is _____
A. walker   B. walks
C. walkest   D. walking

37. The man is the _____
A. older   B. old
C. oldest   D. olds

38. There are many _____
A. cat   B. catted
C. cats   D. catter

39. The woman is _____ than the girl.
A. old   B. oldest
C. older   D. olding

40. The dog is the _____ animal.
A. little   B. littlest
C. littler   D. littles

SIGNED ENGLISH: A FIRST EVALUATION

Harry Bornstein
Karen Luczak Saulnier

and

Lillian B. Hamilton
Gallaudet Signed English Project
Gallaudet College, Washington, D.C.

The English language development of an unselected group of 20 hearing-impaired children taught Signed English was studied over a 4-year period. The children were enrolled in residential and day school settings. Their language development was individually tested annually with the Peabody Picture Vocabulary Test, the Northwestern Syntax Screening Test, and a tailor-made Signed English Morphology Test.

Over the 4 years, the children's receptive vocabulary grew at the rate of 43% of that manifested by hearing children. The vocabulary level reached at age 8 was similar to that reported for comparable hearing-impaired children at age 11 taught by other methods.

There was no apparent syntax development until after the first year. For the succeeding 3 years, however, syntax developed at a steady and, seemingly, accelerating rate.

There was little growth in the children's ability to speechread single word utterances when they were presented orally.

After 4 years all but two children simultaneously spoke and signed every word in the test situation. It is doubtful, however, that the quality of their speech improved very much if any.

After 3 years, mothers were judged, on the average, to have acquired somewhat between a beginner and an average skill in Signed English. Fathers, on the other hand, did not get beyond the beginner's stage.

This is a report of a first evaluation of Signed English, a manual system designed to represent English simply and clearly. Signed English is an educational tool intended to facilitate the learning of English. Since this type of tool can never be separated from its users, this evaluation includes a large amount of qualitatively descriptive information as experimental procedures are virtually impossible to employ in day-to-day school and home settings. It is believed that the reader will better interpret the findings reported herein if he or she knows the circumstances under which this investigation was conducted.

SIGN SYSTEM ENVIRONMENT

In the last decade, schools for the deaf have increasingly used manual communication in the classroom. This change has been most dramatic at the preschool level where signs had previously been excluded as a matter of course (Jordan, Gustason, & Rosen, 1976, 1979). There is little question that this change has been multicaused. (See Furth, 1973 for an extended discussion of possible reasons.) In the main, dissatisfaction with the **results** obtained from an exclusively oral approach became sufficiently widespread for many educators to consider other alternatives. Manual communication was one longstanding alternative which received renewed attention. However, there is little evidence that many schools analyzed their language requirements carefully and matched those requirements against the manual systems that were available. Rather the writers believe that many, if not most, schools began to utilize signs in one of two general ways.

First, many hearing adults have historically communicated with deaf adolescents and adults through the use of a blend of English and the American Sign Language (ASL)[1]. Blends are often found in diglossic language situations, i.e., where members of a minority culture with one language live among a dominant culture which uses a different language. Most of the adult deaf in America appear to live in analagous circumstances, with English and ASL, the two languages serving both "cultures" (Woodward, 1973). Since both deaf and hearing persons are often able to communicate with each other rather well by using a Sign-English blend, many teachers understandably continue to use a Sign-English blend as their manual tool. However, a Sign-English blend is not English, and it would appear that if a child were exposed to a Sign-English blend exclusively then, at best, that blend is what the child would learn.

The second approach, also one with a long history, is to adopt a system derived from the American Sign Language but modified or designed to represent English. The first writer has written extensively elsewhere on these contrived systems (Bornstein, 1973, 1978, 1979). Notwithstanding, the choice of one of the several existing contrived systems often appears to result from accidental encounter with a given system rather than from careful analysis of needs. Sometimes personal taste is the true basis of choice. In this regard, it should be noted that a contrived system invariably will be less graceful and contain more redundant elements than a Sign-English blend. This is all but inevitable, because such systems are designed to represent or parallel a **spoken** natural language. Elements representing inflections for example, are included in a contrived system regardless of need for communication clarity, simply because these are integral parts of English. The writers believe that the task facing system designers is to design a system which balances simplicity and attractiveness against the

---

1. Such blends are termed "pidgins" by linguists. However, since the term is often viewed pejoratively, the term "blend is used in this report .

This evaluation was supported in part by a grant from the Bureau of Education for the Handicapped, HEW. The opinions expressed do not necessarily reflect the opinions or policies of HEW.

Reprinted with permission from American Annals of the Deaf, June 1980, 467-481

need to represent all or most of the important features of English. However, it is naive to believe that any such system will be as fluid and as attractive as either a blend or the American Sign Language.

As noted earlier, several systems have been designed to represent English. Although reviews and logical comparisons of such systems are available (Bornstein, 1973, 1979; Cokely & Gawlik, 1973; Stokoe, 1975; Wilbur, 1976), educational practitioners do not seem to base their choices upon the desiderata described therein.

One reason that logical comparisons between systems may not be effective is that they often focus upon systems fidelity to English. Unfortunately, increased accuracy or fidelity in representing English invariably requires increased system complexity. This increase in complexity generally imposes an added burden upon the learner who, with this type of educational tool, is not only the child but the parent and the teacher as well. Consequently, the question as to which contrived system is best is not a logical but an empirical one. Generally speaking, **"best"** can be defined empirically as that which permits more children to learn more English. The situation is further complicated, however, by the fact that children usually learn their first language in the home from exposure to the language used by the family. If they miss out there, then they must learn from teachers, from other school personnel, or from other children. Thus, the question must be enlarged as to which system can be readily learned by parents and other adults so that they, in turn, can provide an appropriate language environment as early in the life of the child as possible. Further, both parents and child should have materials designed especially for their needs. Consequently, an enormous amount of effort and expense was directed at preparing more than 50 publications for the home and child. These aids are an integral, perhaps the most important, part of the Signed English system. Consequently, comparisons between Signed English and other manual representations of English should not be restricted to the logic of the purely manual aspects of the system. Essentially, when empirical comparisons of effectiveness are made, the techniques designed for learning the manual system are crucial to those comparisons.

At this point it may be useful to describe the logic of the Signed English system and note the major differences between it and other systems designed to represent English. Those readers who might want a full description and comparison should consult these other papers (Bornstein, 1973, 1974, 1975, 1978, 1979).

Signed English is a manual signal which is designed to be a **reasonable** semantic parallel to spoken English. It should be used with speech. Signed English is made up of sign words and sign markers. Each of the sign words in Signed English parallels the **meaning** or **meanings** of a separate word entry in a standard English dictionary. Sign words do not represent sounds or spelling. Similarly, the 14 sign markers included in the system represent the meaning of a selected set of word form changes to indicate tense, plurality, etc. Markers and sign words were selected because of frequent use in English. By design, the basic logic of this system can be represented on a single page as depicted in the figure on the following page.

Signed English is not a language. It is not a substitute for the American Sign Language. It was designed for a different purpose. The basic reason one uses ASL is to communicate with users of that language. Signed English resembles ASL primarily because the overwhelming majority of the signs are taken directly from ASL. When a sign "enters" the Signed

English system, it becomes the semantic equivalent of one given English word. Much of the time, the ASL sign and the sign word have the same meaning. Sometimes they do not. Moreover, sign order and structural characteristics differ as well between ASL and English.

Although Seeing Essential English, Signing Exact English, and Linguistics of Visual English are also derived from the American Sign Language, there are majority differences between Signed English and these other systems. In essence, these systems use signs from the American Sign Language to represent English words and word **parts** which have been sorted according to an arbitrary combination of sound, spelling, and meaning. Because sound is foreign to signs, because English spelling has only a tangential relationship to signs, and because complex and compound English words only sometimes have component sign parallels, these systems contain opposing requirements which are difficult to reconcile. Further, these systems try to include a complete and fully differentiated set of significant word parts, i.e., prefixes, roots, and suffixes (or morphemes) which can be used in unlimited combination. Signed English, on the other hand, employs a **minimum** set of specific and class markers intended to signal the **meaning** of the most common word form changes. Moreover, only one marker is ordinarily used in combination with a sign word. Essentially, this limit is imposed because the motoric requirements and the perceptual demands of unlimited sign combination are judged to be too great (Bornstein, 1979).

In effect, Signed English is as simple a system as can be devised to meet the basic needs of young children, their parents, and their teachers. The system is supplemented with the manual alphabet when the child's language base is sufficiently large enough for him/her to handle greater language complexity.

METHODS

The Design Logic

Ideally, a control group design should be used when assessing the introduction of a tool such as Signed English. One group of children would be exposed to Signed English. A second, similar group would not. If both groups and instructional situations were truly similar, then any incremental change noted for the experimental group could be attributed to the influence of Signed English. This design paradigm was **not** followed for these reasons:

In order to draw comparable samples, it is customary to choose them on the basis of certain attributes, e.g., a limited IQ range, usually around the norm, a degree of hearing loss below given levels, onset of hearing loss by a given age, no additional physical or emotional complications, etc. However, it was obvious that following such a procedure would not allow a description of the utility of the tool for children outside those IQ ranges, or for a later age of onset, or for a slightly smaller hearing impairment, or for what might happen to children who had other problems. Yet, these were the children for whom we wish to know if this tool would be helpful. Clearly, the more variable the subjects included in an experimental sample, the more difficult it is to assemble a comparable group. Another difficulty in employing the usual control design paradigm is that this is a time of great change in the education of the deaf. Schools are frequently changing or modifying their communication techniques (Jordan et al. 1976, 1979). Thus it is almost impossible to be assured that controls

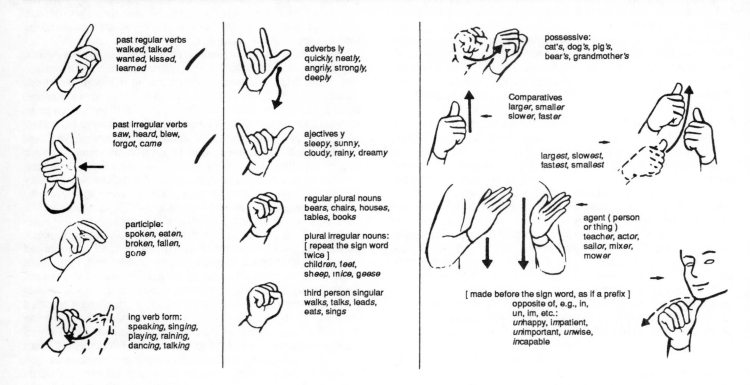

past regular verbs
walked, talked
wanted, kissed,
learned

past irregular verbs
saw, heard, blew,
forgot, came

participle:
spoken, eaten,
broken, fallen,
gone

ing verb form:
speaking, singing,
playing, raining,
dancing, talking

adverbs ly
quickly, neatly,
angrily, strongly,
deeply

ajectives y
sleepy, sunny,
cloudy, rainy, dreamy

regular plural nouns
bears, chairs, houses,
tables, books

plural irregular nouns:
[repeat the sign word
twice]
children, feet,
sheep, mice, geese

third person singular
walks, talks, leads,
eats, sings

possessive:
cat's, dog's, pig's,
bear's, grandmother's

Comparatives
larger, smaller
slower, faster

largest, slowest,
fastest, smallest

agent (person
or thing)
teacher, actor,
sailor, mixer,
mower

[made before the sign word, as if a prefix]
opposite of, e.g., in,
un, im, etc.:
unhappy, impatient,
unimportant, unwise,
incapable

Signed English uses two kinds of gestures or signs: sign words and sign markers. Each sign word stands for one English word from a basic vocabulary of 2500 words used by and with young children. These are words such as mother, house, play, eat, think, etc. These sign words are used in the same order as words in an English sentence.

The sign markers are used when you wish to show that you are talking about more than one thing, show that something has happened in the past, or show the possessive. At this writing, we recommend that you use the 14 sign markers pictured above. All but one of these markers are signed after the sign word. The marker which stands for "opposite of" is the only marker signed before the sign word.

In **Signed English** you use either a sign word alone or a sign word and **one** sign marker to represent a given English word. When this does not adequately represent the word you have in mind, use the manual alphabet and spell the word.

If you use these markers properly, you will be able to offer a better and more complete English model for the child.

in a longitudinal study can continue to serve that purpose throughout the course of the study. In support of this contention, a recent longitudinal study by Moores, McIntyre, & Weiss (1974) amply demonstrates that the most careful and painstakingly assembled treatment groups cannot be maintained as such when schools change their communication and educational philosophies.

Consequently, the basic logic of this evaluation consists of the charting of the English language development of a group of unselected hearing-impaired children and comparing that language development with the generality of hearing children and with already reported studies of other deaf children. For these purposes, two standardized tests and one tailor-made test, designed to measure use of the Signed English marker system, were employed.

Participating Schools and Programs

This study began in the fall of 1974 and was planned originally to continue through the spring of 1977. It was extended still another school year in order to learn further about the language development of the children. Children studied lived in the state of Maryland and came from all parts of the state, i.e., the Baltimore area, and two large suburban areas around Baltimore and Washington, D.C., and from a number of small towns in the coastal and mountainous areas of the state.

The participating programs covered a range of educational services for hearing-impaired children. Three-fourths of the children were taught by the Maryland School for the Deaf. The major components of the schools which figure in this study are the primary departments at the Frederick campus, a residential school, and at the Columbia campus, which has both a day and residential program. Both campuses are also served by a statewide weekly home-visiting program provided without charge to children too young to enter school. Some children from three day classes from Prince Georges County also participated in this study. All of the above are nonselective public programs. Essentially, this means that there was a wide range of cooperation from the families of these children as well as a whole host of problems other than deafness with which these children had to cope.

Sign History of Participating Schools and Programs

The Maryland School for the Deaf began, as a great many other schools have done, with a Sign-English blend and materials that were at hand. This is as it should be, because children must be educated even while tools are being improved or developed. However, sign systems have evolved at this school in very interesting ways. Its parent-infant program, which services both the Frederick and Columbia campuses, depends mainly upon weekly home visits to further the preschool child's linguistic and social environment. It had no sign-learning tools which were deemed appropriate for preschool children and their families. Counselors had neither the sign vocabulary nor the kind of materials that related to family and home activities. Hence they welcomed, and became active participants in, the creation of materials that would meet their needs. The Signed English project owes a great deal to this participation.

The newly established Columbia campus of the Maryland School for the Deaf was staffed largely with a very young faculty. This campus, with few historical constraints upon it, examined very carefully its mission, decided it was to teach English, and chose Signed English from those systems that were available. Several teachers also became involved in the effort. One prepared several scripts for the project, and others made valuable suggestions.

On the other hand, the Frederick campus of the Maryland School for the Deaf historically had used a Sign-English blend. Further, it serves children up through the high school grades. During most of the course of this study, it had a committee engaged in preparing a collection of signs for school use. During the next to the last year of the study, the committee produced a collection of about 750 signs, only a small number of which differed from those used in Signed English. As mentioned previously, the children on this campus range up through high school age, and almost half of them first attended the school at the age of 12. Consequently, a wide variety of Sign-English blends are found here, especially at the upper levels. The language environment at Frederick can, therefore, be regarded as much more complex than that at Columbia. The primary department at Frederick, however, uses most of the materials and most of the signs of Signed English. At this writing, a "final" sign system is still evolving on this campus.

The three day classes in Prince Georges County, Maryland, the last group of participants, chose to use Signed English because the system and materials seemed to best meet their needs. However, participating teachers had learned to sign elsewhere and sometimes used signs other than those found in the Signed English system. Further, since the classrooms were not in the same school, there was less uniformity in these classrooms.

The question arises: do the differences in system usage described above bias the **evaluations** reported herein? The writers believe that the effects on the **evaluation** of using alternate signs for a given English word were rather minor because (a) relatively few signs differ at the age levels we were considering, and (b) before each child was tested, the examiner determined which signs were used by the teacher and substituted accordingly.

Of far greater import to the writers are the **effects** of inconsistent and/or infrequent use of the sign system on language development. Do parents and/or teachers always use the sign system properly or for all the words they speak, and how com-plete is their use of the marker system, i.e., those signs which indicate tense, plurality, etc.? Ratings by teachers of parents' usage of the system indicate otherwise. These ratings will be discussed later in this report. Teachers also rendered self-ratings on their own skills with Signed English which, unfortunately, did not always agree with the judgment of members of the project team. Indeed, project members were able to detect, with very little difficulty, wide differences in the use of the sign system by different teachers. In general, where supervisors and teachers alike showed concern for uniformity and full use, the manual system employed was for the most part much closer to that envisioned by the system designers. When these conditions did not exist, it appeared to project personnel that children did not learn as well. No data were collected to document this matter because to do so might well have destroyed rapport with school personnel.

Special Conditions of the Evaluation

A major problem in education is the amount of time it usually takes for a significant innovation or new tool to become known to, and then adopted by, schools and teachers. Essentially, the process calls for the development of the tool, tryout with appropriate students, and an experimental comparison between an experimental group and one or more control groups. Finally, the evaluated tool is disseminated to the educational community. This is a prudent, orderly way to ensure that the innovation really represents an improvement. But it is **not** the way the Signed English system was evaluated. Here is why:

When the study first began in June 1974, only a half dozen story books and two posters were ready. This was considered inadequate for parents and children. Therefore, production of materials proceeded at a rate of approximately 15 teaching aids per annum. Because the profession seemed to consider a system a **"system"** only if it were presented in a dictionary-like form, it was judged necessary to prepare such a volume. This was entitled *The Basic Preschool Signed English Dictionary* and consisted of approximately 1,100 signs. After 2 years this dictionary was replaced by a larger, revised one, *The Signed English Dictionary for Preschool and Elementary Levels*. This book contains about 2,200 signs. A third, still larger dictionary, is in preparation.

It should be obvious, therefore, that the teaching aids of the Signed English system were being worked upon and developed at the very same time that the system was being evaluated. Even at this writing, the system is still being expanded and revised. Similarly, the teachers began to learn how to use these teaching aids and the system as it developed over the years. It is fairly clear, therefore, that this evaluation was not of a system in optimum condition or use. As an aside, the writers guess that it probably takes several years before a newly introduced manual system can be learned and used efficiently. Indeed, unless the school administration and faculty choose one system, define it properly, and monitor its use carefully, it is probable that a system will never be used well.

In summary, this evaluation was made of a system during the very course of its development and while it was still being learned by teachers. Consequently, it should yield a more conservative estimate of effectiveness than a study that might be started when the system is complete. Unfortunately, such a study might not be available for another 10 years.

Measuring Instruments

The principal group of children studied was a group of 20 children who attended preschool and who would be at least 4 years old before the close of the first school year in 1975. It was thought that 4 years was the youngest age at which a child could be administered an individual language test such as the Peabody Picture Vocabulary Test (PPVT) or the Northwestern Syntax Screening Test (NSST). As it turned out, some such children were not able to achieve even a minimum score on the latter test. This is reported, of course, but procedures for scoring partial success were also developed and, as will be seen, were quite sensitive to emerging language development.

In addition to the principal group of 20, a second group of 17 children came into the school the following year (1976), and a third group of 11 started in 1977. These children served as backup groups primarily because the size of each group was so small. The characteristics and language development of these groups were compared with the primary group to note if there were any major differences. In the main, the groups were roughly similar and performed approximately the same. Correlations between language development and other variables of interest such as demographic variables fluctuated markedly between groups and over time. Such fluctuations seem almost surely to be a function of small samples rather than of the variables of interest.

As noted in the section on design logic, the language performance of these children was to be compared with that of "normal" children. Unfortunately, most standardized tests of language competency have difficulty slopes which are too steep for the hearing impaired. Simply put, such tests are too difficult. After the first few items, the hearing-impaired child is often unable to respond correctly. After a careful review of those available, we chose the PPVT and the NSST as most likely to be sensitive to the level of language competency of these children. Nevertheless, we were not able to escape the fact that the latter test, especially, was still too difficult; therefore, we sometimes resorted to counting correct performance for parts of sentences in order to trace language development. Such scoring did prove useful and yielded some interesting findings.

In addition to language achievement as measured by these two tests, we measured the children's performance in three ways important to those who study the language development of the hearing impaired. First, we compared the size of the children's receptive vocabulary when words were communicated by the simultaneous method and by the oral method. Next, we measured how much vocalization each child used and judged how intelligible that vocalization was. Finally, we described their ability to receive and produce 11 of the 14 markers in the Signed English system. We were not able to devise effective test items for the three remaining markers. The test and analyses will be described below. The tailor-made test is described in Appendix 1.

The children were tested individually each spring (April or May) for four successive years. Each testing session was limited to 40 minutes, although most were much shorter because testing was terminated when the child had reached his or her "ceiling." The same 20 children were tested throughout the 4-year span except for two children, slightly older than the average of the group, who moved from the state in the final year of the study. Their final performance was not measured.

RESULTS

Subject and Family Background

When they entered the several school programs, the participating children had a mean chronological age of approximately 4 years (47.6 months). Their mean better ear hearing loss was 88.2 (S.D. 23.2 decibels). The mean age of onset of deafness was 1.1 months (S.D. 3.3). In effect, the entire sample was prelingually deaf and quite homogeneous on the variables generally considered the most sensitive predictors of language performance and educational achievement.

Information gained about the families of the children revealed that the average age of their mothers was 30.8 years (S.D. 4.8) while that of their fathers was 33.8 (S.D. 4.6). Both mothers and fathers had a mean educational level of 13.5 years (S.D.'s of 3.0 and 2.9, respectively). On an occupational level scale ranging from 1-6, the mean occupational level of the fathers was 4.12 (S.D. 1.69) and that of the mothers, 2.38 (S.D. 2.25). Most mothers were homemakers. Some supplemented that role with nonprofessional jobs. A level of 4 on this scale corresponds to that of technical or skilled craftsman jobs. Two of the 20 sets of parents were, themselves, hearing impaired. None of the remaining families had any previous significant contact with the hearing impaired.

In this latter regard, teachers rated those parents with whom they had some contact on their facility with Signed English. The scale ranged from zero to four. The scale points were: 0 = no use; 1 = no skill; 2 = a beginner; 3 = average; and 4 = very good. These evaluations are summarized over the first 3 years of the study, as noted in Table 1.

The data in Table 1 show that the parents obviously did not advance very much beyond the beginners' level of proficiency even after 3 years of exposure and use. Although one would expect that mothers would acquire more skill than fathers, the difference between means was not statistically significant. However, it is likely that the true difference between mothers and fathers is greater than that shown in Table 1, because the number of fathers rated dropped each year. This usually happened because teachers had insufficient contact with them to be able to rate them. Probably the "missing" fathers were even less skilled than those rated.

As noted earlier, correlations based on N's of 20 and less are subject to wide sampling fluctuation. However, the pattern of correlations between the mothers' and fathers' facility in

Table 1. Mean Judged Facility of Mothers and Fathers in Signed English After One, Two, and Three Years.

| After Year | One | | Two | | Three | |
	Mothers	Fathers	Mothers	Fathers	Mothers	Fathers
Mean	1.94	2.12	2.69	1.91	2.67	2.10
SD	1.04	1.69	1.08	1.45	1.05	1.37
N	18	16	16	11	15	10

Table 2. Receptive Achievement on Peabody Picture Vocabulary Test (PPVR) and Northwestern Syntax Screening Test (NSST) at One Year Intervals. (N=20)*

| Variable | | Mean Scores After Academic Year | | |
	One	Two	Three	Four
Chronological Age (months)	56.6	68.6	80.6	92.2
PVVT (months)	33.8	38.9	46.1	49.2
NSST (percentile for a given year and month range)	no age	20%	25%	25%
	equiv.	3.0-3.11	4.0-4.11	6.6-6.11
NSST Raw Score (total possible: 40)	11.3	18.8	23.9	29.2

* After Year Four, the N fell to 18. The two *missing* children were older than the average of the group.

Signed English and the several measures of English competence for the second and third years showed some positive relationships as high as .40 and .50. Many others were much lower. There was so much sampling variation in these statistics that it seems best to await better estimates from studies with larger samples.

Receptive Measures of Language Development

After being in school for 7 or 8 months, the children had a mean chronological age of 56.6 months or a few months short of 5 years of age (Table 2). At this same time the mean simultaneous communication receptive vocabulary score of the PPVT was 33.8 months or about 2 months short of 3 years. Consequently, there was about a 23-month lag at this age. Nearly 3 years later, the children's vocabulary had grown a little more than a year and a quarter. Their rate of growth in knowledge or words was thus about 43% of that of hearing children. There was a decline in rate of vocabulary growth in the last year as the mean gain was only slightly more than 3 months.

There may be two explanations for this apparent slowing down. First, the difficulty of the vocabulary test appears to accelerate rather rapidly, i.e., later words on the test appear much less frequently in children's texts according to the tabulations recorded in the *American Heritage Word Frequency Book*. Second, and perhaps more important, most of the later

words in the test must be fingerspelled, because there are no signs presently available to represent them. Since these children were only beginning to read, they most probably had not encountered many of the "spelled" words.

The second standardized test, the NSST, presents a somewhat different picture. After the first "year" in school, the children did not perform well enough to merit an age equivalent score. Gains after that first year, however, are much more impressive. Three years later, the children were able to complete nearly three-fourths of the times on the test and score at the 25th percentile of the 72-83 month range. Since the vocabulary on this test is deliberately kept simple, it can be said that children do develop a considerable competence with simple syntax within a restricted vocabulary range.

Expressive Measures of Language Performance

As can be seen in Table 3, the children were not, on the average, able to express a single correct English sentence after their first 7 or 8 months in school. Since the teachers firmly believed that the children were expressing themselves better, project personnel began to measure sentence elements or parts at the end of the second year of testing. Test administration remained unchanged. The examiner simply recorded verbatim all of the children's responses to her statements. The first column in Table 3 shows the number of different sentence elements and how many of each are found in the test sentences.

Table 3. Expressive Performance on NSST at One Year Intervals. (N = 20)*

| Variable | No. in Test | One** | Mean Score After Academic Years | | |
			Two	Three	Four
Sentences	40	0.2	1.8	6.3	11.8
Words	193	--	102.3	147.6	160.6
Form Class Words	103	--	78.0	96.4	96.7
Structure Class Words	90	--	24.3	51.2	64.1
Strings	--	--	11.3	8.4	2.1
Mean Lengths of Utterance	5.0	--	3.5	3.7	4.0
Morphemes	224	--	106.5	157.6	173.4
2 Word Combinations	--	--	1.4	1.2	2.2
2 Word Emerg Sentence	--	--	5.4	3.9	2.7
3 Word Emerg Sentence	--	--	8.2	13.0	14.4
Noun Phrases	75	--	32.9	32.8	44.6
Verb Phrases	46	--	5.1	15.5	21.7
Number of Transformations	19	--	1.3	4.1	5.3
No. Different Transforms	19	--	.8	2.6	2.8
No. Inflections	27		4.2	9.9	13.6
No. Different Inflections	5		1.3	2.7	3.3

* After Year Four, the N was 18.
** Partial scoring began after Year Two

For example, there are about 27 inflections present in the 40 sentences, but only five different kinds are included. Although judgments about what may or may not be an "emerging" sentence might be somewhat subjective, the other sentence elements appear to be objectively measured. Now to the results:

On the complete sentence level, using the conventional way of scoring, the children were not able to earn an age equivalent until the close of their final year, where they fell at the first decile of the 3 years to 3 years and 11 months age range. On the partial sentence level, however, their teachers' intuitive judgments were clearly borne out. The children improved markedly in every index noted. The sharp drop in their use of word strings, a sequence of words with no apparent ordering, is also noteworthy. The results suggest that these children may now be at the threshold of expressing themselves in correct English sentences, albeit very simple ones.

Comparison of Receptive Vocabulary as Transmitted by Means of Simultaneous Communication and Oral Communication

There are two forms (A and B) of the PPVT. Throughout the 4-year period, each child was administered both forms. The first administration of the PPVT, with forms randomly chosen, was solely oral. The remaining form was administered on another day when the test administrator both spoke and signed the vocabulary items. As can be seen in Table 4, there appears to be little growth in the children's ability to comprehend the vocabulary when it is presented orally. Since their scores on the simultaneous communication administration indicate that the children do command a considerable vocabulary, the consistently poor performance on the oral administration reflects their inability to speechread single word utterances effectively.

Amount of Quality of Voice Used

As noted earlier, scoring of sentence parts on the NSST expressive scale did not begin until the second year of testing.

Then the examiner noted on her score sheet which words were expressed manually, orally, or simultaneously. Finally, she made an independent judgment as to the intelligibility of the child's speech. The results shown in Table 5 reveal that in this testing situation, at least, the majority of the words expressed were simultaneously spoken and signed throughout all stages. In the early years, a significant proportion of the words, a third to a fourth, were expressed manually. However, after 4 years, only two children did not express every word simultaneously. One of these children was about 70% manual and 30% simultaneous. The other expressed about half orally and half simultaneously. This last child was the only child judged to have good speech.

The judgments of speech intelligibility were based upon a four-point scale: (1) no voice used, (2) unintelligible speech, (3) intelligible speech, and (4) good speech. The mean score for the group remained at the unintelligible level over the years. There is a slight improvement in the last year, but it is difficult to know whether or not this is a chance phenomenon or whether the examiner had simply learned to know these specific children better. It can be stated unequivocally, however, that children do not stop speaking when taught in a simultaneous communication environment. It is doubtful, nevertheless, that the quality of their speech improved very much, if any. Certainly, it will require a sustained and focused effort to teach this skill to these children.

Reception and Expression of the Signed English Markers

The reader will recall that only five different inflections exist in the NSST. Consequently, a special morphological test was devised in the third year of study to test the ability of the children to express and receive the Signed English markers. The 11 markers tested are listed in Table 6. On the receptive test each child was required to point to one of two pictures after the content was described by the examiner. Because it was a long test, only two items were presented for each marker. "Mastery" meant that the child got both items correct. A similar procedure was obtained for the expressive part of the test. Then, however, the child was required to complete the stimu-

Table 4. Comparison of Receptive Vocabulary on PPVT When Transmitted by Oral and Simultaneous Communication Methods. (N=20)*

| Variable (age in months) | Mean Scores After Year | | | |
	One	Two	Three	Four
Chronological Age	56.6	68.6	80.6	92.2
Simultaneous Communication	33.8	38.9	46.1	49.2
Oral Communication	12.6	17.6	22.8	17.7

* After Year Four, N was 18.

Table 5. Amount and Quality of Voice Used on Expressive Part of NSST. (number of words in test = 193)

| Variable | Mean Scores After Year | | | |
	One	Two	Three	Four
Manual Words Only	--	34.1	32.9	All but two
Oral Words Only	--	3.3	3.1	children were 100%
Simultaneous Words	--	64.9	102.7	simultaneous.
Voice Intelligibility*	--	2.2	2.1	2.4

* Intelligiblity scale: 1 = no voice used; 2 = unintelligible; 3 = intelligible; 4 = good speech.

Table 6. Percent of Students with All (Two) Correct Responses On a Picture Morphology Test.

Sign Marker	Receptive After Year				Expressive After Year			
	One	Two	Three	Four	One	Two	Three	Four
1. regular plural	27	53	75	94	09	12	50	67
2. possessive	18	35	75	78	15	12	50	61
3. ing	27	59	75	100	08	12	25	50
4. regular past	00	06	10	39	08	00	15	39
5. 3rd person	36	65	80	78	00	00	15	11
6. participle	00	06	05	22	00	00	00	17
7. comparative	18	65	90	100	00	00	00	11
8. superlative	00	59	60	67	08	00	05	12
9. agent	18	35	45	89	00	00	00	17
10. irregular plural	00	24	10	39	00	00	00	05
11. irregular past	00	00	10	33	00	00	00	05
N	11	17	20	18	11	17	20	18

lus sentence with the properly inflected last word. Although by simply guessing, 25% of the children could be expected to get two items correct, this did not happen often. When unable to handle the task, the children most often actually did not try to guess. The very large number of zero percents in Table 6 corroborates this observation. Since this test was not developed until after the third year of evaluation, it was necessary to test other children who had been in school for only 1 or 2 years. It will be recalled that 17 children had enrolled 1 year after the experiment began while a second group of 11 children enrolled 2 years later. In effect, therefore, the first three columns represent cross sectional findings. The fourth column is a longitudinal extension of the third year for the principal group of children studied.

The results reported in Table 6 are quite consistent with those found with the standardized tests of language performance. Receptive competence preceded expressive competence by a wide margin. While receptively many markers were at or approached 100% accuracy, only the regular plural, possessive, and "ing" endings could be expressed by half of the children. The patterns of growth in the ability to receive are clearly and roughly parallel to those of hearing children. Hopefully, the same will happen expressively, but because of the lag, more data will be required before this can be regarded as conclusive.

DISCUSSION

The results obtained from the administration of the two standardized tests, the Peabody Picture Vocabulary Test and the Northwestern Syntax Screening Test, and the tailor-made Signed English Morphology Test show that these children are developing some competence in the English language. Not surprisingly, it is a limited competence. Will it continue to develop and to what degree? Obviously, we must wait for these children to grow further to answer this question. Moreover, an acceptable answer may best be obtained by disinterested scientists using carefully drawn and adequately sized samples.

System makers tend to compare the progress of this group with others who may have been exposed to other communication systems. One recent attempt to establish norms for hearing-impaired children who were exposed primarily to fingerspelling in the classroom shows that children got comparable PPVT scores only after they were 12 or more years of age

(Forde, 1977). By this standard, this sample did well. But the truth is that these other children performed in a very limited fashion, and it is of small comfort that the children in this study did considerably better.

Perhaps a better way to look at the problem is to note that the children began to show less progress on the vocabulary test at that point where no signs were available to represent the words in the test. Quite simply, the children were unable to read the fingerspelled words. This suggests two possibilities for remediation. First, more signs could be incorporated into the Signed English system. This is being done. As always, existing signs would be incorporated first, followed by invented signs where appropriate. However, there seems to be a real limit to the number of signs that can be added. The system presently contains about 2,600 signs and will be expanded to perhaps 4,000. At that point, it might be the largest collection of signs published. Beyond that point, the "return" for each new sign would be rather small, because each would parallel a word that is used rather infrequently. Further, each new sign must be learned by hearing adults, and it is not clear how many would seek to learn such signs. The vast majority of parents have demonstrated that they are not near the limits of the current vocabulary.

Second, it seems probable that a more efficient way to further language growth may be to facilitate the children's transition from reading signs to reading print as rapidly as possible. Essentially, those sign words known to the child should be associated with their printed counterparts as early as possible. Along with that transition, reading materials should be structured so that new vocabulary can be learned from context. A more complete statement of this rationale was presented earlier (Bornstein, in press). It will be the starting point of the next sizable phase of the Signed English project.

CONCLUSIONS AND SUGGESTIONS FOR FURTHER STUDY

Perhaps the major reservation in writing a report such as this is the realization that this evaluation is already seriously dated. It will be remembered that the teaching aids which are an integral part of the Signed English system were developed throughout the very course of the evaluation. Indeed, new aids are still being developed at this writing. Similarly, the teachers who used the system were at varying levels of skill in their use of signs and speech. By the time the evaluation was completed, most of these teachers had probably become quite skillful. It is very possible that better results might have been achieved if the teachers had been fully experienced throughout the course of the study.

Regardless of these problems, it was possible to demonstrate that children exposed to Signed English did, indeed, begin to acquire some considerable skill in the use of this English based system. The order of acquisition of sign markers, if not the pace, appeared to be roughly comparable to that noted for hearing children. It still remains to be demonstrated, however, that these children will master the full set of markers although there appears to be no clear reason why this may not happen.

Vocabulary acquisition also is still somewhat indeterminate. The children reached the same vocabulary level of the Peabody Picture Vocabulary Test many years earlier than another rather similar group of deaf children (Forde, 1977). Both groups "paused" at a place on that test where the English vocabulary was not represented by existing signs. Not surprisingly, it appears that further vocabulary growth may be dependent upon the development and use of reading skills rather than signs. The Signed English project will direct its attention to this goal as the next step in its program (Bornstein, in press). The outcome of this effort will be the subject of future reports to the profession.

REFERENCES

Bornstein, H. (1973). Description of some current sign systems designed to represent English. *American Annals of the Deaf*, 3, 454-463.

Bornstein, H. (1974). Signed English: A manual approach to English language development. *Journal of Speech and Hearing Disorders*, 3, 330-343.

Bornstein, H. (1978). Sign language in the education of the deaf. In I. Schlesinger & L. Namir (Eds.), *Sign language of the deaf: Psychological, linguistics, and social perspectives*. New York: Academic Press, Inc., pp. 333-359

Bornstein, H. (1979). Systems of sign. In L. Bradford & W. Hardy (Eds.), *Hearing and hearing impairment*. New York: Academic Press, Inc., pp. 333-361

Bornstein, H. The design of Signed English readers. *Proceedings of Gallaudet Conference on Reading in Relations to Deafness*, Washington, D.C., (in press).

Bornstein, H., Hamilton, L., & Saulnier, K. (1975). *The Signed English dictionary: For preschool and elementary levels*. Washington, D.C.: Gallaudet College Press.

Carroll, J., Davies, P., & Richman, B. (1971). *The American heritage word frequency book*. New York: American Heritage Publishing Co., Inc.

Cokely, D., & Gawlik, R. (May 1973). Options: A position paper on the relationship between manual English and sign. *Deaf American*, pp. 7-11.

Forde, J. (1977). Data on the Peabody Picture Vocabulary Test. *American Annals of the Deaf*, 122, 38-43.

Furth, H. (1973). *Deafness and learning*: A psychological approach. Belmont, Calif.: Wadsworth Publishing Co., Inc.

Goodman, L., Wilson, P., & Bornstein, H. (April 1978). Results of a national survey of sign language programs in special education. *Mental Retardation*, pp. 104-106.

Jordan, I.K., Gustason, G., & Rosen, R. (1976). Current communication trends at programs for the deaf. *American Annals of the Deaf*, 121, 527-532.

Jordan, I.K., Gustason, G., & Rosen, R. (1979). An update on communication trends at programs for the deaf. *American Annals of the Deaf*, 124, 350-357.

Moores, D.F., McIntyre, C.K., & Weiss, K.L. (December 1974). *Evaluation of programs for hearing impaired children: Report of 1973-1974*. Research Report #81. Minneapolis: University of Minnesota.

Stokoe, W.C. (1975). Face to face interaction: Sign to language. *In Organization of behavior: Face to face interaction*. The Hague, Mouton.

Wilbur, R.B. (1976). The linguistics of manual language and manual systems. In Lyle L. Lloyd (Ed.), *Communication assessment and intervention strategies*. Baltimore: University Park Press, pp. 423-500.

Woodward, J. (1973). Some characteristics of Pidgin Sign English. *Sign Language Studies*, 3, 39-46.

APPENDIX 1

The Signed English Morphology Test[2]

The Signed English Morphology Test developed for use with primary level hearing-impaired students ages 4-12 tests their familiarity with the following inflectional word endings and word changes: noun plural, regular (-s); verb, ing; noun possessive (-'s); verb past, regular (-ed); noun plural, irregular; verb, third person singular (-s); adjective comparative (-er); noun agent marker (-er). All of the above listed inflections and word changes can be produced by using the sign markers provided for in Signed English (See Figure 1).

The receptive portion of the test measures the child's ability to perceive an inflected or otherwise "marked" word and assign to it the meaning denoted by the marker. A sentence including the marked word is spoken and signed to the child and he/she must choose one picture of two which best conveys the meaning of the sentence.

The expressive portion of the test surveys the child's ability to express inflected words and word changes in a structured setting. After looking at stimulus pictures, the child is expected to complete the examiner's sentence with the appropriately marked word.

Since this morphology test is designed for hearing-impaired children, the examiner simultaneously says and signs the stimulus material. The child is encouraged to respond accordingly. However, a purely manual or oral response is acceptable. The test should be administered over a 2-day period.

2. The Signed English Morophology Test was developed by Karen L. Saulnier and Virginia Heidinger.

The receptive portion of the test is presented on the first day. The child is comfortably seated at the table directly across from the examiner. A binder containing the colorful and clearly illustrated test items is placed on the table in front of the child. The examiner flips up all the pages within the binder. After establishing eye contact with the child, the examiner exposes the first of four practice items. These practice items may be used in any way necessary to elicit a correct response from the child. Additional "prompt" sentences may be used to insure the child's understanding of the task at hand (e.g., "This is a picture of an apple. This is a picture of two apples. Now, can you show me a picture of 'apples?'" If the child is still unable to respond correctly to the practice item, the examiner may furnish the answer.

When the practice items have been completed, the first of the test items is presented. The key sentences are spoken and signed by the examiner. The child then points to the picture which best illustrates the key sentence. The child's choice is recorded on the response sheet by the examiner.

The expressive portion of the test is administered on the second day. The physical setting and testing procedure is the same as it was for the receptive portion of the test. However, instead of pointing to an appropriate picture, the child's response task is to spontaneously complete the examiner's sentence with the correctly marked word. Again the child is encouraged to both speak and sign, however, either a manual or oral response will be accepted. The child's response is recorded on the response sheet by the examiner. If desired, incorrect and/or incomplete responses may also be noted on the response sheet for future error analysis.

After the entire test has been completed, the results from both response sheets are entered on the tally sheets. This does not give a final score to the test, but it does allow for an item analysis of the markers so that the general characteristics of the child's responses may be more clearly seen.

SIGNED ENGLISH MORPHOLOGY TEST
RECEPTIVE PORTION

Sample Items

A. Which picture is **apples**?
B. The dog has food.
   Show me: The **dog's** food.
C. The cat can walk.
   Show me: The cat **walked**.
D. Show me: The cat is **walking**.

Test Items

1. Which picture is **moons**?
2. This boy will dig.
   Show me: The boy is **digging**.
3. Which picture is **glasses**?
4. This cat has a baby.
   Show me: The **cat's** baby.
5. This boy will push.
   Show me: The boy **pushed**.
6. These mice are small.
   Which mouse is **smaller**?
7. These dogs are brown.
   Which dog is the **brownest**?
8. This dog has a house.
   Show me: The **dog's** house.

9. The girl will talk.
   Show me: The girl is **talking**.
10. This ice cream will melt.
    Show me: The ice cream **melted**.
11. Which picture is **women**?
12. This boy will jump.
    Show me: The boy **jumps**.
13. These pigs are fat.
    Which pig is **fatter**?
14. The boys are sad.
    Which boy is **saddest**?
15. The girl can pull.
    Show me: The girl has **pulled**.
16. Show me: The **painter**.
17. The cat will drink.
    Show me: The cat **drank**.
18. Show me: The **driver**.
19. This cat can walk.
    Show me: The cat has **walked**.
20. These boys will fight.
    Show me: The boys **fought**.
21. Which picture is **feet**?
22. The boy can throw.
    Show me: The boy **throws**.

SIGNED ENGLISH MORPHOLOGY TEST
EXPRESSIVE PORTION

Sample Items

A. This is a bird.
   Here are two (**birds**).
B. The girl can eat.
   Now the girl is (**eating**).
C. This dog can cry.
   Yesterday the dog (**cried**).
D. This girl has a bow.
   Here is the (**girl's**) bow.

Test Items

1. This is a star.
   Here are two (**stars**).
2. The baby can cry.
   Now the baby is (**crying**).
3. This is a cup.
   Here are two (**cups**).
4. The boy has a ball.
   Here is the (**boy's**) ball.
5. This house will burn.
   Yesterday the house (**burned**).
6. This fish is small.
   This fish is even (**smaller**).
7. This fish is the (**smallest**).
8. The duck has an umbrella.
   Here is the (**duck's**) umbrella.
9. The girl can swim.
   Now the girl is (**swimming**).
10. This flower will die.
    Yesterday the flower (**died**).
11. This is a man.
    Here are two (**men**).
12. The rabbit can jump.
    Everyday the rabbit (**jumps**).

13. This snake is long.
    This snake is even **(longer).**
14. This snake is the **(longest).**
15. The dog can pull.
    Now the dog has **(pulled).**
16. The woman can sing.
    She is called a **(singer).**
17. This dog can eat.
    Yesterday the dog **(ate).**
18. This man can build.
    He is called a **(builder).**
19. This flower will open.
    Now the flower has **(opened).**
20. This glass can break.
    Yesterday the glass **(broke).**
21. This is a mouse.
    Here are two **(mice).**
22. The boy can ride.
    Everyday the boy **(rides).**

SIGNED ENGLISH: A BRIEF FOLLOW-UP TO
THE FIRST EVALUATION

Harry Bornstein and Karen L. Saulnier
Gallaudet Signed English Project
Gallaudet University, Washington, D.C.

One year after the first evaluation, teachers rated 18 children on their frequency of use of the Signed English markers. On the average, the group showed a slight improvement in their *use* of the marker system. Six children used the markers significantly better, seven slightly better, and three showed no change. Two children could not be rated.

Additionally, frequency of use of each of the 14 markers was also rated by the teachers. The regular plural and the possessive were frequently used. The ing marker and the regular past were somewhat regularly used. Five other markers were seldom used and five were rarely used. Some possible explanations for these results are offered.

INTRODUCTION

Last year, this journal published a first evaluation of Signed English. This is a brief and limited follow-up to that evaluation. It is concerned exclusively with the expressive use of the sign markers of the Signed English system one year later.

One of the basic tasks in designing a manual English system is how to represent English words over the many and varied forms they may take in English sentences. Signed English accomplishes this by "adding" a separate sign, termed a sign marker, to the singular form of a word or to uninflected forms of verbs and adjectives. The combination of sign and sign marker represents the desired meaning of the target word.

When this strategy is employed, two problems are encountered. First, adding signs requires additional effort and increases time of execution. Clearly, unlimited combinations of signs should hamper the ability of a signer to synchronize his/her speech and signs. Consequently, Signed English limits combinations to a single sign and a single sign marker. Second, as noted above, there are a great many inflections or bound morphemes in English that could be represented. If sign markers were developed for each of these word form variations, these would have to be learned and used by adults, more than 95% of whom are hearing, before they are learned by the children. This is, without question, a difficult learning task. To simplify this task, the Signed English system design takes advantage of the fact that most of these word form changes are used rather infrequently. Only frequent form changes, therefore, are included in the system. The manual alphabet is used to represent infrequent words and infrequent word form changes. Historically, the maximum number of sign markers proposed was 14, later it dropped to 12, and now it is back up to 14. In truth only half of these are frequently used in English. The reduced set of seven markers are especially recommended for adults who are not "linguistically adept" or facile with manual communication.

METHOD

In the first evaluation, a group of 18 unselected children were measured on their ability to receive and express themselves correctly on 11 of the 14 sign markers on a tailor-made picture morphology test. Only 11 markers were tested because the writers were unable to devise items to measure three of the markers. One year later, rather than assessing a child's ability to perform in a testing situation, it was decided to secure ratings of marker **use** from each child's teacher. Teacher ratings are an economical way, in time and money, to obtain informa-

tion about a child's actual day-to-day behavior. However, such ratings may not be as reliable or valid a measure as that which might be obtained from a standardized test situation.

Ratings were rendered by the teacher checking the appropriate number on a four-point scale of usage: 4 = almost always; 3 = frequent; 2 = seldom; and 1 = rarely, for each of the 14 sign markers. The rating scales were drawn on a single page. On a separate page, the teacher was asked to rate **change** in overall use of the entire marker system. This scale ranged from 4 = significantly better; 3 = slightly better; 2 = about the same; and 1 = decreased usage. There was also a space for a teacher to indicate if he/she was not able to make such a judgment.

The students rated were the 18 students who participated longest in our evaluation, i.e., for 5 years. Their mean chronological age was 114.2 months at the time of this rating. A more complete description of them can be found in the first evaluation. However, the final receptive and expressive columns from Table 6, Percent of Students with All (Two) Correct Responses On a Picture Morphology Test, are included in the results section of this report to enable the reader to better understand the current findings.

RESULTS

As can be seen in Table 1, on the average, two markers were judged to be frequently used by these children. These are the regular plural and the possessive. Two other markers fall more than halfway between seldom and frequent use. These are the ing marker and the regular past. Five other markers are seldom used: the 3rd person singular, the irregular plural, the agent, and the comparative. The remaining five markers are rarely used: the participle, the superlative, the irregular past, the adjectival, and the opposite.

The ratings on overall use of the system markers as compared with that of a year ago yielded a mean rating of 3.19 (S.D. = .75), which indicates slightly better use of the marker system than was evident at the end of the previous year. Of the 18 children, six used the markers significantly better, seven slightly better, three showed no change in use, and two could not be evaluated because they had a new teacher. There was a rank order correlation of .68 between the ranked percentage of expressive knowledge of the first 11 sign markers and their ranked frequency of use 1 year later. Thus, an estimate of competence in expressive use of markers appears to be a good predictor of later **order** of frequency of judged use of markers. The order of percentage of correct recognition of the sign markers did not relate as high with the two expressive

Reprinted with permission from American Annals of the Deaf, February 1981, 69-72.

Table 1.

| | After FOUR Years [a] | | After FIVE Years | |
| | Percentage of Students With All (Two) Correct Responses On a Picture Morphology Test | | Teacher Ratings of Expressive Use [b] | |
Sign Marker	Receptive	Expressive	Mean	S.D.
1. regular plural	94	67	3.06	.94
2. possessive	78	61	2.89	.90
3. ing	100	50	2.61	.92
4. regular past	39	39	2.67	1.14
5. 3rd person	78	11	1.94	1.11
6. participle	22	17	1.06	.24
7. comparative	100	11	1.72	.83
8. superlative	67	11	1.39	.61
9. agent	89	17	1.78	1.11
10. irregular past	39	05	1.44	.78
11. irregular plural	33	05	1.83	.71
12. adverbial	NOT MEASURED		1.28	.46
13. adjectival	NOT MEASURED		1.44	.62
14. opposite	NOT MEASURED		1.11	.47

[a] Statistics taken from the first evaluation.

[b] 4 = almost always; 3 = frequent; 2 = seldom; 1 = rarely.

measures. It was .41 with both expressive rankings: the order of correct expressive use in the same year and the order of frequency of use a year later. The principal reason for the reduced size of the latter two relationships appears to be caused by the contrast between high recognition of the comparative, superlative, and agent markers, and the relatively low use of those same markers.

DISCUSSION

This brief study demonstrates that this group of unselected deaf children, on the average, continues to show a slight improvement in their **use** of the sign markers of the Signed English system. Slightly more than a third of the group were rated as showing a significant increase in their usage of the set of sign markers. How praiseworthy these numbers are clearly depends upon the readers' expectations. If one expects significant growth every year for all children, then these findings are disappointing. However, it should be pointed out that pauses or plateaus in language development on the part of deaf children are not unusual. For example, the normative sample employed in the CID Grammatical Analysis of Elicited Language Test shows a plateau at ages six and seven and another apparently appearing at age eight to nine, the age at which testing stopped (Moog & Geers, 1979, pp. 57; 60; 61).

Another possibility is worth considering. Although expressive knowledge of the sign markers lags behind receptive knowledge, the students did show growth in their expressive ability in the first evaluation. However, frequency of use and expressive ability are not the same phenomena. As noted earlier, using a marker requires additional time and effort and often adds little semantic information beyond that supplied by context. It may well be that children will not freely use some markers except where such use brings positive reinforcement, e.g., teacher approval, better test performance, and increased understanding of their language. It is even possible that expressive knowledge might be manifested or used more in

speech and/or in writing where social approval and disapproval may be more evident on the part of adults.

Some comments about the individual markers are in order. How frequently each marker is used by a child is probably a complex function of the general language level of the child, the frequency with which a given marker appears in the language (over all levels), and the expressive value of the marker for a child, i.e., the amount of information which is conveyed by using the marker. In general, the frequency of usage of these 14 markers parallels that found at early stages of language development for hearing children. There are exceptions, however. For example, the third person singular marker is frequently used in English, but not by these children. Why? Possibly because the third person singular marker most often offers redundant information. Context and the appropriate noun form provide the same information, i.e., singularity. As suggested above, using this marker is more of a "sign of literacy" than a means of increasing the accuracy of a child's communication. If so, then other means of "teaching" this aspect of English may need to be emphasized. The obvious ones are, of course, speech, reading, and writing, and these may need to be varied to fit the needs of a given child.

On the other hand, the comparative, the superlative, and the agent markers which are taken directly from the American Sign Language are also not used frequently. Since these markers convey a great deal of information, one must suspect that the general language level of the children and/or the nature of the cognitive tasks presented to them may not afford them enough opportunity to use these markers.

Apart from the specific individual markers, is 14 too many or too few markers? Results of this study clearly show that children of 9 1/2 years of age rarely use half of the 14. The first evaluation revealed that parents did not master the 14 markers. Taken together, these results strongly suggest that 14 sign markers are certainly not too few. Additional sign markers such as are included in the S.E.E. systems, probably have little or no practical educational value, especially since such a convenient tool as the manual alphabet is available for low-frequency words and word form changes. This does not mean that **some** parents and **some** children cannot learn more complex systems. But these are exceptional children and exceptional parents. They are not the vast majority of parents and children whom teachers will encounter and should serve.

It may be that teachers should consider using a smaller marker set with children who appear to have a more limited language aptitude. This suggestion was made when the system was first devised (Bornstein, 1974). It is probably worth considering again.

At this stage of development of manual systems designed to facilitate the learning of English, it appears that further exploration of how to best use them is still very much in order.

REFERENCES

Bornstein, H. (1974) Signed English: A manual approach to English language development. *Journal of Speech and Hearing Disorders, 3*, 330-343.

Moog, J. S., & Geers, A. E. (1979). *Grammatical analysis of elicted language: Simple sentence level*. St. Louis, Mo.: Central Institute for the Deaf.

BIBLIOGRAPHY

Bornstein, H. (1973). A description of some current sign systems designed to represent English. *American Annals of the Deaf, 3*, 454-463.

Bornstein, H. (1978). Sign language in the education of the deaf. In I. Schlesinger & L. Namir (Eds.), *Sign language of the deaf: Psychological, linguistics, and social perspectives*. New York: Academic Press, Inc., pp. 333-359.

Bornstein, H. (1979). Systems of sign. In L. Bradford & W. Hardy (Eds.), *Hearing and hearing impairment*. New York: Academic Press, Inc., pp. 333-361.

Bornstein, H., Saulnier, K., & Hamilton, L. (1980). Signed English: A first evaluation. *American Annals of the Deaf, 4*, 467-481.

DOES SIGNING EXACT ENGLISH WORK?

Gerilee Gustason, Ph.D.
Department of Education
Gallaudet University

Although much discussion has taken place concerning various systems of manual communication, little data has been available on the English skills achievement of students in programs using specific systems. In 1978-79, a study was done of five school programs reporting the use of *Signing Exact English* as their primary reference text. Data were collected from the school programs and parents on age at onset of deafness, age at detection, additional handicaps, age of child when parents began sign classes, whether one or both parents signed at home and type of signs used, hearing status of the parents, number of years in a total communication program, hearing loss, IQ, and standardized achievement test scores in reading and language. Regular classroom teachers administered the screening test portion of the Test of Syntactic Abilities and collected writing samples. Results indicate that a large percentage of parents state they use signs at home, and younger profoundly deaf students are performing above the average of the normative group on the TSA. Students with less profound hearing losses did less well.

Much theorizing and discussion, but little hard data, has been available thus far on the merits of various sign systems used in educational settings with deaf children. Research has shown that a number of school programs have adopted some form of signs in a total communication program over the past decade (see Jordan, Gustason, and Rosen, 1976 and 1979), and other research has indicated that total communication tends to be better understood by the students (the November 1978 Annals provides a good review of research on this question). However, other than anecdotal reports, little information has been available as to the effectiveness of the various sign systems.

One may, of course, present all sorts of caveats. For instance, to what do we refer when we use the term "effective" -- achievement on various tests of scholastic knowledge? English writing skills? a healthy self-concept and relations with family and peers? The variety of end products is matched only by the variety of factors which influence those end products. One may consider, for example, the age of onset of deafness, the age at which deafness was detected, early communication mode, structure of school programs, teacher abilities in a number of areas ranging from communication skills through curriculum development, and the like.

Nonetheless, while the questions and the relevant variables are numerous, some information can and should be sought concerning the impact of communication systems at home and at school. Many schools have reported the use of one of the newer systems of manual communication developed to represent English, and this use seems to be growing (Jordan, Gustason, & Rosen, 1979). In an effort to gather data that might indicate the effectiveness of one such system, *Signing Exact English*, or SEE 2, a study was done in the winter of 1978-79 at five schools reporting the use of that text as their primary sign book reference.

PROCEDURE

The five schools were selected for variety of location and program size. All reported the use of Signing Exact English. The longest period of such use was roughly ten years; the shortest, approximately four years. None of the programs were consistent in the use of this method among school personnel. All of the schools were day programs. School 1, in the South, was a self-contained day school with no main-streaming, encompassing preschool through eighth grade, with a total communication program for some years, a written communication philosophy, and the use of SEE 2 signs for three years. School 2, in the Midwest, had self-contained day classes in a public elementary and junior high school with some mainstreaming using interpreters, and had changed from the oral mode to SEE 2 signs approximately 6-1/2 years previously. School 3, in northern California, had self-contained day classes on the campus of public schools at all grades, preschool through twelve, with some mainstreaming at the elementary level, and had been using SEE 2 signs approximately five years. School 4 in southern California was a self-contained day school on the campus of a regular elementary school for preschool through grade five with some mainstreaming, with the use of interpreters, which had used SEE 2 for nearly ten years, and fed into School 5, which had day classes on public junior high and high school campuses for grades six through twelve with some mainstreaming, which received students from other elementary schools as well that did not use SEE 2 signs.

Data were collected on all students aged seven or older whose parents returned permission slips and questionnaires. From school records were culled the latest achievement test scores in language and reading, hearing loss in the better ear in the speech range, IQ, and date of birth. Parent questionnaires were utilized to obtain information concerning age at onset, age at which the impairment was detected, number of years in the present program, number of years in other programs using total communication, additional handicaps, whether either or both parents signed at home, the hearing ability of the parents, the types of signs used (e.g., Signing Exact English, American Sign Language, or some other type), whether the parents had ever taken a course in manual communication and, if so, the age of the child when the course was taken.

The students' regular classroom teachers administered Form 1 of the Test of Syntactic Abilities (TSA) screening test developed and standardized by Quigley and associates. The picture stimuli from the Myklebust Picture Story Language Test were utilized to elicit writing samples. Demographic data and TSA scores were entered on a computer for analysis. The writing samples of students in a limited group comparable to Quigley's standardization group (90+ DB losses, 80+ IQ, no additional handicaps other than corrected visual deficiencies, and hearing impairment by the age of two) were submitted to

Reprinted with permission from *Teaching English to the Deaf*, Winter 1981, Published by Gallaudet College, Department of English, Volume 7, No. 1.

the English Language Program at Gallaudet College for rating on the five point scale used by that program to assess student writing abilities.

RESULTS

Parental permission slips and questionnaires were returned on a total of 216 students among the five programs. Two students below the age of seven were in classes of students seven years and older and took the tests with their classmates; data on these two are included for information purposes where so indicated. The age range of the students in this sample was four to eighteen years; the DB loss range from 20 to 110+ (with data missing on 19 students); and the IQ range from 64 to 146 (with data missing on 60 students). No use was made of the standardized achievement test scores, since no two schools utilized the same test.

Concerning age of onset, in cumulative percents, 73.6% were reported by parents to be deaf at birth, 77.8% before six months, 81% by one year, 84.3% by two, 85.6% by three. Only 1.9% reported the deafness occurring after age three, but a relatively large 9.3% checked age unknown, and 3.2% did not respond to this question. The hearing impairment was detected by six months for 25.5%, and by one year of age for over half (52.3%) of the students in this study. By 1-1/2, 63.4% were detected, 75% by two, 85.2% by three, 91.2% by four, with 7.9% detected after four years of age and .9% not responding.

Concerning parental use of signs, fourteen of the 216 had deaf parents and were exposed to signing from birth, and two additional students had deaf foster parents, for a total of 7.4% of parents. The remaining two hundred had hearing parents. Both parents are reported signing by nearly half (48.6%) the hearing parents. Thus, in this study 56% of the students come from homes where both parents are reported to be signing. It should be remembered that this is self-reported and that no attempt was made to evaluate parent (or teacher) signing skill. Of the 27.3% reporting only one parent signing, in all cases except one that parent was the mother. A small percent (.5%) reported the use of fingerspelling only, 15.7% reported they did not sign at all, and .5% did not respond. The large percent (83.3%) of students with at least one parent signing at home is notable, especially when student performance on the TSA is considered.

Pearson correlation coefficients were calculated for the total TSA screening test scores with age, IQ, age at onset, DB loss, and total number of years in a total communication program, age of child when parents took their first sign class. Age correlated .19 (significant at the .003 level), .36 with IQ (significant at the .001 level) and .33 with the total number of years in a total communication program (.001 level of significance). No correlation was found between scores on the TSA and either DB loss or age of onset. For students with hearing losses of 90 DB or greater, the correlations with age and IQ were lower: .09 and .32 respectively. The large number of parents reporting the use of signs in general and Signing Exact English in particular (70% reported the use of Signing Exact English, while an additional 6% reported using both that and American Sign Language) made any correlation of type of signs used with scores meaningless. No correlation was found between scores and the age of the child when the parents reported taking their first sign class. No correlation of TSA scores was attempted with standardized achievement tests, since no two schools utilized the same test.

Quigley reports the average percent correct on the TSA screening test for students in his standardization sample to be 53%. Quigley's sample consisted of students aged ten through eighteen with 90+ DB losses by the age of two and IQ of 80 or above, with no additional handicaps other than corrected visual deficiencies. Since this normative group is older (10-18) than the 7-18 age range represented in this study, it was expected that a lower average percent correct would appear. This is borne out with a mean percent correct of 48.3% when all students in the study are summarized, as indicated in Table 1. However, this summary includes all students, regardless of IQ, hearing loss, age of onset, or additional handicaps.

Table 1. Mean percent correct, all students, by age group

Age range	Mean % correct	N
up to 6	55.4	2
7 - 9	38.6	41
10 - 12	48.3	84
13 - 15	52.0	82
16 +	60.6	7
TOTAL	48.3	216

When students are matched to the criteria set by Quigley, the percentages are different. Despite the younger age, the 39 students meeting these criteria averaged 59.8% correct, with students aged 10-12 averaging 63.4%. Table 2 gives the mean percent correct of 86 students in different age groups, and with different hearing losses, meeting the IQ, age of onset, and no additional handicaps criteria.

Table 2. Mean percent correct by hearing loss and age group for all students with 80+ IQ, no additional handicaps, and hearing impairment by age two.

Losses	Age range	% correct	N
90 DB+ losses	7 - 9	56.4	8
	10 - 12	63.4	15
	13 - 15	58.1	16
	TOTAL	59.8	39
60 - 89 DB	7 - 9	40.5	8
	10 - 12	42.1	10
	13 - 15	61.7	13
	TOTAL	49.9	31
15 - 59 DB	7 - 9	40.4	4
	10 - 12	40.0	7
	13 - 15	47.0	5
	TOTAL	42.3	16

For groups with less severe hearing losses, increased age tends to lead to increased scores. It should be noted that as the hearing abilities of the groups **increase**, the mean scores **decrease** at each age level.

Unpublished information furnished by Dr. Quigley on studies conducted with the TSA in Canada and Australia gives a broader perspective for the 90+ DB group. The age ranges, number of students, and mean percent correct in these two studies, the present study, and the normative group are listed in Table 3. Despite the younger age of the group in the present study, these students show the highest mean percent correct.

Table 3. Comparison of mean percent correct among four populations with 90+ DB loss.

	Present study	Normative group	Australian study	Canadian study
Age range	7 - 15	10 - 18	10 - 15	8 - 18
N	39	411	69	140
mean percent correct	59.8	53	35	58

Data from the Canadian study were also available for additional students grouped by degree of hearing loss. Comparison of the students in the present study with those in the Canadian study reveals striking differences for the less profoundly deaf. While in the present study mean scores decreased as hearing increased, in the Canadian study the reverse was true. In this study, students with 90+ DB losses averaged 59.8% (58% in Canada), 60-89 DB losses averaged 49.9% (Canada: 63%), and 15.59 DB loss students 42.3% (Canada: 78%).

There are many factors that may influence the varied scores of students at the five schools of the present study. Differences among the various age groups among schools suggest the need for examining a number of variables, such as school curriculum, parent and teacher sign skill, and the like. Table 4 gives the mean percent correct for all students, regardless of IQ, DB, additional handicaps or age of onset, by age group for each school.

Table 4. Mean percent correct. By schools, by age group, all students.

School	Age range	mean %	N
1	7 - 9	35.9	12
	10 - 12	34.6	28
day school,	13 - 15	46.3	28
no mainstreaming	16+	54.2	1
grades K - 8	TOTAL	39.9	69
2	7 - 9	28.9	11
	10 - 12	62.8	17
day classes	13 - 15	65.7	11
some mainstreaming	TOTAL	54.1	39
grades K - 12			
3	7 - 9	28.3	7
	10 - 12	64.3	6
day classes	13 - 15	50.1	15
some mainstreaming	TOTAL	47.7	28
grades K - 12			
4	Up to 6	55.4	2
	7 - 9	57.7	11
day school,	10 - 12	42.5	25
some mainstreaming	TOTAL	47.6	38
grades K - 5			
5	10 - 12	71.0	8
	13 - 15	53.2	28
day classes,	16+	61.7	6
some mainstreaming	TOTAL	57.8	42
grades 6 - 12			

Compositions were available for rating from 38 of the 39 students in the 90+ DB group. The rating scale utilized in the English Language Program at Gallaudet ranges from a low of 1 to a high of 5, with 3.5 considered the demarcation point between students ready for freshman English courses and those needing additional preparatory work on English writing skills. The mean rating for these 38 students was 1.87, with a range from 1.0 to 3.5. Two students attained 3.5 ratings; one was 11 and one 13 years old.

DISCUSSION

The present study raises far more questions than it answers. Much of the data came from school records or parental self-reporting and was thus uncontrolled. While schools included in this study stated they used Signing Exact English, the consistency of this use among teachers varied a great deal from school to school. In addition, the length of time this mode of communication had been the school policy varied widely. No attempt was made to assess teacher or parental signing skill, or to consider other factors that might be involved such as the language curriculum used by the school, parent socio-economic status, and the like. While no conclusions can be drawn concerning Signing Exact English use per se, it is interesting to note that of those parents responding at all five schools, 56% reported both parents sign at home and an additional 27.3% reported one parent signing.

In addition, the results indicate that profoundly deaf children of these parents in these schools, who met Quigley's criteria, did better than Quigley's normative group. Perhaps most striking is the better performance of the younger students.

The generally better performance of younger students may be understandable in view of the fact that published manual English texts first appeared in 1972, and that teacher signing skills have undoubtedly taken time to develop. Whether these younger students will in fact continue to improve in their English skills is not yet determined.

The comparatively poor showing of students with less profound hearing losses is disturbing. The reasons are not clear, and further research in this area is needed. Administrators at several schools noted that in many cases hard-of-hearing students had entered the programs after failing in oral-only programs and in many cases undiagnosed learning disabilities were suspected. The better-achieving hard-of-hearing students, these administrators felt, were usually mainstreamed. An in-depth study of this question is very much needed.

Another question is whether students whose parents and programs use Signing Exact English develop better English skills than students in total communication programs using other methods of signing. In-depth and longitudinal studies of parent-child communication and relations would also be of great value. A more detailed study to attempt to determine common factors among high scorers on the TSA and a similar study with low scorers, would be of great interest.

The questions are numerous. What emerges from this study is the fact that some schools reporting the use of total communication in general and Signing Exact English in particular have some young profoundly and prelingually deaf students doing better in English than older students.

SIMULTANEOUS COMMUNICATION IN THE CLASSROOM: HOW WELL IS ENGLISH GRAMMAR REPRESENTED?

Gloria Strauss Marmor & Laura Petitto

ABSTRACT

Simultaneous communication as used in classrooms is here analyzed to determine how well it represents English grammar. Samples of the communication used in teaching were collected from two hearing teachers as they conducted regular classes at a large residential school for deaf children. Comparisons were made between teachers' spoken and signed utterances with respect to grammatical construction, including declarative sentences, questions, relative clauses, pronoun use, and verb tense in English, and to such specifics as facial expression, head and body tilt, eye gaze, and use of space in American Sign Language (ASL). Results showed that signed utterances were predominantly ungrammatical with respect both to rules of English and to rules of ASL. The need to institute stricter requirements so that teachers of the deaf become better equipped to use simultaneous communication as well as other forms of communication is made salient by this study. Related issues requiring further research are also considered.[1]

THE PROBLEM

Deaf children for the most part do not master initial reading skills easily, making about as much progress in developing reading comprehension between ages 8 and 18 years as the average hearing child makes between first and fourth grades (Jensema 1975). One major reason, perhaps most crucial, is the deaf child's failure to completely grasp English grammar.[2] Lacking knowledge of the grammatical structure of English, the deaf child faces a serious obstacle in learning to read.

Attempts to provide deaf children with good English language models have been accompanied by controversy (Bender 1970). The oral method of communication with the deaf, which predominated in schools for the deaf in the United States since the first part of this century, urges the use of speech and lipreading and forbids the use of sign language. However, empirical research suggests that too little may be perceived through lipreading alone for the method to provide sufficient grammatical information (O'Neill 1954, O'Neill & Oyer 1961). A strongly advocated alternative method has been simultaneous communication, the simultaneous use of speech and signing. Several systems recently designed to render English more fully encoded in manual signs (e.g. Anthony, Gustason et al. 1972, Bornstein et al. 1973, 1974) are now being used as the signing simultaneous with speaking. This presentation of English through speech and signing simultaneously is at the current time enjoying a sharp rise in popularity among educational programs for deaf persons (Jordan et al. 1976), making it timely to examine whether this approach provides a framework through which teachers can transmit to deaf children enough linguistic information to foster their mastery of the structure of English. The aim of the present study is to analyze the linguistic nature of such simultaneous communication. Specifically our question is, How well does simultaneous communication used in educational programs represent grammatical English?

METHOD

Sources of the data analyzed were two hearing teachers, one male and one female, from a large residential school for the deaf where official school policy was to use simultaneous communication in every aspect of school life. Both teachers had used Manual English in the classroom for more than three years prior to the study (the term Manual English, or MCE, is a convenient cover term for any of the several systems using manual coding). The teachers were judged to have exceptionally good command of Manual English and simultaneous communication by the school administrator who selected them for participation in the research. One one-half hour language sample was taken on videotape of each teacher during a social studies class. Both teachers conducted class in a similar fashion; they lectured, but during the lecture they asked questions and responded to student-initiated questions. During their lectures both teachers spent some time reading from a prepared chart. The chart conveyed information about the topic under discussion in short sentences that the students could read as the teacher read aloud and signed.

The teachers understood that they were to communicate with their classes being videotaped as they did normally. They were told that they would be participating in a study aimed at analyzing simultaneous communication and that their performances would be used for research purposes only and would not be shown outside our research laboratory. Also they were instructed that their identities would be kept confidential. The teachers seemed relaxed during taping, and a school administrator familiar with the signing styles of both teachers viewed our videotaped records and felt that the teachers had used their customary styles for the camera. The pupils were told that the videotapes were being made of the teachers; their behavior was not out of the ordinary. In sum, neither the teachers nor their pupils had much reason to be disturbed by the camera, and evidence suggests that their performance on tape was typical of their normal classroom communication. During filming, both teachers instructed their regular classes of pupils. The first teacher had a class of seven prelingually deaf children, ranging in age from 11.1 to 13.1 (average age 12.24 years), with average hearing loss of 96db in the better ear (range 82-112db). The second teacher's class also contained seven prelingually deaf children, ranging in age from 12.0 to 13.3 years (average age 12.01 years), with hearing losses averaging 97db in the better ear (range 80-113db).

To transcribe the content of the two videotapes, the spoken portion of each utterance was written out verbatim. The simultaneously signed portion of each utterance was rendered in English glosses for each manual sign, with attention to grammatical inflection characteristic of American Sign Language (ASL); i.e., facial expression, head and body tilt, eye

Reprinted with permission from *Sign Language Studies* (1979) 23, 99-136.

gaze, and use of space. In transcribing the signed portion of each utterance the citation form of each sign was given an English gloss and recorded in order of appearance on the transcribed "sign line." This sign line was the pivotal component of the transcription system used, because it conveyed basic meaning (the gloss) augmented by additional "inflectional" information. Such information, which included aspects of ASL thought to be grammatical (Klima & Bellugi 1979, Fischer & Gough 1978), was recorded in raised brackets to the right of the sign. Information about the formation of the sign appeared below the sign line. Clarification of the meaning appeared in brackets after an equal sign (=) on the sign line. All pointing was indicated on the sign line inside parentheses. Symbols used in the transcription are presented in Appendix 1, and examples appear in the following discussion.[3]

Because both teachers freely alternated between lecturing in an unrehearsed fashion and reading aloud from a prepared chart, two analyses were performed, one of "spontaneous communication" and the other of "reading aloud." The spontaneously generated utterances occurring in the first ten minutes of each videotape were examined, yielding a corpus of 183 spontaneously generated utterances for the first teacher, and 116 such utterances for the second teacher. These spontaneously generated utterances were broken down further into "complete sentential utterances" and "all other utterances." To examine the "reading aloud" state, all of the full sentences read aloud by each teacher within the half hour videotaped were analyzed. The first teacher signed and read aloud 31 complete sentential utterances and the second teacher, 11 complete sentential utterances. The analysis of spontaneous communi-cation was restricted to the first ten minutes of each tape in order to keep the number of utterances under examination from becoming too great. Many fewer utter-ances were read than were communicated spontaneously; thus it was feasible to analyze all the reading aloud utterances in each half-hour tape.

The major divisions in the discussion of results below are Spontaneous Communication and Reading Aloud; the first is subdivided into grammatical categories: Declarative Sentences, Question, Relative Clauses, Personal Pronouns, and Verb Tenses. Results for each teacher are presented separately within these divisions.

Spontaneous communication

1 Declarative sentences.
   a. First Teacher.

(A simple declarative sentence is defined as expressing an assertion in one independent clause.) Among the spoken spontaneous utterances made by the first teacher in the first ten minutes there were 96 full sentential utterances (Table 1) and 87 other utterances, analyzed as 33 "fillers," 24 incomplete phrases, 14 ungrammatical phrases, 14 lexical items in isolation, and 2 single-word questions. Of the 96 full sentences 40 were simple declarative sentences. The signing accompanying these 40 declarative sentences was categorized thus:

1 **Exact representations**, i.e., signed utterances that completely and exactly represented the spoken utterances they accompanied

2 **Primary deletions**, i.e., signed utterances that failed to include the subject and/or the main verb and/or the auxiliary verb of the spoken utterance
3 **Secondary deletions**, i.e., signed utterances that included the subject, main verb, and/or auxiliary verb spoken but failed to include some other part of the spoken utterance; these included such deviations from grammatical English as omissions of verb tense marking, plural marking, functors, and articles.

Table 1. Spontaneous communication by teachers.

Type of spoken utterance	No. of spoken utterances	
	1st. tea.	*2nd tea.*
Full sentential	96	38
All other	87	78
Filler (ok, no, right)	(33	(23
Incomplete phrase	24	16
Ungrammatical phrase	14	20
Lexical item in isolation	14	13
Single word question	2)	6)
Total	183	116

Among the signed utterances accompanying the simple declarative sentences spoken by this teacher, 83% showed primary deletions, and 12% showed secondary deletions, leaving exact representation of speech in sign in only 5% of the utterances. Table 2 gives a detailed breakdown of the kinds of deletions made.

Table 2. Sign representation of speech in simple declarative sentence by teachers.

Primary deletions	Teacher 1		Teacher 2	
	No.	*%*	*No.*	*%*
	2	5	0	0
Main verb	10	25	3	25
Subject & auxiliary verb	2	5	0	0
Subject & main verb	12	30	0	0
No signs used	7	18	0	0
Primary delitions	33	83%	3	25%
Secondary delitions	5	12%	8	67%
Exact representations (signs-words)	2	5%	1	8%
	40	100%	12	100%

According to Table 2, subject deletion (omission of the surface structure subject from the signing) occurred in 5% of Teachers 1's simple declarative sentence utterances. In 1a and 1b below (which are respectively transcriptions of the spoken and signed output) subject deletion is illustrated:

1a He just died   from   being an old man.
1b -- ----- DIE --- FROM --- ------ OLD MAN/

In 1b, blanks stand for omitted words or suffixes and '/' for a break in the signed portion of the utterance.[4] Main verb deletions, i.e., omission of the main sentence verb from the signing, occurs in 25% of Teacher 1's utterances and is illustrated here:

2a That's prejudice.
2b THAT -- PREJUDICE/

In deleting from signing the "apostrophe-s" of the contraction **that's**, this teacher omitted the copula, the main verb of the spoken sentence, at least according to school grammar. Interestingly, in the entire 10 minute corpus, this teacher used the copula in 22 spoken, grammatical, utterances and deleted the copula in 91% of the accompanying signed utterances.[5] Sentences 3a and 3b provide an example of "Subject & Auxiliary verb" deletion:

3a He was not killed.
3b -- --- NOT KILL --/

Subject and auxiliary verb deletion occurred in 5% of this teacher's declarative sentences. (Failure in 3b to sign **was** and the **-ed** verb marker, which are obligatory in several of the systems of simultaneous communication, means that this sentence is not marked as a passive; Power & Quigley, 1973, document deaf children's great difficulty in learning the active-passive distinction. Here the teacher's deletion effectively conceals it.)

To illustrate "Subject & Main verb" deletion three consecutive declarative sentences have been chosen from Teacher 1's discussion of the word **assassination**, a vocabulary word in the lesson. The prior context (according to the teacher's spoken output) was, "Do you remember the names of the two Kennedy brothers who were assassinated? Do you remember what their names were?"

4a One was in the Navy.
4b --- --- --- ---   NAVY/
5a His name was John.
5b -- -- --   J-O-H-N/ (fingerspelled)
6a He was the President of the United States
6b -- -- --   PRESIDENT 0-F THE 'UNITED STATES'/

Subject and main verb deletion was typical of 30% of this teacher's simple declarative sentences. Sentence 7b provides another example of subject and main verb deletion. The sign ≠ above the signed representation of 'people' in 7b indicates that the teacher used a sign whose gloss is not the word she spoke:

7a The word assass-   to kill an important   person.
         inate means   ≠
7b -- -- -- -- ------   TO KILL A-N IMPORTANT PEOPLE/

Note that in 7b the article **an** and the noun **people** fail to agree in number. Taking the spoken message into account, it seems that the teacher signed "PEOPLE" while intending to sign "PERSON." The teacher did not correct her error in the sign medium. One might conjecture that had she committed an equally obvious error in her speech she would have corrected it, indicating a differential tolerance of grammatical errors in signing and speaking. The "No signs used" category in Table 2 consists of sentences in which speech is used in the absence of any signing. These were mainly short sentences, generally in reaction to students' comments; e.g., Teacher 1 asked why Hubert Humphrey died: "Why did he die?" and repeated for the class one student's response with the following sequence:

8a He got cancer.
8b --- --- ------   (no signs)

9a That's right.
9b ---- - RIGHT/ (subject & main verb deletion)
10a He did.
10b -- ---   (no signs)
11a He got cancer.
11b -- --- ------   (no signs)

Deletions of all signs occurred in 18% of this teacher's corpus of simple declarative sentences.

Secondary deletions occurred in 12% of the same teacher's simple declarative sentences; e.g.

12a Yes; presidents had mustaches   a long   time   ago.
                                      ≠
12b -- PRESIDENT -- HAVE -- MUSTACHE -- -- PASTMARKER TIME --/

Sentence 12b illustrates the common lack of verb tense marking in the signed portions of simultaneous communication (a topic to be discussed below in detail) and the lack of inflection of the noun for plural. Within this teacher's 40 simple declarative sentences, nouns made plural in speech failed to be inflected for plurality in the signed portions of the same utterances in 63% of the contexts where such inflection was obligatory according to the grammar of spoken English. Other secondary deletions found in the signed portion of the corpus included (a) the deltion of **to** from infinitives, which occurred in 25% of the obligatory English contexts, (b) deletion of articles, which occurred in 91% of the obligatory contexts, (c) deletion of the agreement suffix on verbs for third person singular subjects, which occurred in 100% of the obligatory contexts.

Of the 40 simple declarative sentences, two (5%) were judged to be accompanied by an exact sign representaion. Sentence 13b is one such sentence.

13a That was violence.
13b THAT WAS V-I-O-L-E-N-C-E/

Spontaneous communication.

1 Declarative sentences.
b Second Teacher.

Within the 10-minute sample collected from the second teacher, there were 38 full sentential utterances in speech and 78 other spoken utterances (See Table 2). Of the full sentential utterances in speech, there were 12 simple declarative sentences, and of these only 8% were represented exactly in the accompanying signing; 67% were signed with secondary deletions, and 25% were signed with primary deletions (Table 2). All of the primary deletions were deletions of the main verb; e.g.

14a That's important.
14b THAT -- IMPORTANT/

Secondary deletions included (a) deletion of **to** from infinitives, which occurred in 100% of the obligatory English contexts, (b) deletion of articles, which occurred in 75% of the obligatory contexts, and (c) deletion of the agreement affix for verbs in the third person singular, which occurred in 100% of the obligatory contexts.

Both teachers deviated from grammatical English in the signed portion of their utterances in more than 90% of their

93

simple declarative sentences. Their deviations differed, however; the first teacher made more primary deletions, and the second teacher made more secondary deletions.

Spontaneous communication

2 Questions.
  a First Teacher

In English, questions take four syntactic forms: **wh-** questions, yes-no questions, tag questions, and declarative sentence forms with rising intonation; e.g.

What day is it?   (**wh-** question)
Are you ready?   (yes-no question)
You take sugar, don't you?   (tag question)
You take cream and sugar?   (question intonation)

Of the corpus of 96 full spoken sentential utterances, 25 were questions, of which 11 were **wh-** questions. Table 3 shows the distributional analysis of the kinds of deletions made in the signing accompanying **wh-** questions.

Table 3. Sign representation of speech in *wh-* questions.

Primary deletions	Teacher 1		Teacher 2	
	No.	%	No.	%
Subject	1	9	0	0
Subj., Main and/or Aux. verb	4	36	1	11
Wh- word, Main and/or Aux. verb	1	9	1	11
Wh- word, Subj. and Aux. verb	1	9	0	0
No signs used	2	18	0	0
Subtotal	9	82%	2	22%
Secondary delitions	1	9%	7	78%
Exact representations	1	9%	0	0%
TOTAL	11	100%	9	100%

An illustrative utterance from each category is listed below. The presence (+) or absence (-) of quizzical facial expression (QF) or questioning voice (QV) is shown above the signs in this transcription:

                                    +QV
15a Where did you see that before?   -QF
15b WHERE D-I-D -- SEE THAT PASTMARKER (=
   before) (Subject deletion)
16a What did you learn about a neighborhood?
   -QF
16b WHAT -- -- LEARN ABOUT -- FRIEND + AREA/
                    (Subj. & aux. del.)
      +QV
17a What were their names?
              -QF
17b --- --- ---- NAME --/(Wh- word & main v. del.)
              +QV
18a Why did he die?
            -QF ≠ -QF
18b WHY -- -- HOW/ (Subj., aux., & main v. del.)
              +QV
19a What is that?
19b --- --- ----   (No signs used)
Utterance 18b is one of a limited number of instances of "leak-

age of meaning" in which what is signed expresses an idea that is collaterally related to what is said rather than expressing the same idea as that expressed in speech.

Table 3 shows that the signed portion of 82% of the **wh-** questions contained primary deletions. Secondary deletions were found in 9% of the signing, with deletion of plural noun inflection in 100% of the obligatory contexts, deletion of articles in 80% of the obligatory contexts, and deletion of tense markers.

In the light of Woodward's discussion (1973) of the prevalence of mixing ASL conventions with those of English grammar, an analysis was performed to compute the frequency with which ASL conventions appeared in questions. In four yes-no questions the teacher used head tilt, body tilt, and eye gaze as these would be used to form questions in ASL. However, the questioning facial expression, which is obligatory in ASL questions did not accompany this teacher's sign questions; e.g.

                +QV
20a Do you remember... -QF
20b -- --- REMEMBER...

In sum, a small portion of this teacher's questions were "ASL-like" in form; however, without appropriate facial expression they cannot be considered quite grammatical in ASL.

  b Second Teacher

Of the second teacher's corpus of 38 full spoken sentences, 9 were **wh-** questions. Primary deletions occurred in the signing accompanying 22% of his **wh-** questions. One example:
                +QV
21a How does it hold the plant?
                +QF
21b HOW -- -- HOLD -- PLANT/ (Subj. & aux. v. del.)

Secondary deletions occurred in the signing accompanying 78% of his **wh-** questions. Secondary deletions included (a) deletion of inflection of nouns for plurality, 75% of obligatory contexts, (b) deletion of articles, 100% of obligatory contexts, and (c) deletion of affix for agreement of verbs with third person singular subjects, 100% of obligatory contexts, also (d) deletion of verb tense marking.

The second teacher accompanied each **wh-** question with the kind of quizzical facial expression and head and body tilt that is obligatory in ASL questions. Facial expression of questioning coincided with the signing of the **wh-** word in 22% of the sentences, or came at the end of the sentence, in 56% of the cases. Forward body tilt without quizzical facial expression appeared in 22% of the questions. It is common in ASL to form questions with sign equivalents of **wh-** words at the end of the utterance. The second teacher combined this ASL convention with English grammar, producing the kind of question here:

22a Plants are food for who? +QV
22b PLANT--ARE FOOD FOR WHO/ +QF

These questions were classified as "ungrammatical spoken utterances," yet they serve to show the influence of ASL conventions on the spoken as well as on the signed portion of the second teacher's utterances. There were nine such questions in this teacher's 10-minute corpus.

To compare the use of simultaneous communication by these two teachers, both failed in more than 90% of their questions to reflect English question formation appropriately in the signed portions of their full spoken utterances. The first teacher made more primary deletions, and the second teacher made more secondary deletions. The second teacher also clearly incorporated more aspects of ASL, especially facial expression, into the signed portion of his full sentential utterances.

Spontaneous utterances

3 Relative clauses.

Traditionally, parts of sentences that begin with the relative pronouns **who**, **when**, **which**, or **that** have been called relative clauses. Relative clauses usually contain both a subject and a verb and in this way resemble sentences themselves, although they are actually parts of surface structure sentences. According to generative grammar, a relative clause is a complete sentence in deep structure that has become embedded in the surface structure of another sentence. In 23 the relative clause consists of the underlined portion:

23 The tugboat **that had pushed the ship** returned to dock.

The sentential quality of relative clauses is shown by replacing the relativizing pronoun **that** with the noun for which it stands, **tugboat**; this literally yields one sentence embedded in another.

a First Teacher

Of the corpus of 96 full spoken sentences, 11 contained relative clauses. The nature of the deletions in the signed portion of the utterances is presented in Table 4. These deletions are similar to the deletions found in questions and declarative sentences. Examples of each kind of deletion follow:

24a First word is the word called prejudice.
24b FIRST WORD -- -- -- -- --   PREJUDICE/

We counted sentence 24a as grammatical although the obligatory article **the** fails to begin the sentence. Notably in 24a the relative pronoun **that** and the verb **is** have been deleted in a way that is grammatical in English, so that the underlying relative clause "that is called prejudice" actually appears in speech as "called prejudice." In 24b the verb was omitted from both the relative clause and the main clause leaving no trace of the embedding apparent in 24a.

Table 4. Sign representation of speech in relative clauses.

| *Primary deletions* | Teacher 1 | | Teacher 2 | |
	No.	%	No.	%
Main or Aux. verb	9	82	0	0
Subj. & main and/or aux. verb	1	9	0	0
Subtotal	10	91%	0	0%
Secondary delitions	1	9%	1	100%
TOTAL	11	100%	1	100%

25a Poor people all live together in one place that's called a ghetto.
25b POOR PEOPLE ALL LIVE TOGETHER IN ONE PLACE
THAT -- CALL -- A G-H-E-T-T-O/ (Aux. verb deletion)

The auxiliary **is** and verb marker **-ed** were deleted from 25b, making the predicate of the relative clause ungrammatical.

26a These are the vocabulary words
that we are going to find now in the story.
26b THESE ARE ---'V' WORD --
THAT --- --- FIND NOW IN ---- STORY/
(Deletion of subject and aux. verb)

In 26b the structure of the spoken relative clause "that we are going to find now in the story" was disturbed, because the subject **we** and the auxiliary "are going" were deleted. In addition, **to** was deleted, disturbing the infinitive form "to find." Notably there was not a single instance in which the relative pronouns **who** and **that** (**when** and **which** did not appear in the corpus) were deleted from signing, except where the deletion also occurred grammatically in the spoken part.

Spontaneous communication

3 Relative clauses.
b Second Teacher

Of the second teacher's corpus of 38 full spoken sentences, only one contained a relative clause. In the signing accompanying that clause, the verb, in the third person singular, lacked the obligatory agreement affix.

To compare the use of relative clauses by both, the first teacher used many more such constructions than did the second. Because of the high frequency of primary deletions, the first teacher failed to show the sentential nature of the relative clauses in the signed portions of her utterances.

4 Personal pronouns.

Noun phrases can be replaced in English surface structure by pronouns, and the substitution, whether obligatory or stylistic, reduces redundancy. Pronouns must agree with their referents in four ways: (1) case (subject, object, possessive adjective, possessive pronoun, or reflexive), (2) number (singular or plural), (3) person (first, second, or third), and (4) gender (masculine, feminine, or neuter in the third person singular). In order to accomplish pronoun-referent agreement, English uses a system of 50, in some cases lexically repeated, personal pronouns (Table 5). Artificial Manual English systems (Anthony 1971, Gustason et al. 1972) provide signs for glossing most, if not all, of the 50 instances in Table 5. The sign for 'he', for example, is represented by a fingerspelled "E" signed initially at the temple and subsequently moved forward and slightly to the right. The sign for 'him' is a fingerspelled "M" moved forward from the temple in the same way (Gustason et al. 1972). For these and other pronouns in Manual English, case, number, person, and gender are indicated by signing, as they are in English through choice of lexical item.

In ASL lexical choice does not play the same role that it plays in Manual English. In contrast to English, ASL relies on such conventions as pointing to the referent or to its established locus in the signing space, directing one's eyes toward the referent, using head tilt and body shift to indicate the established location of the referent in the signing space, and pronoun incorporation (Fischer & Gough 1978). To present in one's own Manual English a good model of English pronoun usage, one should choose the appropriate sign from the Manual English pronoun lexicon or perhaps fingerspell the appro-

Table 5. Personal pronouns in English (Adapted from Quigley, Montanelli, & Wilbur 1976).

		CASE	Subject	Object	Possessive Adjective	Possessive Pronoun	Reflexive
	PERSON						
	First		I	me	my	mine	myself
Number							
	Second		you	you	your	yours	yourself
		GENDER					
Singular	Third	Masculine	he	him	his	his	himself
		Feminine	she	her	her	hers	herself
		Neuter	it	it	its	----	itself
	First		we	us	our	ours	ourselves
	Second		you	you	your	yours	yourselves
Plural	Third	Masculine	they	them	their	theirs	themselves
		Feminine	they	them	their	theirs	themselves
		Neuter	they	them	their	theirs	themselves

priate English pronoun. Use of ASL conventions or deletion of pronouns from signing will provide poor models of English grammar for deaf children.

b First Teacher.

With respect to the signing accompanying the 79 instances of personal pronoun usage in the first teacher's full spoken sentences, 25% was signed according to Manual English conventions, 1% was signed according to ASL conventions, 11% was signed using gestures foreign to Manual English and ASL conventions, and 63% was omitted from the signed portion of utterances. This teacher used 18 of the 50 different pronoun types of Table 5 in the spoken portion of her utterances. However, in the signed portion of these utterances, she used only six different Manual English pronouns: "I," "me," "you-ss" (singular, subject), and "you-spa" (singular, possessive adjective form). In one instance she used the ASL convention of pronoun incorporation (Fischer & Gough 1978) by signing "show you-po" (plural object) by moving the sign glossed 'show' in the direction of the persons being addressed.

Accompanying a wide range of spoken pronouns, including "you-ps" (plural subject), "he," "him," "his," and "it," the first teacher used a gesture foreign to both Manual English and ASL, which might be characterized as a "random point" (i.e., pointing in an arbitrary direction and at nothing in particular, rather than pointing at the object or person under discussion or at a previously established locus in the signing space). The random point clearly lacks the linguistic specificity of pointing at the addressee, a gesture used for "you-ss" (singular subject) and "you-so" (singular object) in both Manual English and ASL, or of the "distributive point" used for "you-ps" or "you-po" (plural subject or object) in Manual English (Anthony 1971) and in ASL. Consider the following illustration of the random point as used by the first teacher:

27a . . . people loved him . . .
27b . . . PEOPLE LOVE - (pt: random) . .

In the parentheses, the letters **pt** indicate that the signer pointed, and the word **random** indicates that the signer made a random point rather than pointing at a referent or location. In 27b the object of the people's love is unclear, in part because the random point fails to agree either with its referent in number, case, person, and gender as it must in English, or to indicate the referent's locus in space, as is done in ASL.

Most characteristic of the first teacher's use of pronouns was the high frequency of pronoun omission from the signed portions of her utterances. Because pronouns replace noun phrases in English, pronoun deletion usually results in serious agrammaticality, contributing to the high frequency of subject deletion in declarative sentences (Table 2), in questions (Table 3), and in relative clauses (Table 4).

Spontaneous communication.

4 Personal pronouns.
b Second Teacher.

With respect to the signing accompanying 48 instances of personal pronoun usage in the second teacher's full spoken sentences, 33% was signed according to Manual English conventions, 50% was signed according to ASL conventions, and 17% was omitted from the signed portion. In contrast to the first teacher, the second teacher omitted fewer pronouns from the signed portions of utterances and relied more heavily on the conventions of ASL to form pronouns in the signed portions of his utterances.

The second teacher used 10 of the 50 different pronoun types of Table 5 in speech but used only 3 different pronoun types from Manual English ("I," "you-ss," and "your--pa"). The remaining 7 pronoun types used in speech were glossed according to ASL conventions. Among the ASL conventions used to form pronouns in sign were (1) pronoun incorporation for me, you-plural obj., and her--sing. obj.; (2) directed eye gaze, for you--sing. subj., you-pl. subj., and you-pl. obj.; (3) pointing to the actual referent (you-sing. subj., he, she, and it); and (4) pointing inflected for number, for you-pl. subj., and you-pl. obj. The following sentences show use of directed eye gaze, pointing to the referent, and pointing inflected for number, respectively:

                    +QV
28a Do you remember before . . .
                (+QF, +Rep. EG ➜ child = you)
28b -- -- REMEMBER   PASTMARKER (= before) . . .

The presence of repetition (+Rep.) of the sign meaning 'remember' is indicated above the sign line in this transcription. The record also indicates that the teacher expressed the ASL equivalent of the English pronoun **you** by gazing toward the child being addressed (EG ➜ child).

96

29a She   wants to add something.
29b (pt: → child) WANT -- --ADD SOMETHING/
                                     +QV
30a What do you   think?
                                     +QF
30b -- -- (pt: → class=you - plural) THINK/

In 29b the teacher pointed toward a child and thereby conveyed the equivalent of 'she.' In 30b the teacher pointed in a sweeping motion of all the children in front of her (pt:- → class), and thereby conveyed the plural **you**. In general, deletion of pronouns from the signed portion of the second teacher's utterances occurred only for the pronouns **I**, **me**, and **it**; and 75% of the deletions involved omission of the pronoun **it**.

To compare the two teachers' use of pronouns in the signed portions of their utterances, both formed pronouns according to Manual English conventions in less than half of their signed utterances. The first teacher used only six Manual English pronouns, and the second teacher, only three. In short, the way that the English-speaking person using simultaneous communication might select from a system of some 50 personal pronouns that agree with their referents in number, case, person, and gender was not clearly demonstrated in the signing of either teacher.

Spontaneous communication

5 Verb tense.

In English, tense is represented by an affix that marks the verb as either **past** or **present** (Akmajian & Heny 1975). Past tense is usually indicated by adding the suffix **-ed** to the main verb; however, past tense may be indicated by a vowel change, as in **run/ran**, or by using a different past tense form, as in **go/went**. The form used for the present tense in some languages can depend on the subject of the sentence through subject agreement, so that a tensed verb is conjugated to agree with the sentence subject in person and number. An overwhelming majority of English verbs are not modified for subject agreement, however. In fact, only verbs with subjects in third person singular are conjugated to agree with their subjects, as in **He runs/They run**. This process here will be called **number agreement**.

When an auxiliary verb is used, it is said to carry the tense and dictate the form of the verb immediately following it. The auxiliary of the sentences recorded include (a) the **modals** will/would, shall/should, can/could, and may/ might; (b) the **have auxiliary** have/has/had; and (c) the **be auxiliary** is/am/are/was/were. The modal prevents the verb following it from acquiring tense. Thus the verb following a modal appears in the infinitive, uninflected, or citation form, as in I may **go**. The **have** and **be** auxiliaries require the verb that follows to take the suffixes **-en** and **-ing** respectively. Akmajian & Heny (1972) describe the affixation of the suffixes **-en** and **-ing** as accomplished through an obligatory rule they call "affix hopping."

a First Teacher.

Among the 96 full spoken sentences made by this teacher, there were 126 spoken expressions of tense marking on main verbs (regular and irregular), auxiliary verbs (modals, have, and be), and obligatory affixes on verbs following auxiliaries.

The occurrence of tense in the signed portion of these utterances is represented in Table 6. The table shows that of the 126 spoken expressions of tense, the present tense was spoken in 54% (68) of the utterances, the past tense in 45% (57), and the future tense (will modal with infinitive) in 1% (1). Of the 68 spoken expressions of present tense, 57% were completely omitted from the signed portion of the utterance; 32% expressed tense appropriately; and 10% omitted number agreement; e.g.

Table 6. Verb tense expression in two teachers' signing.

Type of spoken utterance	Teacher 1		Teacher 2	
Expression of tense	126	100%	51	100%
Present tense	68	54%	37	73%
Verb deletion in sign	(39	57)	(13	35)
Number agreement deleted	(7	10)	(7	19)
Signed correctly	(22	32)	(17	46)
Past tense	57	45%	14	27%
Verb deletion in sign	(21	37)	(0	0)
Signed incorrectly	(29	51)	(13	93)
Number agreement deleted	(1	2)	(0	0)
Signed correctly	(6	10)	(1	7)
Future tense	1	1%	0	0%
Signed correctly	(1	100)	(0	0)

31a . . . a person who teaches about God.
31b . . . -PERSON WHO TEACH -- ABOUT GOD/

From this teacher's 57 spoken expressions using past tense the verb was omitted in 37% of the signed accompaniment. In 51% of the instances, the verb was signed without any kind of past tense marking, thereby leaving the verb in present tense by default. The following example shows an agrammatical tense deletion:

32a . . . I decided that 8-B was a good choice.
32b . . .I DECIDE - THAT 8-B W-A-S A GOOD CHOICE/

In all of this teacher's past tense spoken expressions, only 10% of the signed portion had the past tense signed correctly. Interestingly, verbs like **talk** that take the regular past-tense affix **-ed** and verbs irregular in the past like **catch/caught** were not given past tense marking in sign. The 7 verbs that were signed for past tense correctly were instances of **be**, **have**, and modal auxiliaries. Obligatory "affix-hopping" was not supplied in other expressions;

33a . . . words that maybe you have not seen before.
33b . . . WORD- THAT MAYBE (pt: class) HAVE NOT SEE-PASTMARKER (= before)/

In sum, of the 126 spoken expressions of tense, about half were completely omitted from the signed portion, and of those rendered in sign only 23% were expressed entirely correctly.

b Second teacher

There were 51 spoken expressions of tense among the second

teacher's 38 full spoken sentences, including main verbs (regular and irregular), auxiliary verbs (**be**, **have**, and modal), and all obligatory affixes. Table 6 shows that 73% (37) of the spoken expressions of tense occurred with present tense and 27% (14) with past tense. Among the former, the verb was deleted in sign in 35% of the cases, signed without the obligatory agreement affix in 19% of the cases, and signed correctly in 46% of the cases. Among the 14 utterances spoken in past tense, 93% of the second teacher's signing was without any past tense marking and thus appeared inappropriately in the present tense. Only in one instance was the verb--the verb in this case was **have**--signed correctly in the past tense. Thus of 51 spoken expressions of tense in this teacher's grammatical spoken sentences, only 35% were signed correctly.

To compare the teachers with respect to expression of verb tense in signing, both fail to sign the verb tense correctly in the majority of instances. It is worth note that deaf children have great difficulty with verb tense and agreement affixes in written English (Quigley, Montanelli, & Wilbur 1976).

Use of American Sign Language

Analyses of question formation and personal pronoun use indicate that the communication of both of these teachers was influenced to some extent by the conventions of ASL.

a First teacher.

Accompanying the first teacher's 96 full spoken sentences, 3 instances of ASL usage (excluding pronouns and questions) occurred; one example:

34a That's all.
34b 'ZERO'/

The teacher made the sign for "zero," which in ASL can mean 'none' and 'nothing' as well as 'that's all.' Using an ASL idiom, utterance 34b carries the same meaning as 34a. Among the utterances classified as "All other" in Table 1 (p. 92) there were no occurrences of ASL.

b Second teacher.

Accompanying the second teacher's 38 full spoken sentences, 11 instances of ASL usage were found; e.g.

35a Okay; watch Debbie.
          (IX: you → at me, you → at 'her'/Debbie)/
35b O-K LOOK

The teacher did not sign LOOK in citation form but inflected it for person (IX):(see Appendix). Instead of moving the hand near his eyes, the teacher moved it from the addressee to self (you→at me) and then from self toward the second child, Debbie. Before the final movement the orientation of the signing hand was changed so that the teacher's palm faced outward from his body toward Debbie (you->at 'her'/Debbie). This sign conveyed the meaning 'look at me and from me to Debbie' (or 'watch Debbie not me'). In this signed utterance the teacher used one lexical item to convey more than one proposition in a way that is tyical of ASL and of course not typical of English.

Of the material falling in the "All other" category of Table 1 (p. 92), 12 of this teacher's utterances were signed in ASL; e.g.

36a Help.
          (IX: each one of you → me plurality)
36b HELP/

The teacher signed HELP as in ASL signing; i.e., inflecting the movement and location of the sign (IX:). Initially the signing hands were held away from the signer's body, then moved inward toward the signer, conveying 'You help me.' Also the sign was repeated consecutively in horizontal rays in front of the signer's body, thus conveying 'each of you.' In its entirety the sign conveyed 'Each of you help me' as the parenthesized notation in 36b indicates.

To compare the two teachers, the first used aspects of ASL in the signed portion of only 3% of her full spoken sentences. The second used ASL constructions in the signed portion of 29% of the signed utterances accompanying his full spoken sentences and in 15% of the signed utterances classified as "All others." ASL constructions were used infrequently in the signing of both teachers, with the second using more of them than did the first.

Interestingly, knowledge of ASL influenced the teachers' use of spoken English in some instances; e.g., the second teacher found a child, David, daydreaming instead of attending to discussion contributed by another, Debbie. He signed and said:

```
                                                      +QV
37a David; right or wrong? -- dreaming; what she say?
37b ⌈EG: David        ⌉ RIGHT--WRONG (pt:→ch.= Debbie),
    {gesture: hits desk}
    (mime: teacher mimics David; looks around)     +QF
    DREAM, (pt:→ch.= David)WHAT(pt:→ch.=Debbie)SAY/
```

Utterance 37a contains several ideas, but none of them are expressed in well-formed English. Had the teacher used full English sentences to convey the meaning of 37a, he might have said, "David, is Debbie right or wrong?" Instead, the teacher seems to have interpreted a well--formed ASL utterance into speech in 37a. While speaking thus (37b), the teacher hit his desk and looked at David. He then signed RIGHT WRONG in succession and pointed to Debbie, meaning 'Is Debbie right or wrong?' The teacher then imitated a person daydreaming as if to say, 'You are daydreaming again.' Finally he pointed to David, signed WHAT, pointed to Debbie and signed SAY, meaning 'David, what did she say?' The second teacher made 78 spoken utterances classified as other than full spoken sentences. Of these 12 seemed to be utterances in which ASL conventions governed both sign and speech. No such instances appeared in the first teacher's language corpus of spontaneous utterances.

Reading aloud

a First Teacher.

The first teacher read 31 full spoken sentences aloud from a chart, of which 81% (25) were simple declarative sentences. Some 64% (16) of these simple declarative sentences were represented exactly in signing. Recall that only 5% of this teacher's declarative sentences were signed exactly during spontaneous communication. Among the remaining 9 read aloud sentences (36%) there was one instance of primary deletion in signing and 8 instances of secondary deletion. The former consisted of an instance of subject deletion; the latter consisted of deletion of articles, which occurred in 17% of the obligatory contexts; deletion of inflection for plural nouns, which occurred in 32% of the obligatory contexts; deletion of prepositions, which occurred in 5% of the obligatory contexts; deletion of the possessive affix on nouns, which occurred in 100% of the obligatory contexts; and deletion of past tense markers.

One **wh-** question was read aloud and represented exactly in sign and without any ASL facial expression or body tilt. Three sentences with relative clauses were read aloud, one of which was represented exactly in sign; the other two were represented correctly in signing except that past tense markers were deleted.

Although this teacher deleted pronouns from the signed portion of her spontaneous utterances 63% of the time, there were no pronoun deletions in the signed portions of the utterances she read aloud. Of the pronouns read aloud, the three **he**, **his**, and **him** occurred in the spoken portion 89% of the time; these pronouns were fingerspelled rather than signed 75% of the time. In the signed portions accompanying spontaneous speech, fingerspelling was used to represent the pronouns **he**, **his**, and **him** only 14% of the time.

In the utterance corpus derived from reading aloud there were 38 spoken expressions of tense, of which 87% (33) were past tense and 3% (1) was in the future tense. Among the past tense verbs, 1 (3%) was deleted in sign, and 7 (21%) were signed inappropriately in the present tense. The remaining verbs in past tense (76%) were signed correctly. All of the verbs spoken in present and future tense were signed appropriately. Thus in contrast to this teacher's spontaneous utterances where tense was expressed appropriately in sign only 23% of the time, 79% of the expressions of tense were correct in signing when reading aloud.

Reading aloud

b Second teacher.

The second teacher read aloud 11 full spoken sentences of which 10 (90%) were simple declarative sentences. Some 7 (70%) of these were represented exactly in signing. In the remaining 3, inflection for noun plurality was inappropriately deleted from the accompanying signing. Deletion of plural markers occurred in 29% of the obligatory contexts. Deletion of plural inflection also occurred in the single **wh-** question read aloud from the chart. The teacher used one pronoun, **you**, which he inflected for plurality, as Anthony (1971) recommends and as is done in ASL. Moreover, he made 13 spoken expressions of tense, all of which were represented correctly in sign.

In sum, both teachers conveyed English grammar better in their signing when reading aloud than when communicating spontaneously. It is as if the written word prompted them not to ignore what the teachers considered subordinate words in sentences. Alternatively, being relieved of the need to generate the content of their sentences at the time of presentation, they had perhaps more available attention with which to focus on making signed utterances correctly.

DISCUSSION

In recent years educators have tended to turn their backs on pure oralism and to accept simultaneous communication, a form of communication that combines oral communication with Manual English (Jordan et al. 1976). The hope of those initiating the change was that deaf children would learn the English language more effectively if reception did not depend so heavily on lipreading. Believing that manual representation of English would make English more accessible, these educators established Manual English in the classroom. Their decision may well turn out to have been a wise one. Nevertheless, the danger that confronts all innovations is that they will fail because of improper implementation. The role of "applied research" in education, and of the present study specifically, is to determine how well implementation is proceeding. Our research has yielded surprising and unsettling results in that it suggests that simultaneous communication, as it currently is used in schools, may do little to bring English grammar to deaf children.

Simultaneous communication should, in theory, better present the structure of English to deaf children than did lipreading. The reason is ostensibly that in lipreading the child does not perceive every word in the utterance, but because simultaneous communication should present all words both orally and manually, the child should have a better chance of perceiving grammatically complete utterances. Our results suggest that there may be essentially less difference between what deaf children receive through lipreading and through simultaneous communication than might have been expected. Hart and Rosenstein's description (1964) of the deaf child's reception of linguistic structure through lipreading is instructive.

> In lipreading--the chief avenue through which the deaf child develops language---the child does not perceive every word in an utterance, but rather catches the key words, or even only the root parts of words (e.g., **boy** instead of **boys**, **walk** instead of **walked**). The words that are ignored are words that are not understood, as well as function words (e.g.,**to**, **the**, **at**, **for**) that tie the communication together (1964:680).

Our data show that deaf children in classrooms where Manual English is used, like the child dependent on lipreading, in many instances perceive key words or root parts of words only, missing function words and other obligatory parts of English grammar. Moreover, in the case of primary deletions, even the key words may be missing. For the child in the Manual English classroom, the difficulty lies perhaps not so much with his or her ability to receive language but with the unsophisticated use of Manual English on the part of the teacher.

In the present study we examined the way in which Manual English was used in the classroom by two experienced teachers, looking closely at five major aspects of English grammar: declarative sentences, questions, relative clauses, pronouns, and verb tense. Uniformly across all linguistic constructions we found the teachers' signed utterances to be predominantly ungrammatical. Specifically, declarative sentences and questions were signed incorrectly more than 90% of the time. Relative clauses were ungrammatical in all instances, and pronouns and verb tenses were handled inappropriately about two-thirds of the time. In light of these results, one must ask "How can the students absorbing these utterances gain anything but a distorted picture of what English grammar is?" If deaf children are learning such poor English, one should not be surprised that they fail to read adequately.

Analysis of simultaneous communication must be extended in the future to a wider sample of teachers and schools. Informal observation, however, suggests that the present results will not be atypical of simultaneous communication used in schools across the country at this time. The source of the poor grammar in the Manual English signing--at least in our sample--was not the mixing of the grammars of English and ASL, because neither teacher used much ASL, and in fact the first teacher seemed unacquainted with it. Instead, grammatical errors stemmed from gross omissions of obligatory words and morphemes from signing. Different patterns of omission emerged from the signing done by the two teachers. As just one of many possible examples, the first teacher made predominantly primary deletions; the second teacher, however, made predominantly secondary deletions. Given our scoring procedure, the difference reflects frequent omissions of subjects and verbs by the first teacher and omissions of verb tense and plural markers and functors and articles by the second teacher. Although the pattern of omissions made by the second teacher would probably interfere less with the communication of ideas, his signing nonetheless failed to provide an accurate model of English grammar. We found the percentage of total utterances by both teachers that were signed entirely in correspondence with the rules of English grammar pitifully small. Neither teacher signed more than 10% of his or her utterances in accord with the rules of English grammar. The main problem in both cases was the omission from signed utterances of words and morphemes that one is obliged to use in English.

Why did these teachers make such extensive omissions from their signing? There are several plausible answers to the question. First, Bellugi and Fischer (1972) have found that the rate of articulation for speech alone is near twice the rate of articulation for signs alone. When speech and signing are used simultaneously, the rate of speech articulation averages 1.65 times faster than that for signs. The teachers observed here perhaps deleted signs to obtain simultaneity. If so, however, simultaneity might be achieved with less grammatical disturbance if teachers spoke more slowly and were able to coordinate this speaking with a faster more expert rate of signing.

Second, simultaneous production of English in two modalities, speech and manual signing, may overload the human intellect. In other words, casting a thought simultaneously in both an oral and a manual vocabulary may tax to excess the capacities of the human mind. Aspects of our findings are consistent with the notion of overload. For instance, both teachers conveyed English grammar better in their signing when reading aloud than when communicating spontaneously. If simultaneous communication were to result in intellectual overload, then removing one mental task, namely deciding on the content of the discussion, should leave more intellect available to handle correctly the grammatical properties of the utterance. As support for a hypothesis that there is cognitive overload, simultaneous communication requires its user to encode consciously in gestural signs all the grammatical affixes that are obligatory in the spoken portion of the utterance. Thus hearing teachers must analyze each utterance for grammatical patterns, such as subject-verb agreement, when such analysis does not require conscious analysis in oral discourse. Moreover this unusual analysis must be carried on in conjunction with decisions about meaning, selection of vocabulary from two different lexicons (oral and manual), and overall sentence structure. Those interested in pursuing research necessary to test the overload hypothesis might begin by training a group of expert signers, with years of experience, to represent each aspect of English grammar manually as well as orally. The training should be followed by much supervised practice

of the kind typical of practice in learning to play a musical instrument while simultaneously singing. Only after expert signers have been given a chance to adjust to the rigorous demands of putting all properties of English spoken grammar in manual form while speaking can we begin to explore the notion of overload. If simultaneous communication were in fact to overload the processing powers of the human intellect, one might find, for example, that effective training led to elimination of primary deletions but not of secondary deletions. In any case, the overload hypothesis has yet to be tested.

Third, it is also quite possible that the teachers in this study neither received adequate training in Manual English during their years of preparation for their careers nor received adequate on-the-job training. Our research suggests that if simultaneous communication is to be used in schools for deaf children, the communication skills of teachers may well be in need of improvement. To upgrade the Manual English used by teachers, the analytic techniques developed in the present study could be adapted for use with individual teachers to provide feedback as to the correctness of the language model they provide for their pupils. It would be well worth while for teachers to videotape and analyze their own simultaneous communication techniques. In-service filming and linguistic analysis may go a long way toward upgrading a teacher's use of simultaneous communication.

A simple breakdown of the kinds of ungrammatical signed utterances, along with a conscious choice of a way to eliminate these errors from the signed portion of utterances, would undoubtedly yield important improvements. Thus, for example, a teacher who habitually omits pronouns in signing (as did the first teacher in this study) may, upon realizing the error, resolve to fingerspell each pronoun, so avoiding the extra burden of trying to recall the correct form of pronoun sign in the particular Manual English system in use. With awareness of a personal weakness in Manual English expression, a teacher can choose from many methods of remedy. There certainly is more to evaluating teachers' manual language skills than testing how many signs teachers know. Attention must be paid to how well English grammar is represented in the signed portions of utterances. It is also important for teachers to present as wide a range of English constructions as is appropriate to their pupils' stage in acquiring English. The teacher observed here used many simple declarative sentences and few grammatical complexities, such as relative clauses. Russell, Quigley, & Power (1976) show that deaf children often misunderstand the meaning of complex grammatical constructions. Appropriate and consistent use of such constructions in the context of classroom discussion should help deaf students become acquainted with them.

The findings reported here suggest that simultaneous communication requires further consideration, discussion, and research. Any method of communication as currently used by schools and educational programs for deaf children has at the very least two main goals, namely to provide a means by which the deaf child can communicate, while at the same time to provide examples of English grammar from which the child can learn English grammatical structure. To determine how well simultaneous communication meets these goals more empirical research is needed.

First, it would be important to determine if in fact a high level of accuracy in the signed portions of utterances is feasible, inasmuch as the joining of two fundamentally different expressive modalities may overload the intellect. Second, the effect of simultaneous communication on the deaf pupil must also be investigated. Simultaneous communication may be so cumbersome a method compared to American Sign Language that the overtaxed learner may lose motivation to learn the system and thus fail to master it. For example, deaf children who know American Sign Language know that often what one can communicate in ASL with one or two signs (in combination with other, non- manual devices) requires perhaps a half dozen signs to put in simultaneous communication. Consider the statement, "She is weak minded," which requires five signs in Manual English but only two in ASL (i.e., a sign for 3rd person singular plus the sign WEAK made with fingertips touching the head at the temple). Future investigation might seek to enumerate what features, if any, of simultaneous communication tax the learner, and in addition might delineate which cognitive processes (such as short-term memory in sentence integration) might be influenced. Simultaneous communication is only one means by which to reach the dual goals of offering deaf children a communication system and provision of exposure to English grammar in order to facilitate their reading and writing. An alternative might be to begin to teach children about the give and take of communication with American Sign Language--which may be more appropriate to the visual mode of perception and so more congenial to them; then after the child has learned to communicate in ASL, English might be taught as a second language. For the latter process, simultaneous communication might be used as one of several tools for presenting the structure of English grammar. As linguistic research makes American Sign Language easier and easier to teach to hearing and deaf people (see, e.g., Klima & Bellugi 1979), the latter plan becomes increasingly practical. With respect to motivation, much of the child's desire to learn language is born of his or her wish to become part of a social unit. Since there is no natural community of language users for any invented manual system, and since its use is most often restricted to the classroom and interaction with the teacher, the child's interest in learning the method may be less than desirable, and less than might be the case with American Sign Language, which has a large community of users. Moreover, it may be the case that the best deaf pupils, those who achieve the greatest mastery of Manual English, may grow up outside any language community, having access neither to hearing society nor to deaf society, where currently American Sign Language predominates.

Third, it is widely assumed that if deaf children are taught with simultaneous communication, they will learn English better, but more research is needed to test whether simultaneous communication facilitates acquisition of English better than do alternative methods of instruction. Longitudinal research comparing the English language skills of children being taught to use "exact" Manual English and children being taught to use alternative systems, such as American Sign Language perhaps with English taught as a second language, would be useful in evaluating the merits of using simultaneous communication in the classroom.

NOTES

[1]This research was supported in part by Alcohol, Drug Abuse, and Mental Health Administration National Service Award 1F3 MH 05453-02 from the National Institute of Mental Health to Gloria Strauss Marmor, and by a grant from the Rehabilitation Services Administration, Department of Health, Education, and Welfare, to the Deafness Research and Training Center, New York University. We are grateful to Jerome D. Schein of the Center, and to Dennis Cokely of Gallaudet College.

[2]This is amply documented; see Cooper 1967, Cooper & Rosenstein 1968, Charrow 1975, Fusfeld 1955, Goda 1964, Hart & Rosenstein 1964, Heider & Heider 1940, Myklebust 1960, Russell, Quigley, & Power 1976, Sarchan-Deilly & Love 1974, Simmons 1962.

[3]Part of the transcription notation was developed while the second author was at the Salk Institute and the University of California; she is grateful to Ursula Bellugi and Edward Klima.

[4]Sentences showing primary deletions are counted as such. They were not counted as secondary deletion sentences if they also showed such deletions, but were included in the tally of obligatory contexts; e.g., article deletion in 1b was not counted as secondary deletion in Table 2 but was counted in the tally of obligatory contexts on page 107.

[5]Deaf children lag behind hearing children in learning when to use and when not to use the verb **be**. Prelingually deaf children of age 10 tend to judge sentences like "the girl sick" to be correct in written English despite the omission of the verb **be**, a mistake that few hearing 10-year olds would make (Quigley et al. 1976). By her frequent omission of the verb **be** in Manual English, the first teacher is buttressing the common misimpression among her deaf pupils.

APPENDIX: TRANSCRIPTION SYMBOLS

(pt:)	Information about pointing, especially pronouns, is enclosed in parentheses.
➔	Indicates direction of signer's pointing, from signer to referent.
Random	Pointing that does not use signing space systematically.
CS, RS, LS	Denote location of eye gaze and pointing (central space, right front of signer, left front, respectively).
EG	Used to denote eye gaze.
QF	Used to denote quizzical facial expression with sign.
H/BT	Head and/or body tilt; most frequently during ASL question formation.
+QV	Indicates that speaker-signer used question intonation.
(+) SIGN	Indicates feature accompanying sign; or use of two signs to render one English word; e.g.'neighbor + hood' as FRIENDAREA.
(-)	Also above sign line, means feature did not occur
----	Shows that signing did not appear with the spoken material directly above the blank in the transcript.
/	Indicates a break in the signed portion of utterance.
S-I-G-N	Indicates fingerspelling.
≠	Indicates difference of signed item from spoken item.
SIGNSIGN	Indicates that two spoken words are rendered by one sign.
{ }	Indicates simultaneous expression of two mes-

sages, usually by different signs with right and left hands.

I   Indicates that the sign was inflected by ASL conventions; for ASL inflection, see Klima & Bellugi (1979).

X   Indicates that the signed verb was inflected for-person; see Fischer & Gough (1978).

Rep   Indicates that a sign or action of a sign was repeated.

PASTMARKER
      Indicates that the ASL sign denoting past time was used. The specific intended meaning (as determined by the context and spoken portion of the utterance) appears in parentheses adjacent to the PASTMARKER entry, as in PASTMARKER (= Before).

REFERENCES

Akmajian, A., & Heny, F. (1975). *An Introduction to the Principles of Transformational Syntax.* Cambridge, MA: MIT Press.

Anthony, D.A. (1971). *Seeing Essential English*, Vols. 1 & 2 Anaheim, CA: Anaheim Union School District.

Baker, C. (1978). How does 'Sim Com' fit into a bilingual approach to education. Paper, second National Symposium on Sign Language Research & Teaching, San Diego.

Bellugi, U., & Fischer, S. (1972). A comparison of Sign Language and Spoken Language, *Cognition, 1*, 173-200.

Bellugi, U. (Edward S. Klima & Ursula Bellugi) (1979). *The Signs of Language.* Cambridge, MA: Harvard.

Bender, R. (1970). *The Conquest of Deafness.* Cleveland: Case-Western Reserve.

Bornstein, H. (1973). A Description of Some Current Sign Systems Designed to Represent English, *American Annals of the Deaf, 118*, 454-463

Bornstein, H. (1974). Signed English: A Manual Approach to English Language Development, *Journal of Speech & Hearing Disorders, 39*, 330-343.

Charrow, V. (1975). A Psycholinguistic Analysis of "Deaf English," *Sign Language Studies, 7*, 139-150.

Cooper, R. L. (1967). The Ability of Deaf and Hearing Children to Apply Morphological Rules, *Journal of Speech & Hearing Research, 10*, 77-86.

Cooper, R.L., & Rosenstein, J.(1966). Language Acquisition of Deaf Children, *The Volta Review, 68*, 58-67.

Fischer, S., & Gough, B. (1978). Verbs in American Sign Language, *Sign Language Studies, 18*, 17-47.

Fusfeld, I. S. (1955). The Academic Program of Schools for the Deaf, *The Volta Review, 57*, 63-70.

Goda, S. (1964). Spoken Syntax of Normal, Deaf, and Retarded Adolescents, *Journal of Verbal Learning & Verbal Behavior, 3*, 401-405.

Gustason, G., Pfetzing, D. & Zawolkow, E. (1972). *Signing Exact English.* Rossmoor, CA: Modern Signs Press.

Hart, B. O., & Rosenstein, J. (1964). Examining the Language Behavior of Deaf Children, *The Volta Review, 66*, 679-682.

Heider, F., & Heider, G. (1940). Comparison of Sentence Structure of Deaf and Hearing Children, *Psychological Monographs, 52*, 42-103.

Jensema, C. (1975). *The Relationship between Academic Achievement & the Demographic Characteristics of Hearing Impaired Children & Youth.* Washington: Office of Demographic Studies.

Jordan, I. K., Gustason, G. & Rosen, R. (1976). Current Communication Trends at Programs for the Deaf, *American Annals of the Deaf, 121*, 527-532.

Klima, E. S., & Bellugi, U. (1979). *The Signs of Language.* Cambridge, MA: Harvard University Press.

Myklebust, H. R. (1960). *The Psychology of Deafness.* N.Y.: Grune & Stratton.

O'Neill, J. J. (1954). Contributions of the Visual Components of Oral Symbols to Speech Comprehension, *Journal of Speech & Hearing Disorders, 19*, 429-439.

O'Neill, J. J., & Oyer, H. J. (1961). *Visual Communication for the Hard of Hearing.* Englewood Cliffs, NJ: Prentice-Hall.

Power, D. J., & Quigley, S.P. (1973). Deaf Children's Acquisition of the Passive Voice, *Journal of Speech & Hearing Research, 16*, 5-11.

Quigley, S. P., Montanelli, O. S. & R. B. Wilbur (1976). Some Aspects of the Verb System in the Language of Deaf Students, *Journal of Speech & Hearing Research, 19*, 536-550.

Russell, W. K., Quigley, S.P. & Power, D. J. (1976). *Linguistics & Deaf Children: Transformational Syntax & its Applications.* Washington: A. G. Bell Assn.

Sarachan-Deily, A. B., & Love, R. J. (1974). Underlying Grammatical Rule Structure in the Deaf, *Journal of Speech & Hearing Research, 17*, 689-698.

Simmons, Audrey A. (1962). A Comparison of Type-Token Ratio of Spoken & Written Language of Deaf & Hearing Children, *The Volta Review, 64*, 417-421.

Wilbur, R. B., Montanelli, & Quigley, S. (1975). Pronominalization in the Language of Deaf Students, *Journal of Speech & Hearing Research, 19*, 120-140.

Woodward, J. C. (1973). Some Characteristics of Pidgin Sign English, *Sign Language Studies, 3*, 39-46.

THE GRAMMATICALITY OF MANUAL REPRESENTATIONS
OF ENGLISH IN CLASSROOM SETTINGS

Thomas N. Kluwin, Ph.D.
Researcher, Educational Research Lab
Gallaudet University, Washington, D.C.

This study examined the ability of teachers to produce grammatical manual representations of English under normal classroom conditions. Three groups of teachers--inexperienced signing hearing teachers, experienced signing hearing teachers, and deaf teachers--were observed three times using a live-observation system. Twenty-three teachers were observed with an inter-coder reliability of .896. Differences in teachers' ability to use separate signs for English grammatical endings and the use of ASL-like signing were found.

The general conclusion of the study is that increased experience leads to increased use of natural language features in classroom communication.

The use of a manually coded form of English for the education of hearing-impaired children rests on an unproven assumption and a mathematical difficulty. The unproven assumption is that the presentation of all educational information to the child in the form of a manual representation of English will lead to the acquisition of English. Superficially, this is a reasonable assumption, but two problems plague the acceptance of this position. The first is that there is no conclusive evidence that such a system actually works the way it is supposed to work (Moores, 1972). The second is that there is no evidence to suggest that the recipients of the system perceive the signs used in the same fashion as those who propose their use (Reich & Bick, 1977).

The mathematical problem introduced by the attempt to manually encode English is that under normal conditions, spoken language can be produced at a rate much faster than a manual encoding system can represent it (Bornstein, 1979). This is not to say that it is impossible to have simultaneous communication using a system with a perfect correspondence between spoken English and the manual system, but the difficulties inherent in such systems preclude their use as efficient forms of communication for effective classroom interaction. Very seldom have writers faced the unusual constraints that morphemically-based systems impose on teachers, parents, and children (Bornstein, Saulnier, & Hamilton, 1980).

Since the systems cannot be 100% efficient in matching one code to the other, some kind of reduction must be taking place. Recent work has indicated that a wide range of deletions take place (Marmor & Petitto, 1979; Reich & Bick, 1977). The logic of such systems suggests and quantitative research supports the position that the systems are inefficient forms of classroom communication. The question that must be asked now is under what conditions and for what categories of users are the systems the least effective. If it could be demonstrated that experienced users of such systems are able to use these systems with minimal amounts of major errors, then it is possible through suitable training programs to increase the effectiveness of the language source and to truly examine the most basic question, that is, the assumption that such systems are effective in teaching English. If it is shown that even experienced users of these systems are unable to use them grammatically, then the question of their practicality as instructional systems is in doubt.

Several writers have claimed that a process of **pidginization** occurs in classrooms where such systems are used (Woodward, 1973). The teacher and the children negotiate a mutually intelligible pidgin consisting of ASL or home signs, some signs from the system approved by the school policy, and English word order (Bornstein, 1979). For example, except for the definite determiners, determiners are dropped; prepositions and adverbs are incorporated into the verb sign; and copula verbs are not used. In essence the child is exposed neither to ASL nor English but to a compromise of the two that meets the demands of the situation. Since this is a pidgin, it is not regularized across very many users, thus the child may be exposed to as many varieties as he or she has teachers (Bornstein, 1979; Bornstein et al., 1980). The child is doubly deprived in such a case since he or she neither learns English nor ASL.

While evidence exists that various kinds of deletions occur in the manually coded English of teachers using simultaneous communication, previous work does not provide sufficient information to generalize these findings to the entire field of classroom use of simultaneous communication (Marmor & Petitto, 1979). The effects reported could be the result of several things. For example, administrator perceptions of teachers' behavior are notoriously colored by a variety of factors, thus the use of administrator selected subjects in the Marmor and Petitto (1979) study makes the results suspect. There was also no report of control for subject matter or lesson content. There is considerable evidence of teacher behavior in other areas being related to the content of the instruction (Dunkin & Biddle, 1974). Finally, the subjects selected were neither randomly nor broadly chosen. Variation in teacher behavior could be ascribed to any number of causes. What is needed is a study of a larger number of teachers selected over a number of different programs, backgrounds, and abilities.

METHOD

Three observations were made of 23 teachers from the secondary programs of three schools for the deaf on the East Coast. When possible, each teacher was observed in two of his or her classes.

A live observation instrument was used that attempted to reflect the major syntactic categories of English, the more important morphological features of English, and some ASL features. Total deletions were cases where a teacher spoke a word but did not sign it. Tense errors were coded when an inappropriate sign was used or when there was no indication of the tense of the verb. The same rubric applied to the other kinds of morphological errors. The most liberal interpretation was always applied to the coding system. If some form of grammatical marking was used, it was coded as correct.

Reprinted with permission from *American Annals of the Deaf*, June 1981, 417-421.

Table 1. Categories of Live Observation System.

Feature	Error Categories				
Verb					
Modals	Total deletion				
"to have"	Total deletion	Tense error			
"to be"	Total deletion	Tense error			
Main verb	Total deletion	Tense error			
Noun					
Subject/					
Object	Total deletion	Number error			
Pronoun					
Subject/					
Object/					
Possessive	Total deletion	Indexing	Number error	Case error	Form class error
Adverb	Total deletion	Manner incorporation			
Adjective	Total deletion	Comparative deletion			
Preposition	Total deletion	Verb incorporation			
Determiner	Total deletion				
Conjunction	Total deletion				

Indexing is the ASL device for indicating pronominal relations. The signer establishes the locale of the individual and his or her identity and then points to that locale instead of signing a specific pronoun. **Incorporation** is also an ASL feature in which two English grammatical categories are combined into one sign. For example, prepositional direction is often incorporated into the verb.

Three coders used the live observation system and were able to attain an inter-coder reliability of .867 as determined by the calculation of a Cronbach's alpha (Cronbach, Gleser, Nanda, & Rajaratnam, 1972). The trade-off in the study was between a higher degree of information and a higher degree of reliability. Some initial categories were eliminated during practice sessions because it was difficult to achieve reliability within them. Table 1 presents the categories used in the study.

Each teacher was observed in each grammatical category, e.g., modals within the verb phrase, for 30 seconds. There was a 15-second break, and the next category was coded. Such a procedure permitted the rater to continuously watch the teacher and to code during the 15-second break. It took slightly less than 5 minutes for each complete cycle through the observation form. Generally seven to nine cycles of observation were completed during the 45- to 50-minute class periods. Coders did not code during test administration nor during other kinds of procedural activities. If the teacher stopped talking for more than 60 seconds, the coder stopped and waited for the teacher to begin again before coding proceeded. Observations with less than three cycles through the observation form were eliminated and rescheduled.

Table 2. Background Information for Teachers.

		Teaching experience (years)	Signing experience (years)	Class size
Inexperienced	Math/Science (3)	10.333 (4.163)	2.000 (1.000)	6.545 (1.695)
	English (2)	3.000 (0.000)	2.000 (1.414)	6.000 (1.732)
Experienced	Math/Science (8)	11.125 (5.866)	5.875 (1.885)	7.152 (1.349)
	English (5)	10.800 (1.483)	7.400 (2.074)	7.000 (1.549)
Deaf	Math/Science (3)	8.677 (4.509)		7.500 (2.507
	English (2)	9.500 (4.950)		6.333 (1.033)

SUBJECTS

The subjects for the study were 23 hearing and deaf teachers at three schools for the deaf on the East Coast. One school used a specific sign system for representing English, one advocated "total communication," and the third had recently changed from oral methods to "total communication." The teachers were divided into two groups by subject matter and three groups by experience and degree of hearing ability.

The teachers were classified as Reading/ English or Math/Science (see Table 2).Teachers with four or more years of classroom signing experience were defined as "experienced teachers." Deaf teachers were kept as a single group. No effort was made to control the ability level of the classes. The teachers were all volunteers, and they selected the class or classes in which they wished to be observed. Because of the lack of control over class selection, the unequal distribution of subject matters across schools, and unequal number of observations overall; only the experience of the teachers and the subject matter were considered as pertinent variables.

RESULTS

In general, neither subject matter nor school made any difference in the signing behavior of the teachers. The clear factor in the teachers' classroom signing was their degree of experience in the use of manual communication. Although "stylistic" differences were noted between subject matters, the obser-

vation form did not permit the capturing of those differences. ASL features were indexing, incorporation of adverbial manner in the verb sign, and incorporation of the preposition in the verb sign.

Deaf teachers deleted far fewer signs and used more elements of ASL while the inexperienced hearing teachers did the reverse. The experienced hearing teachers were the middle group in all cases. There were no effects of experience in the general class of grammatical errors. A two by three Chi square, type of error by signing experience, was calculated for the number of errors per hundred ASL intrusions versus deletions. A Chi square value of 12.944 with two degrees of freedom was significant at the .01 level.

Major grammatical categories such as noun subjects, noun objects, and main verbs, which do not have special ASL forms, were less likely to be deleted as the signing experience of the teacher increased. However, prepositions and pronouns which differ greatly between ASL signs and contrived English representations showed quite different patterns. Prepositions showed an unusual pattern in that the more experienced hearing teachers deleted 10 times the number of prepositions as did the less experienced teachers. The deaf teachers deleted half as many prepositions as the experienced hearing teachers.

What occurs with experience is that intrusions from the natural language structures increase in the contrived systems, i.e., the ASL rule which incorporates the preposition into the verb tended to increase with signing experience. The experienced teachers appeared to be in a transition from deleting preposi-

Table 3. Group Means for Major Syntactic Categories.

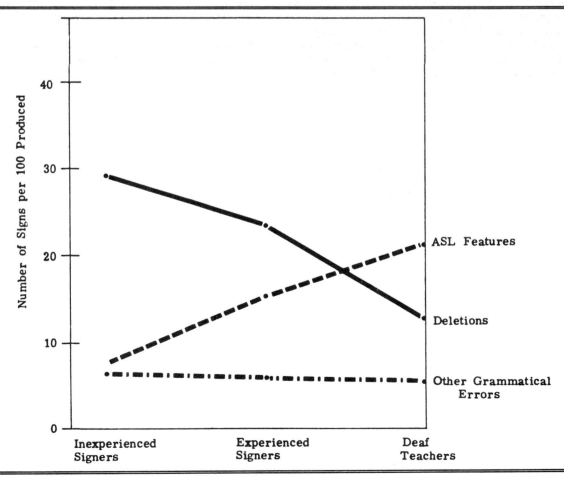

tion signs to incorporating them. Pronoun usage exhibited a similar trend. Pronoun sign deletions increased with experience, but at the same time case errors and the use of indexing increased. Clearly, with increasing experience there was the tendency to incorporate the more efficient, and as communicatively meaningful, natural features. With experience, two things occurred within the contrived signing systems. First, the cumbersome elements that were based on written English structures were deleted. Later with increasing contact with the natural language, the more efficient natural language elements were introduced into the classroom signing.

DISCUSSION

Faced with the multiple demands of the classroom, two general principles seem to be at work in the signing behavior of teachers of the deaf. First, function takes precedence over form. Teachers were more interested in trying to communicate than in the form of the communication. Second, experience is definitely a factor in the quality of the communication that takes place. It is apparent from the results that there are natural language alternatives to the limitations of the representational systems, and that, with experience, teachers will use them.

Classroom teachers as a group, even the most experienced, do not generally conform to the assumptions of the systems for manually representing English. If the purpose of using such systems is to provide deaf children with a model for reading and writing English, then clearly the consistency of the behavioral model is in serious question.

We should confront the real issue: Why do we want teachers to sign in classrooms in the first place? The function of signing in classrooms for the deaf should be to enhance the potential for deaf children to acquire the content being presented. Starting with the results of this present study, a new or modified system of classroom communication should be developed that is based on the actual needs of the child in the classroom situation and principles of natural language use.

REFERENCES

Bornstein, H. (1979). Systems of sign. In L. J. Bradford & W. G. Hardy (Eds.), *Hearing and hearing impairment*. New York: Grune & Stratton, Inc..

Bornstein, H., Saulnier, K., & Hamilton, L. (1980). Signed English: A first evaluation. *American Annals of the Deaf, 125*, 467-481.

Cronbach, L., Gleser, J., Nanda, H., & Rajaratnam, N. (1972). The dependability of behavioral measurements. New York: John Wiley & Sons.

Dunkin, M. J., & Biddle, B. J. (1974). The study of teaching. New York: Holt, Rinehart & Winston.

Marmor, G., & Pettito, L. (1979). Simultaneous communication in the classroom: How grammatical is it? *Sign language studies, 23*, 99-136.

Moores, D. (1972). Communication: Some unanswered questions and some unquestioned answers. In T. O. Rourke (Ed.), *Psycholinguistics and total communications: The state of the art*. Silver Spring, Md.: National Association of the Deaf.

Reich, P. A., & Bick, M. (1977). How visible is visible English? *Sign Language Studies, 14*, 59-72.

Woodward, J. (1973). Some characteristics of pidgin Sign English. *Sign Language Studies, 3*, 39-46.

MOTHERS LEARNING SIMULTANEOUS COMMUNICATION:
THE DIMENSIONS OF THE TASK

M. Virginia Swisher and Marie Thompson
Department of Special Education
University of Washington

The simultaneous communication of six mothers to their hearing-impaired children was studied to determine the extent to which the signed message matched the spoken message. From samples of 100 utterances, a mean 40.5 utterances were signed fully. Although the mean size of the samples was only 389 morphemes, approximately 18% of the spoken morphemes were deleted, on the average. These results indicate that we have underestimated the difficulty of simultaneous communication for parents and that our training methodology needs to be reevaluated. Training programs for parents need to be based on a realistic assessment of demands of the task and of parents' situation as language learners. A first approximation of such an assessment is presented, with recommendations for changes in the way sign training for parents is conducted.

The principal challenge in using simultaneous communication is to sign all of the words that are spoken, including especially the small grammatical words and endings known as functors, which are always difficult for deaf children to learn. For young children with normal hearing, the spoken language input provided by their primary caregivers is generally considered to be of critical importance to language development, and studies of this input have found it to be highly grammatical and tailored to the child in various specific ways (Broen, 1972; Cross, 1977; Newport, Gleitman, & Gleitman, 1977; Snow, 1972). One of the hopes for using Manually Coded English (MCE) in the context of Total Communication has been that the codes would enable the deaf child to receive visible linguistic input that would be functionally the same as the input to normal-hearing children. This would allow the deaf child to acquire grammatical English in an analogous way and with comparable success. The notion that the input would be the same assumes both that the individual signed sentences would be as complete as the spoken ones and that the overall corpus would be equivalent to input to hearing children in both quantity and quality. The data we will report indicate that these assumptions are incorrect in many cases and that we may have underestimated the task parents face when learning to sign. Evidence from the study will be presented, followed by a discussion of the many aspects of learning to sign, and of parents' lives, that may make developing sign fluency difficult. Finally, specific changes will be recommended for the manner in which sign training for parents is conducted.

METHOD

The principal research question was how complete mothers' simultaneous signing is with respect to their speech. In order to investigate this question, a search was conducted for mothers who had learned to sign after their child had been identified as hearing impaired, who had been taught to use simultaneous communication, and who had been signing with their child for a minimum of 2 years. The child was required to be of normal intelligence, to be prelingually deaf, and to have a hearing loss of 70 dB or greater in the better ear.

Six mothers and children were found who met these criteria. The mothers had been using simultaneous communication for an average of 3 years. The sign codes used were Signing Exact English (Gustason, Pfetzing, & Zawolkow, 1980) and Manual English (*An Introduction to Manual English*, 1972). All of the mothers had been introduced to sign language in the course of an early intervention program (for 0- to 3-year-olds) in western Washington (Thompson, 1982). They had subsequently had an average of three sign courses each. Mothers who were signing only casually were not included in the sample on the grounds that they would not have represented a fair test of how completely mothers can sign when they make an effort. The children were from 4.5 to 6 years of age at the time of the study and had a mean hearing loss of 95 dB (range 70 dB to no response at any frequency). All of the children used hearing aids, and all but one had used them since the time of identification.

Mother-child communication was videotaped in the home on the third of a series of visits in which child language data were being collected for another study. One hundred consecutive utterances of mother to child were selected for transcription. Both the spoken and signed messages were transcribed into English for comparison in the spirit of the Marmor and Petitto (1979) study of teachers' performance. Deletions of signs with respect to the spoken message were counted, excluding spoken fillers such as **oh, well**, etc. The number of fully signed utterances was counted, with **fully signed** defined as utterances containing no deletions or sign errors. Sign errors were defined with respect to the texts for Signing Exact English and Manual English. The number and percentages of total morphemes deleted were also calculated.

RESULTS

Completeness of Signing

On the average, just 40.5 utterances per 100-utterance sample were signed in full, with a range of 29 to 61. There was a mean of 69.3 deletions per sample (range 26 to 102), out of samples whose mean size was 389 morphemes (range 310 to 575). In most cases a deletion was the omission of a morpheme from the signed message; however, when a whole utterance was left unsigned, only one deletion was counted. The ratio of deletions to total morphemes per sample ranged from 8% to 25.8%, with a mean of 18%. These figures provide a conservative approximation of the percentage of spoken morphemes that were not signed.

It was determined that the principal grammatical category

Reprinted with permission from *American Annals of the Deaf*, July 1985, 130:212-217.

deleted was the functor. This fact is not surprising for a number of reasons. First, English is a stress-timed language, and functors are spoken more quickly than content words because they are not stressed. In a phrase such as **to the store**, the preposition and article will normally be spoken more rapidly than the noun; this means that there will be less time in simultaneous communication to fit in the corresponding signs. In a phrase such as **in the sun**, the hands must move a considerable distance, when compared to the movements made by the speech articulators. Such naturally determined differences in rate frequently lead to difficulties in synchronizing sign and speech. Second, the class of functors known as bound morphemes, including the inflectional endings on nouns and verbs, requires the simultaneous signer/speaker to concurrently analyze the words she or he is saying, concentrating on the form of language when she or he would normally be focusing only on meaning. The need for such an analysis may be a serious stumbling block to language processing. Moreover, when the spoken ending does not occupy a syllable of its own, as in the word **runs**, the signer is faced with the difficulty of inserting a sign without there being time for it in the stream of speech. Finally, signers of MCE may tend to delete functors because they carry less information than content words and may not be crucial to conveying the message.

The bound morphemes as a group were signed only about 50% of the time, with -ing being signed the most frequently (65%), followed by -s plural (56%), the past markers (40%), the -s present (29%), and the possessive (28%). Functors that occupied a full syllable in the spoken message (e.g., -ing) were signed significantly more consistently than nonsyllabic functors such as the -s ending.

Quantity of Material Input

The high rate of deletions in the samples occurred despite the fact that the average mean length of utterance (MLU) of the group was only 3.89 morphemes. Only one mother had an MLU of more than four morphemes, and the person who made the fewest deletions had an MLU of only 3.1. Although mothers may keep their utterances short partly in response to their children's language level, one cannot escape the suspicion that the difficulty of signing English may also contribute to short utterances. Unfortunately, when sentences are kept very short, both the quantity and quality of linguistic information available to the child are limited. The range of linguistic complexity used by the mothers, and the extent of variation of their communicative skill are demonstrated in the examples of utterances provided in the Appendix.

As noted earlier, the mothers in our sample had been signing for an average of 3 years each and had continued to try to upgrade their skills by attending sign classes. Taking into account the motivation, amount of experience, and training of these mothers, their performance indicates that we have underestimated the task we have given parents and that we may have to reevaluate our methodology for teaching them sign language.

DISCUSSION

The Demands of Simultaneous Communication

In order to improve instruction to parents, the first consideration needs to be determining the demands of simultaneous communication. Although MCE is not a different language

from English, there are several ways in which simultaneous communication requires language-learning skill. Most obviously, the signer must learn a new lexicon, that is, signs that correspond approximately one to one to English words. As in learning a foreign language, the signer must learn to retrieve these symbols rapidly and directly, without translating from English. On the other hand, as mentioned before, MCE requires the separate signing of noun and verb inflections, which necessitates a translation process, an immediate conscious analysis of the words being said. While saying a word ending in an /s/ or /z/ sound, one must be aware of the sound; analyze whether the sound represents a plural, a possessive, a contraction of **be**, a third-person singular present ending, or nothing (as in **princess**); and retrieve the correct sign (/s/ or contracted /s/) to represent the ending. During learning, this conscious analysis and retrieval must go on at the same time the signer is concentrating on meaning and doing sentence and discourse planning of the message. From this perspective, the task of learning to sign simultaneously with speech is anything but trivial.

Given these language-processing requirements, it may be enlightening to consider the situation of hearing mothers learning to sign from the perspective of a hypothetical ideal situation for learning a foreign language. In this situation, the learner would be immersed in the target language. She would have multiple sources from whom to learn new vocabulary, and she would be exposed to words in many different contexts and many different styles of speech. She would also need to produce the language in a number of different situations in order to survive, for example, buying groceries, shopping, asking directions, and interacting socially with peers. Further, her desire to be integrated into the dominant society would provide strong motivation toward the development of native-like language production.

The Language-Learning Environment of Mothers

There is a dramatic contrast between this ideal and the actual situation of mothers learning to sign. These hearing mothers are not immersed in a culture of signing adults (indeed, there is no culture of adults who use MCE as their first language); rather, they are immersed in the culture of their own first language, with little exposure to the target language. More often than not, when the child is young, the mother's source of sign vocabulary is a single sign teacher and a sign book, with occasional group interaction. There is little notion or possibility of developing a signing skill adequate for communication on the mother's own cognitive level. In addition, the amount of teaching time is usually limited to 1 or 2 hours a week. Against this meager amount of input stands the rest of the mother's life, including other children, a husband who is unlikely to learn to sign beyond the beginner's level (Bornstein, Saulnier, & Hamilton, 1980; Hatfield, 1983), and her own activities. A certain amount of organization is required for getting to class even one night a week, and if the mother lives in a rural area, she may have to drive a great distance.

In addition to these practical issues, we need to remember that mothers of deaf children, unlike teachers of the deaf, are not a population selected for having academic skills or college degrees. The necessity of analyzing language form to decide what ending to choose for an /s/ sound or an "-er" ending may be a baffling addition to a new world that includes the jargon of audiologists and teachers, the intricacies of hearing aids, and the difficulties of trying to communicate with a hearing-impaired child. Again, unlike most teachers, parents have been forced by circumstances to learn to sign. Parenting a deaf child is not a profession that they have chosen, and the need to sign is thrust upon them whether or not they have the language aptitude, the intelligence, or the physical coordination to acquire the skill easily. In addition to this lack of choice, they may have deep, unresolved conflicts about having a child with disabling conditions, and these conflicts may affect their disposition to learn. Deciding to acquire sign language implies some degree of acceptance that the child is disabled and that the condition is not going to go away. Furthermore, the decision requires overt demonstration of this acceptance to the world at large. The mother who signs to her child in public will surely be watched and may well be approached by interested bystanders whether she is gregarious by nature or not. A part of her life that may feel very private is necessarily made public for the sake of her child.

Another facet of the mother's learning situation is that the hearing-impaired child is usually the only person with whom she signs on a daily basis. This may be an impediment in several ways. First, the need to sign conflicts with physical care-taking and other household activities; in order to sign completely, the mother must stop what she is doing. This may limit how many utterances she addresses to the child, as well as how completely she signs them. Second, what the mother signs is likely to be affected by the communicative feedback she gets from the child, and this may influence her to simplify her language. For example, if the child does not respond to a question, the mother may rephrase and ask a reduced version of the original. Because producing reduced signed English sentences is also much easier physically than producing full ones (unlike spoken language, where the difference of effort is negligible), there is a double pressure to keep the mother from practicing and becoming fluent at signing complete sentences. It takes a considerable effort of will and motivation for a mother to try to overcome these natural impediments. But if she does not become fluent, she is not in a position to make adjustments toward greater complexity in her signed utterances as her child develops language, and the ability to make such adjustments may be very important (Furrow, Nelson, & Benedict, 1979).

Given the magnitude of the task and the many pitfalls we have described, it becomes less surprising that the mothers in our sample do not succeed in signing everything. Indeed, one must respect the mothers for doing as well as they do. However, the deletion rates are a real source of concern, particularly because deaf children have trouble learning the very elements the mothers tend to omit. In addition, moderate fluency is not adequate if parents are to keep ahead of their children and provide increasingly complex input. Parents need to be provided with better training to help them perfect what is, in fact, a very difficult skill.

RECOMMENDATIONS

It becomes apparent, upon considering the overall language-learning situation of mothers, that development of sign fluency represents a major hurdle and that achieving completeness is only one part of the problem. It is also clear that there is no magic answer to the difficulties. Parents' skills are not likely to improve without a major commitment of time and effort, and this in turn will require a substantial investment of money to support intensive training programs. Further, what is needed is not more of the same. The training available in the past has often been ill-adapted to parents' needs as well as insufficient in quantity. Frequently sign classes focus heavily on the teaching of vocabulary with only minimal practice in encoding or decoding real communication. In community sign classes, even the vocabulary offered may be remote from the language that mothers need to use on a day-to-day basis, and communication practice is unlikely to be related to children because of the diverse nature of class membership. Clearly mothers should not be urged simply to take more sign classes. Rather, intensive programs need to be devised that are geared specifically to helping mothers use sign language with young deaf children.

Recommendations touch three areas: first, providing many hours of practice in which mothers can build fluency by communicating using the codes; second, giving mothers instruction in using MCE in an interactive way that responds to the interests of the child; and, third, providing training aimed at completeness per se.

There is no substitute in language-learning for time on task, and learners of sign need intensive practice. In the authors' view, the best way to become fluent in any language is through communication using that language. In addition, mothers of hearing-impaired children need to experience successful two-way communication using a signed form of English. They need to see that it is possible to communicate across the barrier of hearing loss. Therefore, the following is recommended:

* Practice with older deaf children who have been using coded English systems in school for several years. This will help mothers realize that their signs are actually recognizable to someone who knows the language, and it will give them the experience of real dialogue in which they do not (as with the young deaf child) have to carry most of the conversation themselves. It will also let them see that their signing can become more fluent and effortless as they find themselves being understood.
* Regular practice with deaf adults who are willing to use MCE, for the same reasons.
* Consistent practice with fluent instructors of MCE and with other parents of hearing-impaired children.

The experience of using language communicatively is also the best way for the child to develop language. Consequently, there is a need to ensure that mothers are signing to children in an interactive, responsive way. One problem with the necessity of signing English is that the unaccustomed effort of translation may cause the mother to perform more for herself than for her child. She may concentrate on encoding sentences using the signs she knows, rather than gearing her conversation to her child's interests. The effort to sign completely increases this tendency to sign for the sake of signing. Part of the remedy for this is to help mothers build a flexible vocabulary and to develop their signing to the point of real fluency, as mentioned previously. Mothers also need help coping with the problems of trying to communicate with prelingual children who do not provide much feedback. Some mothers may end up signing to themselves because they do not see that their children are attempting to communicate, even though they do not yet use language. Snow (1979) has observed that normal Motherese is typically "directed by the child's activities" (p. 374). Research has also shown that one important factor in the rate of child language acquisition is the proportion of the

109

mother's comments that are related to her child's previous utterances (Cross, 1978). Mothers of young deaf children often need to be shown the ways in which their children are communicating nonverbally and shown how to tune in to their children's interests. It may also be necessary to teach them to comment on those interests at an appropriate language level, to use normal Motherese in simultaneous communication.

Finally, at the stage when parents are on their way to fluency in producing sign and are using it communicatively with their children, emphasis on completeness should be introduced. At that point, the following is recommended:

* Periodic videotaping to give parents feedback on what they are actually signing and to increase their awareness of what they are omitting;
* Periodic practice in signing without speaking, particularly at the stage when parents are ready to begin adding functors to their signing. We believe that this strategy is important for three reasons: (a) It would allow parents to concentrate on only one type of linguistic planning and to focus their attention on the signed message alone; (b) it would remove the auditory feedback of speech, which, as Baker (1978) observed, lends the impression that a complete message has been transmitted, though all elements may not have been signed; and (c) it may help make parents conscious of what signed message the child is actually receiving.

Clearly, parents are extremely important providers of language input, both because of the nature of their relation to their children and because of the amount of time they spend with them. If the signed input parents provide is not complete, the chances that hearing-impaired children will develop grammatical English will certainly be diminished. It has been suggested that planning programs to help parents become skilled requires realistic assessment both of the demands of simultaneous communication and of the pressures in mothers' lives that operate against the development of fluency. It is our hope that the data and analysis presented here will contribute to a more realistic view and will support the need for a greater commitment of resources to train parents in giving complete, fluent input to their hearing-impaired children.

REFERENCES

Baker, C. (1978). How does "sim com" fit into a bilingual approach to education? In F. Caccamise (Ed.), *Proceedings of the Second National Symposium on Sign Language Research and Teaching* (pp. 13-26). Coronado, CA.

Bornstein, H., Saulnier, K., & Hamilton, L. (1980). Signed English: A first evaluation. *American Annals of the Deaf, 125*, 467-481.

Broen P. (1972). *The verbal environment of the language-learning child.* (Monograph of American Speech and Hearing Association, No. 17).

Cross, T. G. (1977). Mothers' speech adjustments: The contributions of selected child listener variables. In C. Snow & C. A. Ferguson (Eds.), *Talking to children: Language input and acquisition* (pp. 151-188). Cambridge, England: Cambridge University Press.

Cross, T. G. (1978). Mothers' speech and its association with rate of linguistic development in young children. In N. Waterson & C. Snow (Eds.), *The development of communication* (pp. 199-216). Chichester, England: Wiley.

Furrow, D., Nelson K., & Benedict, H. (1979). Mothers' speech to children and syntactic development: Some simple relationships. *Journal of Child Language*, 6, 423-442.

Gustason, G., Pfetzing, D., & Zawolkow, E. (1980). *Signing exact English.* Los Alamitos, CA: Modern Signs Press.

Hatfield, N. (1983). *An investigation of bilingualism in two signed languages: American Sign Language and Manually Coded English.* Unpublished doctoral dissertation, University of Rochester, Rochester, NY.

An Introduction to Manual English. (1972). Vancouver: Washington State School for the Deaf.

Marmor, G. S., & Petitto, L. (1979). Simultaneous communication in the classroom: How well is English grammar represented? *Sign Language Studies, 23*, 99-136.

Newport, E., Gleitman, H., & Gleitman, L. (1977). Mother, I'd rather do it myself: Some effects and non-effects of maternal speech style. In C. Snow & C. A. Ferguson (Eds.), *Talking to children: Language input and acquisition* (pp. 109-149). Cambridge, England: Cambridge University Press.

Snow, C. (1972). Mothers' speech to children learning language. *Child Development, 43*, 549-565.

Snow, C. (1979). Conversations with children. In P. Fletcher & M. Garman (Eds.), *Language acquisition* (pp. 363-375). Cambridge, England: Cambridge University Press.

Thompson, M. (1982). Home instruction for hearing-impaired children and their families. *Hearing Aid Journal, 35* (1), 28-32.

APPENDIX

Extracts from Communication Samples of Two Mothers*

Mother B.

Do you think he is sad?
DO --- THINK HE IS SAD

Mother C.

How many kitties?
HOW FIRE CAT--

---

* The first sentence of each pair is the mother's spoken utterance. The sentence in capital letters represents what the mother signed.

He even looks a little proud.
HE EVEN LOOKS A LITTLE PROUD

I think he looks proud, to have an
I THINK HE LOOK----PROUD TO HAVE A

alligator for a friend.
ALLIGATOR FOR----FRIEND

Where will he uh put the alligator?
WHERE HE WILL HE PUT THE ALLIGATOR

Can you sign that?
----- -----   SIGN THAT

And Ginny----Ginny wants pictures of you
----GINNY GINNY WANTS PICTURE-----OF YOU

signing, so other children can learn
SIGNING SO OTHER CHILDREN CAN LEARN

how to sign too.
HAVE TO SIGN TOO

That does not look like our stove.
THAT DO----NOT LOOK LIKE OUR STOVE

How many?
HOW FIRE

Turkey?
TURKEY

What?
WHAT

What is the horse
WHAT IS THE HORSE

doing?
DOING

Is the little
IS YOUR/THE LITTLE

horse eating?
HORSE EATING

Debby wants a big
DEBBY WANT-----A BIG

horse? OK.
HORSE OK

CHARACTERISTICS OF HEARING MOTHERS' MANUALLY CODED ENGLISH

M. Virginia Swisher
University of Pittsburgh

THEORY & USAGE

The theory of using Manually Coded English (MCE) in simultaneous communication is that every spoken word and inflection should be signed, so that the deaf child can see a complete representation of English sentences. The research of Marmor and Petitto (1979) has shown however that some teachers delete large amounts of the spoken message when they sign. Given the importance of maternal input for the development of language, the completeness of mothers' representation of English may be even more important than that of the teacher. It has been hoped, at any rate, that the use of MCE by hearing mothers would help deaf children learn English as naturally and effortlessly as do normally hearing children. The purpose of my research was to investigate the signing of hearing mothers to their deaf children to find out how consistently they were signing what they said.

The children who were being signed to in the Marmor and Petitto study were 11 to 13; those in the present study were approximately seven years younger. From the armchair it seemed probable that utterances to younger children would be shorter and simpler both in lexicon and in syntax, and that signing to them might therefore be easier and easier to do completely. The results showed that there were indeed fewer deletions than in the Marmor and Petitto data. However, the signing was far from complete, and in the end the brevity and linguistic simplicity of the utterances of several of the mothers became a cause for concern in their own right, since the mothers' communications seemed to be limited by their signing skills. In other words, both deletions and short utterances seemed to be responses to the difficulties of simultaneous communication using MCE. After outlining the procedures and results of the study, I will discuss the characteristics of MCE as they relate to Slobin's four charges to Language.

The six mothers in the sample had all been signing for a minimum of two years, and the mean was three years. They were not beginners. All had been introduced to sign language during an early-intervention program, and they had subsequently had a mean of three sign courses each. They each had one hearing-impaired child; these children were between four and one-half and six years of age and were of normal intelligence or above. They were selected to have a hearing loss dating from before age two of at least 70 dB in the better ear; the mean loss was 95 dB.

Figure 1. Utterances signed & utterances with major & minor deletions.

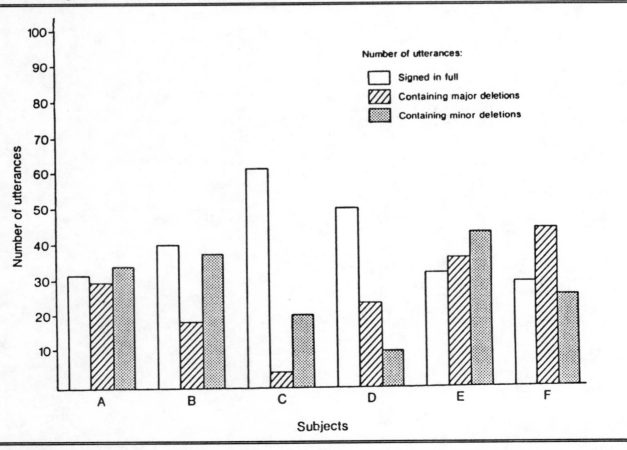

Reprinted with permission from Stokoe, W. & Volterra, V. (Eds.). (1985). *SLR '83: Proceedings of the international symposium on sign language research*, pp.38-47. Silver Spring, MD: Linstok Press.

The mothers and children were videotaped at home. Taping was done on the third of a series of visits in which child language data were being gathered for another study, and this guaranteed a certain amount of social interaction with the experimenter before the taping was done. The mothers had been asked to elicit a sample of the child's best language for the larger study, and it was hoped that this would to some degree decrease their attention to their own signing.

One hundred consecutive utterances of the mother to the child were selected, and both the signed and spoken messages were transcribed into English and compared, in the manner followed by Marmor and Petitto. As the study developed, however, many changes were made in those experimenters' rules for counting deletions, so that the deletion types were finally renamed.

Deletions from the signed messages were categorized as major, minor, and "other." Major deletions (Table 1) eliminated subject, main verb, modal verb, object, and forms of the negative. Minor deletions (Table 2) dropped out of signing functors, including prepositions, articles, bound morphemes, and the like.

The main results by subject are shown in Figure 1. Because an utterance might contain both a major and a minor deletion, the three columns do not sum to 100. There was a mean of 40.5 fully signed sentences per 100-utterance sample. As Figure 1 indicates, some mothers made more major deletions and some made more minor deletions. It should be noted that the great majority of deletions, both major and minor, were of functors.

In order to have a complete picture of the mothers' performance, two more pieces of information are required; i.e., rate of speech and mean length of utterance. In brief, Subjects B and E spoke rapidly and fluently and approximately twice as fast as Subject C, who averaged more than a half second per morpheme. The MLUs ranged from 3.1 morphemes per utterance for Subject C to 5.75 mpu for Subject B. Only Subject B had an MLU of more than four morphemes; the mean was 3.89.

There was a mean of 69 deletions per sample. This should be compared with the number of morphemes per sample, which ranged from 310 to 575, with a mean of 389. Approximately 18% of the morphemes per sample were deleted, and for individual subjects the percentage was as high as 26%.

Table 1. **Examples of major deletions.**

A. Deletion of Subject

> It won't start now.
> -- WON'T START NOW

B. Deletion of Main Verb

> I want you to tell me about Halloween.
> I ---- YOU TO TELL ME ABOUT HALLOWEEN

C. Deletion of Modal Auxiliary

> Can you see yourself?
> --- YOU SEE YOURSELF

D. Deletion of Direct Object

> Can you sign that?
> CAN YOU SIGN ----

E. Deletion of Negative

> Do not look at the book now.
> DO --- LOOK AT THE BOOK NOW

Table 2. **Examples of minor deletions.**

A. Deletion of Bound Morphemes

1. Past marker

> Did you like that story?
> DO-- YOU LIKE THAT STORY

2. -ing ending

> Is he going to be very sick?
> IS HE GO---- TO BE VERY SICK

3. Third person singular present -s

> The alligator wants a worm.
> THE ALLIGATOR WANT-- A WORM

4. Plural

> Chickens can eat worms.
> CHICKEN-- CAN EAT WORM--

5. Possessive

> Did you go to Santa's store at school?
> DID YOU GO TO SANTA-- STORE AT SCHOOL

B. Articles

> The fireman came?
> --- FIREMAN CAME

C. Prepositions

> Look at the wind.
> LOOK -- THE WIND

D. Auxiliaries

> Did you draw?
> --- YOU DRAW

E. Infinitive marker

> What do you want to be?
> WHAT DO YOU WANT -- BE

Table 3. **Some Factors Affecting Amount of Deletions by Mothers**

I. Characteristics of the mother

A. General intelligence
B. Language aptitude
C. Conscious knowledge of grammar
D. Commitment to modeling English
E. Ongoing self-monitoring
F. Physical coordination
G. Motivation/drive

II. Characteristics of the codes and bimodal production

    A. Discrepancy of production rates of sign and speech
    B. Stress-timing of English: less time for functors than content words
    C. Manual codes based on written English, not spoken
    D. Spoken contractions requiring additional sign

III. Immediate communicative and linguistic factors

    A. Pressures of communicative situation (e.g., child doing something dangerous)
    B. Whether mother's hands are occupied (requiring one-handed signing)
    C. Complexity of idea the mother is trying to express
    D. Whether lexical items in sentence are familiar to mother
    E. Spatial and temporal relations of signs to each other
    F. Temporal relations of signs to spoken words

IV. Mother's estimation of the child's receptive skills

    A. General level of child's comprehension
    B. Child's familiarity with ideas being expressed
    C. Child's familiarity with vocabulary mother is using

WHAT'S HAPPENING?

One question of interest is what kind of task simultaneous communication is: Are mothers signing MCE encoding meaning directly in sign, or are they doing a word-by-word simultaneous translation of their spoken utterances? The fact that the great majority of deletions were of functors may indicate that mothers are to some extent encoding meaning directly. In some cases the mothers also tended not to start signing until uttering the first content word of the sentence; as in

"Is it big?" or "Is he eating?"
  BIG   EAT

This suggests a concentration on lexical meaning. Of course, a competing explanation is that in these cases the mother's motor planning for sign lags behind her planning for speech. Deletions of functors undoubtedly also occur because functors are of less duration than content words, so that it is harder to fit the signs in.

In other cases it was clear that the mothers were translating word for word. Evidence for this occurred when they hesitated in speech as they tried to retrieve the correct sign. There was a mean of 6 hesitations in speech per sample, in addition to mid-sentence pauses, which were not tallied. These phenomena are not characteristic of normal Motherese.

Another unusual aspect of the mothers' speech was the occurrence of a small number of ungrammatical or pidginized spoken utterances in four of the samples. This is also in contrast with normal Motherese, which has been found by Newport and others to be "remarkably well-formed" (1976:190). E.g., the mothers in this study were saying things like "We have shower?" and "The man -- mad" and "Numbers one, two, three, you." Mothers may have simplified their speech because shorter utterances seemed less laborious to sign, or because of a conscious or unconscious estimation that they are easier for children to understand. It is also possible that some mothers may fall into a stereotyped foreigner talk of the "Me Tarzan, you Jane" variety. One of the mothers formed negative commands by saying "No" plus the lexical item, as in "No book" and "No touch."

Another unusual feature of both the signed and spoken messages was a strong tendency for mothers to use full rather than contracted forms of the verb be, which gave their speech a stilted quality; e.g., "What is he doing?" instead of "What's he doing?" Four of the mothers used full forms nearly seven times as often as contracted forms, and the category (forms of be) was signed 91% of the time by the group as a whole -- more that all the other functors.

It may be that mothers choose to say full forms when they can because they are easier to sign simultaneously than are contracted forms. When the signing of a set of 13 selected functors was examined, it was found that functors which occupied a full syllable in speech were signed significantly more consistently than those that did not. In other words, functors such as prepositions, pronouns, articles, and full forms of the copula and auxiliary be tended to be signed more consistently than those non-syllabic forms, the -s ending for the plural, the third person singular, the possessive, contracted forms of be, and past tense. Bound morphemes as a group were signed about 50% of the time, ranging from 65% for the -ing to 28% for the possessive.

Deletions are undoubtedly multiply determined; i.e., there are many factors that will intersect to determine how much a mother deletes in general and whether she deletes at a given moment. These factors may be grouped in four categories: (1) general characteristics of the mother, which are more or less stable; (2) characteristics of the codes and the bimodal production; (3) linguistic and communicative pressures that affect immediate processing; and (4) adjustments to the child. Examples of these factors are given in Table 3.

MCE AS LANGUAGE

Although MCE is not a natural language, it must meet the same pressures of processing and communication as must a natural language. It is therefore appropriate to consider the codes in relation to Slobin's four Charges to Language (1975). He has suggested that languages must meet four requirements in order to function as "a full-fledged human language" (Slobin 1975:3). These are:

> Be clear;
> Be humanly processible in ongoing time;
> Be quick and easy;
> Be expressive.

The theory of simultaneous communication, speech with MCE, is of course that spoken English will be completely represented in sign and therefore what the codes transmit should be equally as clear and expressive as English. However, it seems clear that MCE has problems in meeting the second and third requirements; and if breakdowns occur because of this, none of the requirements will be met.

According to Slobin, his second charge, "Be humanly processible in ongoing time," means that "Language must conform to strategies of speech perception and production (ibid.). MCE must conform to those and at the same time to strategies of manual production and visual reception. The mothers' deletion rates and hesitations provide evidence that MCE is difficult to produce manually and to coordinate with speech production. This is certainly not surprising, given that signs take longer to produce than words and that unstressed and non-syllabic functors must be inserted between lexical items. But in addition, the process is made difficult by the conscious analysis of English that must be performed; e.g., first the analysis of whether a final /s/ sound represents a plural, a possessive, a third person singular, or the contraction of "it is;" and then the necessity of retrieving the appropriate "S" sign for it. This kind of processing must go on at the same time the mother is retrieving and producing the correct lexical items, responding to immediate communicative pressures, doing sentence and discourse planning, and so forth. Clearly this is an enormous amount to be asking of cognitive processing, since thinking and encoding can be difficult enough when only one production modality is involved. On many grounds we should not be surprised if mothers delete morphemes or simplify their utterances.

As to the visual perception of MCE, Bellugi has informed us that deaf people report difficulty in processing complete messages in MCE (1980), and she suggests that the limits of visual short-term memory may prevent efficient clausal processing of linearly presented material. In addition, MCE may be difficult to make sense of visually because of its use of separate signs for affixes: These signs are equally as prominent to the eye as are the lexical signs, and they are apt to be equally stressed in performance as well. This may make it harder to synthesize mentally than either the same information presented to the ear or than information being conveyed by a modulation of a root sign, as in ASL. In general it seems that MCE tends to use the visual medium in a way that often does not make visual sense. When parts of the message are hard to synthesize visually, the difficulty of retaining and integrating long strings of visual information may be increased.

Problems of speech perception and production may also arise because of the need to coordinate speech and sign. As we have seen, mothers become dysfluent in their speech when they try to remember a sign or correct an error. If they choose to slow down communication for the sake of signing, this will change their speech production. As speech becomes slower, stress is likely to be more equally placed on content words and functors, and other essential linguistic features, like information contours, may be altered as well. This may mean that the child ends up with less information about the constituent structure of sentences and with fewer syntactic clues to meaning.

Slobin's third charge to Language is, "Be quick and easy," and again the mothers' deletion rates are evidence that MCE is not easy to do completely. Dysfluencies of speech and sign likewise indicate difficulties of performance, and the use of simplified utterances constitutes further indirect evidence.

Slobin remarks that the third charge "allows for human weakness and perversity." He goes on to say that "We seem to blur and smudge phonology whenever possible, to delete and contract surface forms, to conflate underlying forms and surface expression" (ibid.). As far as speech is concerned, MCE tends to prevent such changes, because: (1) It represents written rather than spoken English (e.g., it does not have signs for spoken forms such as "gonna"); and (2) It requires the user to match individual signs to individual words. The need to sign simultaneously with speaking seems to keep mothers from speaking casually (quickly and easily), and in fact communication may in general become an effort, unless the mother has the drive to practice until she has made the breakthrough into

real fluency.

As far as sign is concerned, MCE users are forbidden to "blur and smudge" surface forms because of its obligation to match signs to speech. That is to say, MCE is prevented from evolving into an efficient sign system, and from engaging in the process of assimilation that occurs in spoken languages and in natural signed languages. In fact, MCE is in an awkward limbo, for it must serve as a language and yet cannot change as languages always do. Unless it can evolve in the direction of efficient production in the modality it uses, it is probably doomed to deletion.

As Slobin observes, our tendency to blur and smudge language forms is a natural response to the human communicative system, to the need to get information across before people get restless or take over the floor themselves. It may also be a response to our perceptual limitations, whether auditory or visual. MCE seems to ignore these considerations altogether, and to forget that the purpose of language is communication, and not the other way around. The need to get information across quickly is even greater with young children, who have shorter attention spans and presumably less ability to store and integrate information. The fact that, unless a signer works to become highly skilled, MCE tends to be slow and cumbersome may mean that the child loses both semantic and syntactic information through inattention, the turning of the head, or the flickering of the gaze. Deletions of perception may be added to deletions of production.

In general, communication systems need to flex according to the receptive and productive needs of their users. If they do not, we can expect the kinds of breakdowns represented by deletions, hesitations, and simplified utterances. The fact that MCE has not evolved in and for the modality in which it must be transmitted may prevent it from achieving the purpose it was intended for.

NOTE: The research reported here was supported by a grant from the University of Washington Graduate School Research Fund to Dr. Marie Thompson.

REFERENCES

Bellugi, U. (1980). Clues from the similarities between signed and spoken languages. In U. Bellugi & M. Studdert-Kennedy (Eds.), *Signed and spoken language: biological constraints on linguistics form*, Dahlem Konferenzen. Weinheim: Verlag Chemie GmbH.

Marmor, G. S., & Petitto, L. (1979). Simultaneous communication in the classroom: how well is Englis grammer represented? *Sign Language Studies, 23*, 99-136.

Newport, E. (1976). Motherese: the speech of mothers to young children. In N. Castellan, D. Pisoni, & G. Potts (Eds.), *Cognitive Theory*, vol. 2. Hillsdale, New Jersey: Lawrence Erlbaum Associates.

Slobin, D. I. (1975). The more it changes: On understanding language by watching it move through time. *Papers and Reports on Child Language Development,* no. 10.

INTERPRETERS ENTERING PUBLIC SCHOOL EMPLOYMENT

Gerilee Gustason
Professor, Department of Education
Gallaudet University, Washington, D.C.

A survey of interpreter training programs was conducted in the fall of 1983 to determine the number of trainees entering the field in 1984 and the percent typically obtaining employment in public elementary and secondary schools. Interpreter training program directors were asked to list areas of need or concern in the preparation of educational interpreters. Results indicated that approximately 37% of the trainees are obtaining employment in public school settings, and a need is perceived for clarification of the role and responsibilities of such an interpreter and for training specific to this setting.

In 1979, a nationwide survey of programs for the hearing impaired (Jordan, Gustason & Rosen, 1979) indicated that 37% of the children in these programs were mainstreamed for one or more classes; interpreters were provided for only 24% at the preschool level, 33% at the elementary level, and 41% at the secondary level. In the fall of 1982, according to the April 1983 directory issue of the *American Annals of the Deaf*, 16,346 students, or 35% of the total reported, were mainstreamed or partially mainstreamed. These findings have led to some concern about the provision of support services for mainstream students in general and provision of educational interpreters in particular.

In an attempt to discover the number of interpreters going from training to the public school setting, a questionnaire was sent in the fall of 1983 to 57 interpreter training programs. The programs were listed in the April issue of the *American Annals of the Deaf*, and a directory published by the Registry of Interpreters of the Deaf. This questionnaire asked the number of interpreter trainees the institution expected to graduate in 1984, the percent of their trainees that typically accept employment in various settings (public elementary and secondary schools, post-secondary institutions, community service agencies, free lance interpretation, etc.), and needs or concerns in the area of educational interpreting as perceived by the program director. A copy of the program curriculum was also requested.

RESULTS

Responses were received from 42 of the 57 programs, or 74%. Of those, two programs were no longer training interpreters, and the remaining 40 programs expected to graduate a

Table 1. **Program and Trainee Statistics for Interpreters Entering Public Schools.**

% Trainees entering public schools	Programs	1984 graduates	
0	1	5	
1	2	18	
5	2	57	
6	1	7	
10	6	56	
15	1	11	
20	3	35	
25	3	66	
30	3	26	Average
35	1	12	number of 1984
40	2	12	graduates = 12
	Subtotal (25)		
50	4	60	
60	2	33	
70	4	41	
75	1	15	
85	1	20	
90	1	11	Average
99	1	12	number of 1984
100	1	4	graduates = 13
	Subtotal (15)		
Average % = 37	Total 40	501	Average number of graduates = 12.5

Reprinted with permission from *American Annals of the Deaf*, October 1985, 265-266.

total of 501 new interpreters. The percent reported going into educational interpreting positions in public elementary and secondary schools ranged from none to 100%, with an average of 37%. Twenty-five programs that reported less than 45% of their trainees entered the public schools, whereas 15 noted that between 50% and 100% entered such employment. Average program size was 12.5 graduates (see Table 1).

More than half (22) of the responding programs mentioned the need for a clearer definition of the role and responsibilities of the educational interpreter in the public schools, with respect to expectations, ethics, and job descriptions. One-fourth (11) spoke of the need for increased awareness and understanding among school personnel about the interpreter's role, and a nearly equal number (10) mentioned the range of communication philosophies used in schools as a complicating factor in interpreter training.

The need to develop good sign skills in several modes (American Sign Language and the sign system expected by the schools) was mentioned by seven program directors. Nine felt that, although it would be difficult to find time for such training, there was a need for coursework or a specially designed curriculum involving preparation in education of deaf students, tutoring, familiarity with provisions of Individual Education Programs, aide responsibilities, developmental psychology, and other education-related areas. Five noted a need for the interpreter to understand the information being taught in the public school classroom as well as the technical signs and vocabulary specific to the level of the student.

Four mentioned the need to upgrade the job status and pay to justify more extensive training, and an equal number mentioned the need for more training materials and the opportunity to observe skilled educational interpreters. Three commented that the students themselves sometimes need preparation in the use of an interpreter, including instruction in signs, and two mentioned the lack of research--especially with young children--that would aid preparation efforts.

Not all programs sent a copy of their curriculum, so it is not possible to document the amount of training presently provided in educational areas or English-related sign systems. However, of the 18 programs that did provide outlines of their curriculums, seven offered at least one course in educational interpreting or an education-related area. Five included work on a manual English sign system. It should be noted that the 1979 study (Jordan, Gustason, & Rosen, 1979) indicated that, in the programs using Total Communication, a manual English sign book was reported most used by 67% of the preschool programs, 62% of the elementary, 51% of the junior high, and 41% of the high school programs.

DISCUSSION

Based on the present survey, it would seem that more than one-third of the graduates of interpreter training programs are obtaining employment in public elementary and secondary schools as interpreters, interpreter tutors, and interpreter-aides, many with minimal or no training related to child development, educational aide or tutoring skills, or the sign systems used by the schools. Interpreter training program directors perceive a strong need for clarification of the role of the educational interpreter. With 37% of the interpreter trainees obtaining employment in the public schools, it seems clear information on job descriptions is needed in order to develop more appropriate training.

REFERENCES

Jordan, I. K., Gustason, G., & Rosen, R. (1979) An update on communication trends at programs for the deaf, *American Annals of the Deaf, 124*, 350-357.

Tabular summary of schools and classes in the United States, October 1, 1982, (1983) *American Annals of the Deaf, 128*, 210.

EDUCATIONAL INTERPRETING FOR ELEMENTARY-AND SECONDARY-LEVEL HEARING-IMPAIRED STUDENTS

Esther G. Zawolkow
Consultant, Interpreting Services

Sadie DeFiore
Interpreter, County Department of Education
Orange County, CA

Drawing on direct experience, the authors indicate special considerations in interpreting for hearing-impaired children in mainstream programs, including the variety of roles and responsibilities that may accompany this service. Excerpts are presented from interpreter guidelines developed by one countywide mainstream program. The authors urge that more attention be given to preparation, evaluation, and certification for educational interpreting at the elementary and secondary levels.

As a vocation, educational interpreting has a recent history, beginning in the 1960s with the postsecondary movement that has led to more hearing-impaired students' being educated on regular college campuses.

Educational interpreting at the elementary and secondary levels came into its own with the passage of Public Law 94-142 in 1975, which has led to many younger hearing-impaired students being partially or fully mainstreamed in their local public schools. It is unlikely that these major movements could have occurred without the services of interpreters.

Unfortunately, no national statistics are available regarding interpreters and their services in educational settings, but it is likely today that more interpreting takes place in the classroom than in any other environment. One survey conducted in 1978 among 600 elementary and secondary programs for hearing-impaired students reported that 37% of the students enrolled in these programs were mainstreamed for one or more of their classes. Of these students, 41% at the high school level, 35% at the junior high level, 27% at the elementary level, and 24% at the preschool level had the services of an interpreter (Jordan, Gustason, & Rosen, 1979).

Many of these students were in residential programs, day schools, or day classes that used total communication, and they were mainstreamed for only part of the day. There was a growing need for educational paraprofessionals who could accompany the students to their mainstreamed classes and take on not only interpreting duties, but other functions as well. A new job category appeared: the educational interpreter/tutor or interpreter aide.

Educational interpreting introduces many elements not common to freelance interpreting for hearing-impaired adults. This is more evident in interpreting for younger students at the elementary and secondary levels than for students at the postsecondary level.

Interpreting situations differ from school to school. For instance, an educational interpreter in a rural area may interpret for only one student, with no other support services available. The interpreter may be part of a program for hearing-impaired persons on the campus where the student is mainstreamed or may be hired by parents rather than a school. He or she may be hired from an interpreter referral agency to come in for one or two classes and report back to the agency. The situations vary by locality, which may raise questions of roles and responsibilities.

ROLES AND RESPONSIBILITIES

In the absence of clear, nationally developed guidelines and standards, some programs have begun to develop their own. Among these are the interpreting services guidelines developed by an educational team in Orange County, California, and formally adopted in 1983 by the Orange County Board of Education.

The statement of purpose from the Orange County guidelines states that,

> **The interpreter's primary function is to act as the facilitator of communication between hearing-impaired students and their mainstream teachers. The interpreter is included as a member of the educational team. The interpreter is unique, in that the position is an extension of the student and the student's relationship with the teacher; at the same time, that position is also an extension of the teacher and the teacher's relationship with the student.**

The Orange County guidelines concentrate on the secondary level. Interpreting with younger children includes some different variables. For example, Zawolkow (1983) pointed out that younger children--kindergarten through second grade--often look to the interpreter as a parent figure.

Depending on the students' age, grade level, and experience, interpreters may need to remind them about homework, assist hearing students in accepting and understanding hearing-impaired children, function as liaisons between the program for the hearing-impaired students and the regular teachers, tutor hearing-impaired students and possibly hearing students in the class, and so on. The Orange County guidelines include the following among additional duties of interpreters:

1. When not interpreting, interpreters may be called upon to tutor students (hearing impaired or hearing) during class time under the direction of the regular teacher.

2. Interpreters will be available to interpret before- or after-school tutoring sessions of the teacher and hearing-impaired students where possible.

3. When not interpreting, interpreters may function as classroom aides, assisting the regular teacher as requested.

4. Interpreters may remind the regular teacher when a note-taker is needed for hearing-impaired students.

5. Interpreters should keep the (special resource) teacher

Reprinted with permission from *American Annals of the Deaf*, March 1986, 26-28.

informed of the progress of the hearing-impaired students, as members of the educational team.

6. If an interpreter suspects that a student is having difficulty understanding the course content, he or she should inform the teacher. If such problems arise, interpreters should work with the regular and special resource teachers to determine whether the problems are related to course content or to the interpreting service.

This list, although not all inclusive, is illustrative of the duties interpreters may be asked to perform at the elementary and secondary levels. Comprehensive guidelines should also include special responsibilities of regular teachers and responsibilities of hearing-impaired students themselves (Mitchell-Caccamise, 1982a, 1982b).

Interpreters may be working with different levels and skills in English in the same class and may need not only to interpret but also to explain material again. Sign-to-voice interpreting skills may be important for full participation of hearing-impaired students in the class. In addition, many school programs use some form of Manual English and expect interpreters to follow school policy. Interpreters may need to deal with students who have grown up with such a communication modality, have excellent English skills, and need word-for-word transliterating; students who have come into the program from a background of American Sign Language; students who have come from oral programs; or students who have limited exposure to any education. Interpreters must be able to communicate effectively with them all (Murphy et al., 1980).

Some consistency regarding preferred mode of communication for interpreting in the classroom situation should be developed, but rigidity should be avoided. For purposes of illustration, the Orange County guidelines state,

This is a total communication program where Signing Exact English (SEE 2) and Signed English are the preferred signing systems. However, if a student needs clarification in understanding a concept, developing a concept, or understanding topical issues, the interpreter may use other systems with which the student may be familiar, e.g., ASL, PSE, CASE, any combination of those, or gestures.

Within the context of total communication, oral/aural communication should, of course, also be a part of interpreters' repertoire, including oral interpreting in some situations.

After-school activities may run the gamut from pep rallies to club meetings, from driver education to sports and athletic teams. Christmas programs and artistic interpreting are often important, as are public relations skills with hearing children, parents, and the regular teachers. Yet, although interpreters sometimes function as parent substitutes, teacher aides, tutors, assistant coaches, and the like, they are not parent, teacher, or coach, and role delimitations may be hazy.

Much could be said about interpreters' attitudes. If fully recognized by their colleagues as members of the educational team, they are likely to respond in kind. Interpreters' positive professional attitude does a great deal to establish a healthy educational climate for hearing-impaired students in a mainstream program. Thus, it is important that interpreters understand and subscribe to the educational goals of the program in which they work.

Interpreter attitudes may be detected quickly by hearing-impaired students. For example, if an interpreter shows a lik-ing or, conversely, a disliking for a specific subject in the curriculum, students will probably sense this, and it may influence their own feelings toward the subject. Roles and responsibilities are more easily indicated in guidelines than are attitudes.

WHAT TO DO?

Interpreters will find themselves faced with situations that must be handled with tact, diplomacy, and care in order not to jeopardize the success of the mainstreaming experience. For example, how does an interpreter react when faced with the following situations?

1. In a physical education class, a hearing-impaired student is not sure what to do; the teacher asks the interpreter to be that student's partner until the student is more comfortable.

2. The teacher is not sure how well a hearing-impaired student understands the material that has been taught and asks the interpreter what grade the student should be given.

3. Some hearing-impaired students are talking between classes about cutting class. Should it be reported? If the interpreter knows a student is at school but that student does not appear for the class being interpreted, what should the interpreter tell the teacher when asked if the student is in school?

4. An interpreter notices a hearing-impaired student cheating. What should the interpreter do? What if a hearing student is cheating?

5. Some hearing-impaired students are talking about getting drugs. What should an interpreter, who sees them, do?

6. The students are doing individual seatwork, and a number are asking the teacher for assistance. No one is needed to interpret, but the interpreter cannot leave the class because he or she might be needed at any moment. The teacher asks for assistance with the hearing students. How does the interpreter respond?

These few examples show clearly that interpreting in a secondary or elementary classroom places special demands and ethical considerations upon interpreters. How these situations are handled may make the difference between success and failure of a hearing-impaired student, not just educationally but socially and psychologically as well.

PREPARATION AND SKILLS

It is clear that what is expected of educational interpreters working in elementary and secondary settings is not identical to what is expected of free-lance interpreters who work with deaf adults. A major need today is for special training and evaluation of educational interpreters. Evaluation and certification by the Registry of Interpreters for the Deaf (RID) do not include the area of educational interpreting (unlike legal and artistic interpreting); nor is the Code of Ethics of the RID always clearly applicable in elementary and secondary classrooms, due to the difference in interpreting tasks and other educational responsibilities of interpreters.

Few, if any, interpreter training programs appear to be meeting the need for training in handling such situations. What is clear is the importance of adding to interpreter training and evaluation to cover the areas described here, including (a) judgment in handling complicated situations in the school environment; (b) public relations skills; (c) information on deafness and education needed to function effectively as a liaison; (d) skills in Manual English, in ASL, in re-explaining, and in tutoring and aiding students; (e) artistic skills; (f) knowledge of child development; and (g) ability to function as a member of an educational team.

Free-lance interpreting is without question an important field. Educational interpreting with elementary and secondary school children is also important and needs increased attention.

To help ensure the success of mainstreamed hearing-impaired students, interpreters, teachers (both special and regular), principals, speech pathologists, audiologists, psychologists, parents, and instructional aides must function as one unit to provide these students with the optimum learning experience.

REFERENCES

Guidelines for mainstream interpreters for the hearing impaired. (1983) Orange County, CA: Orange County Department of Education.

Jordan, I. K., Gustason, G., & Rosen, R. (1979) An update on communication trends at programs for the deaf. *American Annals of the Deaf, 124* (3), 350-357.

Mitchell-Caccamise, M. (1982a) *Guidelines for secondary classroom interpreting.* Baton Rouge, LA: Louisiana School for the Deaf. (working paper)

Mitchell-Caccamise, M. (1982b) *Guidelines for students in the mainstream program.* Baton Rouge, LA: Louisiana School for the Deaf. (working paper)

Murphy, H., Hughes, V., Zawolkow, E., Culton, P., Caccamise, F., Rinaldi, A., DeVries, R., & Mitchell-Caccamise, M. (1980) Interpreting settings. In F. Caccamise, R. Dirst, R. DeVries, J.Heil, C. Kirchner, S. Kirchner, A. Rinaldi, J. Stangarone, (Eds.), *Introduction to interpreting.* Silver Spring, MD: Registry of Interpreters for the Deaf.

Zawolkow, E. (1983, February) Interpreter's insights: Elementary and secondary educational settings. *SEE What's Happening,* 2 (1), Los Alamitos, CA: Modern Signs Press, Inc.

LONG-TERM EFFECTS OF MANUAL CODES ON ENGLISH SKILLS

Martha Gaustad, Ph.D.
Department of Special Education
Bowling Green State University
Bowling Green, OH

ABSTRACT

This study examined the imitation, comprehension, and production of twelve language features by groups of deaf subjects who were instructed through manually coded English. Their performances were compared with those of hearing subjects and also with their own follow-up scores from three years later. Results showed early deficits in the English skills of deaf subjects but steady improvement of scores on all tasks over time. Implications for intervention with manual English codes are discussed.

Over the last fifteen years systems of manually coded English (MCE) have been implemented as one means to facilitate language acquisition by prelingually deafened learners, the great majority of whom (95%) have hearing parents. This objective reflects both the importance of language to all aspects of life, and the long-standing English language deficits of the deaf population. Research completed to date has revealed generally positive results of TC programming, especially regarding academic achievement (Brasel & Quigley, 1977; Chasen & Zuckerman, 1976; Moores, Weiss & Goodwin, 1978; Weiss, McIntyre, Goodwin & Moores, 1975). Other studies, which have dealt more directly with linguistic aspects of MCE instruction so far have produced equivocal results (Crandall, 1978; Raffin, Davis & Gilman, 1978; Zorfass, 1981). This is especially true concerning the relationships of chronological age and length of program attendance to MCE gains.

The studies cited above have provided evidence of mastery of certain features of MCE by deaf children but at a delayed pace in comparison with existing data on hearing children. The results have also demonstrated the need for longitudinal monitoring of representative samples of MCE learners, comparative testing of deaf and hearing users of English (preferably with the same tasks) and the evaluation of multiple component MCE skills, (e.g., comprehension and production). These kinds of data are necessary to resolve questions regarding classroom policies for MCE use.

This paper reports on a two-part longitudinal study of English skills of deaf students in existing programs whose instruction relied upon manually coded English (closest in overall form to SEE II). The evaluation instrument sampled a variety of basic grammatical features under each of three performance conditions. During Part 1 the performance of three groups of deaf subjects who used MCE was compared with that of three groups of normal hearing subjects who used oral English. In Part 2 a subset of deaf subjects from the original sample was retested three years later and those scores compared with their original scores. Using the patterns of performance produced by the hearing children as a reference, the effectiveness of MCE can be measured by improvement in the comparative performance of deaf children over time.

METHOD₁

Subjects/Programs

All subjects, hearing and deaf, were selected on the following criteria: (a) intellectual ability within the normal range, (b) average language ability (within their respective populations), (c) no identified learning or behavior problems, (d) at least one year of attendance in a preschool program with a structured language-oriented curriculum. In addition, it was required that deaf subjects have: (e) severe to profound hearing loss at the speech frequencies (75 dB ISO or greater, better ear), and (f) prelingual onset of deafness.

In order to obtain a practical comparison of English language skills between deaf and hearing subjects it was necessary to compensate somewhat for the lag in diagnosis and consequently in language exposure experienced by most deaf children. Specific age levels for corresponding groups of hearing subjects were determined by subtracting a language lag, estimated to be at least two years (Raffin, et al., 1978) from the age levels selected for deaf subject groups. Like the procedure of using mental age rather than chronological age as a matching factor, here the attempted match is "linguistic age" (3, 4, and 5 years respectively, for both hearing and deaf groups).

Programs for the deaf were selected from separate regions of the United States in order to obtain a broader sample of subjects. A total of 39 deaf subjects in the three age ranges of 60-71 months, 72-83 months, and 84-95 months were identified. These subjects represented all of the deaf children meeting the above criteria at three large residential/day schools, one in the Northeast and two in the West. The programs from which deaf subjects were selected (a) had had MCE programs in effect for a minimum of three years at the start of the study, (b) provided parental instruction in manual communication, and (c) stipulated use of MCE in all activities and by all persons interacting with the deaf children. Forty-five hearing subjects, fifteen in each of three age levels, 36-47 months, 48-59 months and 60-71 months, were identified in two separate preschool programs. Demographic data for all subject groups can be found in Table 1.

Fifteen deaf students, all subjects from one of the schools included in Part 1, participated in Part 2. At the time of follow-up, these subjects were aged eight, nine or ten. In comparison with the entire deaf sample these subjects were on the average, about one month older, had hearing losses about five decibels worse and possessed approximately eleven months more MCE experience. In other words these children started MCE almost a year younger than the deaf sample as a whole. Only one subject of this group had deaf parents.

Materials

This study employed a modified version of the Imitation, Comprehension and Production (ICP) measure developed by

Table 1. Demographic Data for Groups of Hearing and Deaf Subjects.

	Hearing			Deaf				
N	Age in mos. mean (range)	N	Age in mos. mean (range)	Age of onset	Hearing loss mean (range)	Time in prog. mean (range)	Cases of Parental deafness
15	44.0 (40-48)	10	66.3 (62-71)	birth (N= 6)	98 dB (85-108)	27 mo. (12-48)	0
15	53.7 (49-59)			infancy (N= 3)			
15	64.4 (60-71)			22 mos. (N= 1)			
		15	77.8 (73-83)	birth (N= 9)	93 dB (75-110)	34 mo. (18-63)	0
				infancy (N= 4)	2 Ss < 85 dB		
				29 mos. (N= 1)			
				16 mos. (N= 1)			
		14	89.7 (84-95)	birth (N=10)	93 dB (78-108)	39 mo. (12-72)	4
				infancy (N= 3)	1 Ss < 85 dB		
				24 mos. (N= 1)			

Fraser, Bellugi and Brown (1963) to study syntactic performances of young normal hearing children.

The ICP measure was selected because it highlights English features which MCE systems were specifically designed to make more perceptually salient for the deaf, contrasts that are otherwise demonstrably difficult for deaf individuals to make and which account for a large portion of the total English language errors produced by deaf children and adults (Cooper, 1967; Crandall, 1978).

Different random orders of a set of 48 test items were employed for three performance tasks: imitation, comprehension, and production. Each test item was composed of "minimal pair sentences" differing only on the grammatical feature to be examined (e.g., The boy writes./The boys write.). The item set for this study contained 12 subtests: mass/count nouns, singular/plural third person present indicative, singular/plural with is/are, present/past tense, present/future tense, affirmative/negative, active/passive voice, direct/indirect object, possessive pronouns, conjunctions, adjectives and prepositions.

Procedures

For the imitation task each hearing subject was presented from audio cassette with one test sentence (of a contrasted pair) at a time and then imitated what she or he had heard. Each deaf subject had the test sentences presented one at a time by the examiner using MCE simultaneously with speech. Then the child imitated the examiner's performance. For the comprehension task, each hearing subject was again presented with test sentences one at a time from the audio cassette. This time the child responded by pointing to that picture of a minimally distinctive pair which corresponded to each sentence. For deaf subjects the only difference was that the sentence presentation again involved MCE. Response procedures were the same as for hearing subjects. Another order of the same pictures (also alternated for left-right position) was used during the production task. The examiner pointed to one picture at a time and the subject provided a description for that picture. This procedure was identical for hearing and deaf sub-

jects except that responses of deaf subjects included signing.

At least a half day separated administration of the imitation and comprehension measures and two days separated the comprehension and production measures. The responses of the subjects were recorded in writing by the examiner and recorded on audiotape (hearing) and videotape (deaf).

Scoring

Each sentence pair was scored as one item which resulted in a possible score of 48 for each of the ICP tasks. If either or both sentences were incorrect the item received a score of zero. In evaluating responses of deaf subjects, the complete oral and manual output was considered (i.e., on occasions subjects had signed but had not vocalized or vocalized in the absence of signing some portion of an utterance).

RESULTS AND DISCUSSION [2]

Statistical analyses of the ICP scores examined differences between hearing and deaf subjects on the basis of (linguistic) age and the performance of deaf subjects over time. Further analyses were performed to determine the contribution of chronological age and time in an MCE program to the ICP scores of deaf subjects and to changes in those scores over time. Finally, ranking analyses were used to estimate the comparative difficulty of the ICP subtests for hearing and deaf subjects and to evaluate the stability of the ranking for deaf subjects over time.

Deaf-Hearing Differences

The first objective of this study was to evaluate differences between the performances of deaf and hearing subjects. Mean scores by hearing condition and age level for each of the ICP tasks are presented in Table 2. Generally these results show that long-term improvement toward control of basic English grammatical features is possible when students are provided with direct, visual access to English through manual codes. The greatest deficits appear on the imitation task where the

Table 2. ICP Means* for Hearing and Deaf Subjects during Parts 1 and 2 of the Study.

Part 1

Condition	*Age (hearing / deaf)* Imitation 3/5	4/6	5/7			Summary (Grand Means)		
Hearing	34.5	40.0	41.2			*Imit.*	*Comp.*	*Prod.*
Deaf	12.8	19.6	28.3					
	Comprehension							
Hearing	23.5	33.0	35.4		Hearing	38.6	30.6	12.9
Deaf	24.4	25.5	27.8		Deaf	21.0	26.0	6.0
	Production							
Hearing	8.9	13.7	15.9					
Deaf	3.3	5.3	8.8					

Part 2
(Deaf subjects only, one group)

Task	*Part 1*	*Time* *Part 2*	*Mean*
Imitation	23.4	34.6	29.0
Comprehension	24.9	34.0	29.5
Production	7.1	17.1	12.2
Mean	18.5	28.6	23.6

*Possible Score: 48

scores of deaf subjects are far below those of younger hearing subjects. But the actual improvement over time is also greatest with imitation. Steady though slower rates of improvement are also evident for deaf subjects on the comprehension and production tasks at all age levels and over time.

In particular, scores of hearing subjects were usually higher than those of deaf subjects indicating that the lag in linguistic development of deaf subjects was not completely accounted for by group matching on estimated levels of language exposure. However, this linguistic age variable did have a consistent effect within both hearing conditions. Older subjects, both hearing and deaf, generally outperformed younger ones.

The apparent differences between performances of hearing and deaf subjects were not consistent across age levels and tasks. Figure 1 is a graphic representation of these interaction results. Information for both groups is presented by task and, for deaf subjects also covers both time periods.

The varied pattern of results for deaf vs. hearing subjects on the imitation task can probably be attributed to a ceiling effect for the oldest, most linguistically sophisticated group of hearing subjects. The items tested by the ICP consist mostly of grammatical features that are nearly mastered by normal hearing subjects by school age. So the oldest hearing subjects in this study were able to do very well and their scores show that all but the most difficult features on the 48-item imitation task had been mastered. By contrast, the scores of deaf subjects steadily improved but did not approach mastery by the oldest age level.

On the other hand, the comprehension task requires a simple pointing response to redundant cues contained in the stimulus [the DOG (singular) digS (singular)]. So, on this task, the relationship between the variables of age and hearing condition is different than it was for imitation. The deaf subjects, by virtue of their comparatively greater chronological age, may have had a cognitive advantage over their linguistically experienced but younger hearing counterparts. Thus, perhaps for different reasons, the younger deaf subjects were as able as the hearing youngsters to use redundant information in comprehension performance. This comparative advantage disappeared with increasing age of the hearing subjects.

Overall, the production task was very difficult for both hearing and deaf subjects. Therefore, the advantage of hearing was consistent across all age levels and the advantage of greater age was consistent under both hearing conditions.

Part 2 of the study concerned only deaf subjects, all the students from one program collapsed into a single group. These subjects' scores from Part 1 of the study were compared with their scores obtained during Part 2. The means for Part 2 scores are also contained in Table 2. Overall, the results showed that time was a significant factor in subjects' performance. As a group these deaf subjects continued to demonstrate increasing MCE skills three years after the original measurement, and means of their Part 2 scores, except for imitation, surpassed the overall means of ICP scores for hearing subjects during Part 1 of the study.

Effects of Time in MCE Program

The second objective of the study was to establish the relative impact of age and time in an MCE program on the actual scores obtained by deaf subjects. Would students in MCE programs longer do better no matter how old they were or would older students always do better? To answer this question chronological age in months and number of months in an MCE program were used as statistical predictors of the three ICP scores. Overall, these analyses indicated that both age and time in a program influenced scores, though to different extents, and that the effects of both factors diminish over time.

More specifically, age significantly predicted only the imitation scores of the deaf subjects, that is, the older they were the better they performed. On the other hand, time in a program (regardless of age), was a significant predictor of both imitation and production. On these two tasks, with longer MCE exposure, even younger subjects performed better than older subjects with less program time. Neither age nor time in a program significantly predicted comprehension scores. The interaction of factors of age, conceptual ability and linguistic knowledge described earlier may explain this inability of either age or program time to predict comprehension scores.

When the same analysis was performed on the differences in ICP scores between Part 1 and Part 2 all results were statistically insignificant. Neither chronological age nor time in an MCE program predicted any ICP difference score for the group of fifteen follow-up subjects.

The ability of age to predict imitation scores of deaf subjects throughout the primary grades may indicate the level of difficulty for the task of manual as opposed to oral imitation. Processing demands for manual imitation may be greater as a result of the greater time required to produce manual signals. Bellugi and Fischer (1972) determined that it takes approximately one and a half times as long to produce a sign than it does a spoken word. For this reason the imitation items, when presented to deaf subjects, may seem longer and may tax the capacities of these beginning language users to receive and hold the stimulus in mind long enough to reproduce it. The fact that they also have to switch viewpoints from objective (model signing) to subjective (self signing) in order to accomplish this task may only make the processing problem worse. The importance of age for imitation performance can then be explained by developmental factors such as are involved in normal increases in the length of a child's utterances over time and in the mastery of perceptual-motor coordination by normal hearing children for similar tasks (e.g., "Simon Says"). These findings indicate the need to research more intensively the issue of manual language processing by very young versus older deaf children, and the ways in which component skills are addressed in school curricula.

A particularly noteworthy finding of the study is the value of time in an MCE program in predicting the quality of spontaneous language production early in the intervention process. Whether these results mean that MCE intervention is also most effective at younger ages is not possible to determine from this study because subjects who began MCE use at ages eight or above were not included in the sample. But it does indicate that full use of MCE codes (including derivational endings, etc.) may have a greater impact early in the intervention process than if complex elements of vocabulary are introduced only with advanced students after they have mastered MCE basics (e.g., inflectional endings).

The effects of time in an MCE program are illustrated by the comparison of two children who participated in Part 1 of the study. They both had two hearing parents and attended the same school (not the follow-up school). Subject AS was a female, sixty-two months of age, who had been exposed to MCE at home and school for thirty months. Her mean length of utterance (MLU), calculated on production responses, was 4.51 and her ICP scores were 30, 33, and 8 respectively. BL was a male, sixty-three months old, who had only been exposed to MCE for twelve months. His MLU was 1.87 and his ICP scores were 6, 19, and 4 respectively. Even if gender

Table 3. Guttman Rank Orderings of ICP Subtests by Hearing Condition for Parts 1 and 2 of the Study.

| Contrast | Part 1 | | Part 2 | |
	Hearing	Deaf	Deaf Follow-up Ranking (Part 1)	Subjects
Affirm. / Negative	1	1	1	1
Preposition	2	4	4	7
Present / Past	3	9	8	8
Adjective	4	7	6	4
Present / Future	5	6	5	5
Sing. / Plural-Is / Are	6	8	9	6
Possessive	7	3	3	2
Active / Passive	8	11	10	10
Mass / Count	9	2	2	3
Conjunction	10	5	7	9
Sing. / Pl.-Pres.Ind.	11	10	11	11
Dir. / Indirect Object	12	12	12	12

plays some part, the differences between the children's performances are remarkable. MCE intervention seems to affect "expressiveness" generally as indicated by MLU but, also, effects the grammaticalness of the linguistic output.

Subtest Difficulty

The last analysis examined the relative difficulty of the ICP subtests for both groups of subjects. Over time, these results show the establishment of a clear pattern of difficulty in the acquisition of the ICP's twelve grammatical subtests by deaf subjects. The advanced conceptual ability and delayed language ability of the deaf subjects as compared to the hearing subjects in this study may be the source of differences between the groups regarding the relative difficulty of grammatical features.

The Guttman Scaling procedure (SPSS; Nie, Hull, Jenkins, Steinbrenner, & Bent, 1970) is special because the scale it produces is considered to be unidimensional and cumulative. This means that a scalable ranking might be said to represent an acquisition order with the easiest items learned first, etc. Table 3 presents the subtest rank orderings for hearing and deaf subjects during Part 1 of the study. Neither ordering met the statistical criteria for a reliable Guttman scale. There was much individual variability and no strong general pattern of performance. Since neither the hearing nor deaf results from Part 1 were scalable more definitive conclusions are not possible.

However, analysis of the follow-up group's later performance did produce a significant finding. Table 3 also contains rankings of subtest difficulty for the follow-up deaf subjects during Parts 1 and 2 of the study. Like the results for the larger deaf sample the ranking produced by follow-up subjects during Part 1 also did not represent a scalable ordering. But the ranking for their subtest scores three years later, during

Part 2 of the study, met the Guttman criteria and thereby established a reliable order of difficulty for the ICP features. In other words, while the pattern of grammatical errors for these deaf students varied widely and unpredictably at ages five through seven, by the time they had completed the primary grades the pattern of errors was very consistent.

When the actual rankings of the follow-up subjects (Part 1 and Part 2) are compared with those of the entire deaf sample and the hearing subjects from Part 1, it can be seen that, in general, where differences exist between the follow-up deaf group and the entire original deaf sample the rankings of the follow-up subjects are more like the hearing rankings. It may be worthwhile to recall here that these subjects had had earlier, not just longer, exposure to an MCE system than did the deaf sample as a whole.

Grammatical Variation

During production, hearing subjects (with the exception of some younger ones) usually responded to the **relationships** within the pictorial stimuli with some form of language construction. This was less likely to be the case as the difficulty of the subtest increased. The youngest deaf subjects and those with the least signed English experience sometimes were completely lost for a description of the relational contrast (present-past, singular-plural, etc.). When this occurred both deaf and young hearing subjects resorted to naming the components of the pictures or, with more sophistication, provided a fuller description but of the **content** rather than the relation depicted (e.g., "Two boys walk a dog," for a possessive picture). More often for deaf than hearing subjects, the same sentence was produced for both pictures of a contrasting pair. These behaviors indicate a greater lack of control in deaf subjects of the English syntactic structures which are necessary to express relational concepts.

Table 4. Exemplary Responses of Deaf Subject Al to Corresponding Contrast Items on the Imitation and Production Tasks.

Type of Contrast	ICP Item Contrasts	Part 1 (age 5) Imitation Responses	Production Responses	Part 2 (age 8) Imitation Responses	Production Responses
Sing./Pl.,3rd Pers.	the girl waves	girl wave	girl is waving	the girl waves	the girl is wave
Present Indicative	the girls wave	the girl wave	the girl are waving	the girls wave	the girl are waving
Sing./Pl. with	the deer is sleeping	the deer sleeps	deer is sleep	the deer is sleeping	the deer is sleeping
Is/Are	the deer are sleeping	the deer are sleeping	deer is sleep two	the deer are sleeping	the deer are sleeping
Active/Passive	the girl is pushing	the girl pushing	the girl is pushing	the girl pushing	the girl is pushing boy
	the girl is pushed	the girl pushing	the boy pushing at girl	the girl is pushing	the boy is pushing girl
Pres. Progressive/	the boy is jumping	the boy is jump	the boy are jumping	the boy is jumping	the boy is jumping the truck
Past	the boy jumped	the boy is jump er	the boy are jump stop	the boy is jumped	the boy jumped the truck
Pres. Progressive/	the mommy is sweeping	the mommy sweeping	the mother was sweeping	the mother is sweeping	the mother is sweeping
Future	the mommy will sweep	the mommy sweep	the mother was get sweep	the mother will sweep	the mother will sweep
Affirm./Negative	the girl is reading	the girl reading	the girl want book read	the girl is reading	the girl is reading
	the girl is not reading	the girl not read	the girl not read book	the girl is not read	the girl is not reading
Possessive	his bicycle	bicycle	the boy have a bicycle	h-i-s- bicycle*	h-i-s- bicycle
	their bicycle	their bicycle	the boy's bicycle	their bicycle	their bicycle
Direct/Indirect	the man throws the	the man throw doll	the man throw bear	the man throw doll	the man is throwing bear
Object	doll the bear	bear		the bear	t-o doll
	the man throws the	the man throw doll	the man throw bear doll	the man throw bear	the man is throwing doll
	bear the doll	bear		doll	t-o bear

* h-i-s - fingerspelled

125

The overall grammaticalness of the utterances produced by hearing and deaf subjects is also indicative of dissimilar levels of competence. Most of the utterances used by hearing subjects, whether phrases or sentences, were grammatically well constructed. They often, however, were simpler alternatives to the construction required for the item to be scored as correct. This evidence would lead to the conclusion that simpler structures had been mastered, and in some instances there was active movement toward mastery of the more complicated construction. In contrast, deaf subjects while communicating effectively through other means, produced many more syntactically incorrect strings than did hearing subjects. In general, the more complexity involved in a construction the more likely it was that deaf subjects would replace it with some other expressive device. Take the instance of how plural concept was rendered by young deaf subjects during Part 1 of the study. Various subjects manipulated the noun, the verb, or a modifier to express a plural meaning but rarely, if ever, was more than one device used in the same utterance. For clarity sake the same subject matter is carried throughout these examples: **sheep sheep jump, sheep jump jump, two sheep jump, both sheep jump, some sheep jump, sheep all jump, sheep jump two**. The next examples are more advanced in that they employ standard English plural conventions but still demonstrate the inclination to manipulate only a single morpheme: **sheeps jump, sheep jumps** (contrasted with **sheep jump**), **sheep are jump**. Some of these examples were shared by more than one deaf subject. When hearing subjects used modifiers like **two**, **some**, or **both** they were used appropriately and in combination with standard plural morphemes.

The difference between communicative ability and specific skill in English can be seen in the performance of one deaf subject who participated in both parts of the study. Table 4 contains actual item responses from one subject which are exemplary of his other responses as well as of the many variations produced by most of the deaf subjects somewhere in the course of ICP evaluation.

AL was 71 months old and had been exposed to signed English for 36 months at the original time of testing. Both of his parents were hearing and he lived at home. His obtained MLU was 5.31 and it is apparent from his responses that he was well into the task of learning English grammar, yet had mastered little of it. His MLU and the content of his productions indicate that though AL's syntactic skills were imperfect he managed to encode much of the meaning, or semantic content, presented to him.

If AL's responses from Part 2 imitation and production are compared with each other and with his responses from Part 1, differences and improvements in his performances are apparent: (a) Overall, his responses became more complete and more correct with time; ten of the sixteen production examples were grammatically acceptable English utterances compared to five for Part 1 production; (b) Responses on imitation and production tasks were more alike during Part 2 than during Part 1, indicating some stability in his control of English structures; (c) AL still omitted some features: 3rd person _s, occasionally _ing, and sometimes medial **the**, especially in more complex utterances such as those containing both direct and indirect objects or passive constructions; (d) He still added information not contained in the ICP stimulus utterance (e.g., truck, boy) but the additions served to increase content information, not to replace syntactic elements; (e) Even when AL's responses did not meet the ICP scoring objectives they were, much more often then during Part 1, grammatically acceptable

English alternatives for expressing the specific content (e.g., substituting progressive for indicative, active for passive or attempting prepositional phrases for indirect objects). This behavior is typical of the response of older hearing subjects to difficult constructions during Part 1.

Figure 1. Mean ICP scores for age groups of hearing and deaf subjects (Part 1) and deaf follow-up subjects (Part 2).

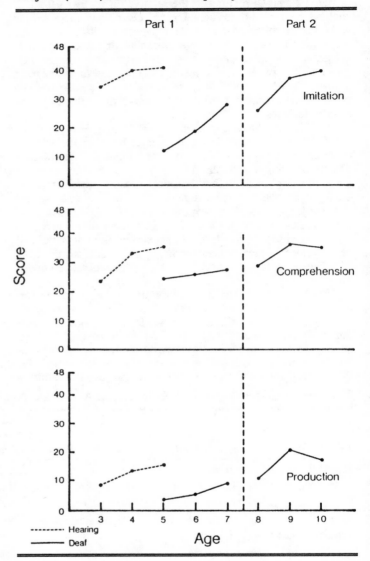

SUMMARY AND CONCLUSIONS

In summary, due to comparatively advanced conceptual development of deaf subjects as they begin to learn English, and what appears to be very flexible early vocabulary, deaf youngsters are able to construct syntactically simpler expressive alternatives to complex English forms. In contrast, very young hearing language learners with perhaps less lexical (conceptual) flexibility and having comparatively greater exposure to conventional English syntax are less likely to arrive at such idiosyncratic constructions. They may, therefore, accommodate language redundancies, etc., earlier in the acquisition process than do delayed language-acquirers such as these deaf subjects. The actual alternative devices which come to be used (see **sheep jump** examples presented earlier) may be individually specific and directly related to the signed language modeled for a deaf child (ASL and English) and the actual vocabulary items s/he acquires earliest. This early lack of control of English syntax and morphology seems to decrease with an increase in exposure to MCE. Subjects with longer MCE experience (like AL) behave in a linguistic fashion more closely resembling that of hearing subjects in overall scores, types of errors, and grammaticalness of their productions.

Though this study has demonstrated that manually coded English provides access to basic English morphology, the gains in skill over time are not uniform across language features. The scope of the study does not permit an explanation of the processes by which the eventual ordering of grammatical subtests was attained. Some of the changes in order over time (e.g., relative improvement in Singular/Plural-Is/Are) may be indicative of particular content instruction which occurred in the meantime. But inhibitory factors may also be operating. There is reason to be concerned about features which consistently appear at the bottom of such rankings and on which little to no improvement is noted. Knowledge of some forms (e.g., negative, mass, count, possessives) may develop naturally out of everyday interactions through manually coded English. Other forms may not be expected to develop in this way, especially if persons interacting with the children are only marginally competent in manual communication or if the forms themselves have simpler or shorter conversational alternatives (e.g., active for passive voice). Acquisition of relatively difficult forms may be facilitated by changes in present manual coding of these forms (e.g., distinction of present indicative __s from plural __s). It may also be necessary to alter implementation procedures or formal language instruction for young signing learners to ensure adequate and earlier exposure to difficult forms (e.g., parallel use of active and passive forms in discussions during ongoing school activities) and special attention to aspects of the task of imitating signing. Moores et al. (1978) also reported from observations of school programs that complex constructions were restricted to print rather than being used in face-to-face communication. Greater and perhaps more systematic consideration needs to be given to language curricula in conjunction with MCE usage.

In general it is apparent, especially from subtest results, that caution needs to be exercised with regard to the breadth of signed content that is presumed to be available within the deaf child's MCE environment.

REFERENCES

Bellugi, U., & Fischer, S. (1972). A comparison of sign language and spoken language. *International Journal of Cognition, 1*, 173-200.

Brasel, K., & Quigley, S. (1977). Influence of certain language and communication environments in early childhood on the development of language in deaf individuals. *Journal of Speech and Hearing Research, 20*, 95-107.

Chasen, B., & Zuckerman, W. (1976). The effects of Total Communication and oralism on deaf third-grade "rubella" students. *American Annals of the Deaf, 121*, 394-402.

Cooper, R. (1967). The ability of deaf and hearing children to apply morphological rules. *Journal of Speech and Hearing Research, 10*, 77-86.

Crandall, K. (1978). Inflectional morphemes in the manual English of young hearing-impaired children and their mothers. *Journal of Speech and Hearing Research 21*, 372-386.

Fraser, C., Bellugi, U., & Brown, R. (1963). Control of grammar in imitation, comprehension and production. *Journal of Verbal Learning and Verbal Behavior, 2*, 121-135.

Gaustad, M. (1986). Longitudinal effects of manual English instruction on deaf children's morphological skills. *Applied Psycholinguistics, 7*, 101-128.

Gustason, G., Pfetzing, D., & Zawolkow, E. (1972). *Signing exact English.* Silver Springs, MD: Modern Signs Press.

Moores, D, Weiss, K., & Goodwin, M. (1978). Early education programs for hearing-impaired children: Major findings. *American Annals of the Deaf, 123*, 925-936.

Nie, N., Hull, C., Jenkins, J., Steinbrenner, K., & Bent, D. (1970). *Statistical package for the social sciences.* New York: McGraw-Hill.

Raffin, M., Davis, J., & Gilman, L. (1978). Comprehension of inflectional morphemes by deaf children exposed to a visual English sign system. *Journal of Speech and Hearing Research, 21*, 387-400.

Weiss, K., McIntyre, C., Goodwin, M., & Moores, D. (1975). *Characteristics of young deaf children and intervention programs* (Research Report #91). Minneapolis: University of Minnesota, Research, Development and Demonstration Center in Education of Handicapped Children.

Zorfass, J. (1981). Metalinguistic awareness in young deaf children: A preliminary study. *Applied Psycholinguistics, 2*, 333-352.

ACKNOWLEDGMENTS

Substantial portions of this article are reprinted, with permission, from *Applied Psycholinguistics, 7*, 1986, p. 101-128.

ADDRESS FOR CORRESPONDENCE

Martha A. Gaustad, Ph.D., Associate Professor, Department of Special Education, Bowling Green State University, Bowling Green, OH 43403.

NOTES

1. Additional details regarding the subjects and testing materials can be found in the tables and appendices of the original article: Gaustad, 1986.

2. A complete description of the statistical procedures and results can be found in the original article. Only a summary and explanation of the findings are presented here.

SEE-2 IN THE CLASSROOM: HOW WELL IS ENGLISH GRAMMAR REPRESENTED?

Barbara Luetke-Stahlman, Ph.D.
Learning, Development and Special Education
Northern Illinois University
DeKalb, IL

Many educators believe that the failure of the majority of hearing impaired students to learn to read above a third or fourth grade level (Quigley & King, 1985) and achieve well academically (Boatner, 1965; Trybus & Karchmer, 1977; Wrightstone, Aronow, & Moskowitz, 1963) is a result of an inability to completely comprehend English grammar. Yet, teachers and parents who use a simultaneous communication method called Signing Exact English, SEE-2 (Gustason, Pfetzing, & Zawolkow, 1972), are hopeful that the hearing impaired student's ability to comprehend English will be enhanced if the child receives grammatically correct English input. The little research as to the effectiveness of the systems which has been done to date (Bornstein, Saulnier, & Hamilton, 1980; Gilman & Raffin, 1975, reported in Raffin, Davis, & Gilman, 1978; Gustason, 1981; Washburn, 1983) is inconclusive and raises many questions.

Aside from the issue of whether or not the invented systems are effective, Marmor and Petitto (1979) and Kluwin (1981) have questioned whether teachers are able to accurately sign all that is spoken in the classroom. In the former study, two teachers were unable to simultaneously voice and sign grammatically corresponding English utterances with a high degree of consistency. Kluwin (1981) did not provide specific information on deletions but stated that teachers did not generally conform to the assumptions of the systems for manually representing English. The aim of the present study was to analyze the accuracy of teachers and parents motivated to use SEE-2 with hearing impaired subjects and compare it to the research reported concerning signed English.

METHODOLOGY

Subjects

Four hearing teachers working in two different educational facilities and three hearing parents whose hearing impaired children were enrolled in one of these programs served as subjects for the study. (Unaided PTA results for the children were 67 dB, 108 dB, 103 dB, and 100 dB. Aided averaged PTA results were 37 dB, 65 dB, 52 dB, and 60 dB, respectively.) The teachers and parents were highly motivated to provide this system of input to their students and children and their decision to use the system was strongly supported by the school administration.

Procedure

Language samples were collected from all subjects. Two 10 minute language samples were collected from Teachers 1 and 2, respectively, who worked at a private, preschool facility. Two 20 minute language samples (10 minutes in a group set-

ting and 10 minutes working individually with a student) were taken of Teachers 3 and 4 who worked with grades K-6 in a public school classroom. Parent samples were taken from data collected for another study (Luetke-Stahlman & Moeller, unpublished) and consisted of five 10 minute videotaped samples collected from each parent in a structural play environment in the sixth session of the data collection period. All teachers and parents were asked to communicate with their students or children as they did normally and were told that the purpose of the sample was to analyze their ability to simultaneously communicate with hearing impaired children. Subject characteristics appear in Table 1.

Table 1. Subject Characteristics

Subject Identification	Type of School or Child	Time (No of Utterances) *	Years Signing SEE-2
Teacher 1 Joni	Private preschool	20 min. (110)	2.0
Teacher 2 MaryPat	Private preschool	20 min. (118)	6.0
Teacher 3 Debbie	Public K-3rd grade	10 min. (208)	6.0
Teacher 4 Ruth	Public 4-6th grade	10 min. (137)	6.0
Parent 1 Renelle	3 year-old deaf son	10 min. (111)	3.0
Parent 2 Larry	4 year-old deaf son	10 min. (58)	3.5
Parent 3 Char	4 year-old deaf son	10 min. (78)	3.5

* Marmor and Petitto (1978) utilized two 10 minute language samples, analyzing 183 utterances for Teacher 1 and 116 utterance for Teacher 2.

Observational Systems

All utterances occurring in a sample were transcribed by the author. A bimodal transcription system was utilized such that the spoken portions of utterances were transcribed in lower case letters and signed portions in upper case letters. Morphological markers were transcribed as they coincided with the oral English morphology. For example, an utterance in which sign accurately augmented voice according to SEE-2 rules was transcribed as follows:

The boys had a wonderful day at the museum.
THE BOYS HAD A WONDERFUL DAY AT THE MUSEUM..

If the "S" marker, articles, and -FUL suffix had been deleted and the subject had signed BUILDING instead of "museum" the utterance would have been transcribed as follows:

The boys had a wonderful day at the museum.
BOY HAD WONDER DAY AT BUILDING.

American sign language characteristics (i.e., facial expressions, head and body referencing, eye gaze, use of space, etc.)

Table 2. Results of Language Sample Coding.

Subject	Total Utterances	MLU	SEE-2 Consistency	Semantic Intent Ratio	IJC
Teachers					
1. Joni	110	5.4	77%	80%	91%
2. MaryPat	118	7.2	89%	100%	100%
3. Debbie	208	5.3	71%	85%	77%
4. Ruth	137	7.7	84%	92%	81%
5. Elena	55	6.6	82%	91%	--
6. Kim	102	8.3	80%	96%	--
Parents					
1. Renelle	58	5.9	70%	79%	96%
2. Larry	78	10.6	77%	85%	99%
3. Char	111	6.4	85%	92%	99%
Mean:	108	7.0	79%	89%	

were not transcribed as the subjects had little if any exposure to that language.

The Coordinator of Aural Rehabilitation at the private preschool facility transcribed at least 100 utterances from each of the four teachers and all parental utterances. Interjudge reliability scores were computed. In addition to the analysis of SEE-2 consistency, the semantic intactness of each utterance was also coded. For this analysis, the taxonomy from Bloom and Lahey (1978, Appendix B) was utilized. If, for example, a subject would have signed

She gave me a litt
POINT SHE GIVE

The utterances would
signed SEE-2 utterance
meaning. To compute
semantic intent ratio, the

correct (or intact u
total number of utterance

was used. Mean-length-ut
all language samples. 1
English "parts of speech"
by Marmor and Petitto (1978).

.....ing five
.... to those completed

RESULTS

Data from this study as compared to Marmor and Petitto (1978) is reported in Table 3. Interjudge reliability for all analyses was above 80%. The SEE-2 consistency ratio (averaged at 79%), semantic intent ratio (averaged at 89%), and MLU for each sample are reported in Table 3.

DISCUSSION

It is strikingly apparent from this data analysis that teachers and parents **are** able to accurately sign what they speak if

Table 3. Data Comparison.

Form	Marmor & Petitto (1978)					Session 6: Luetke-Stahlman & Moeller (in press)				
	Subject	N	Primary Deletions	Secondary Deletions	Correct	Subject	N	Primary Deletions	Secondary Deletions	Correct
Wh-Questions	T$_1$	11	82%	9%	9%	Teacher 1	17	0	0	100%
						2	24	0	1	96%
	T$_2$	9	22%	78%	0%	3	37	0	3	92%
						4	21	0	1	95%
						Parent 1	5	1	0	80%
						2	10	0	0	100%
						3	17	0	0	100%
Declarative	T$_1$	40	83%	12%	5%	Teacher 1	41	0	7	98%
						2	43	0	0	100%
	T$_2$	12	25%	67%	8%	3	76	19	7	66%
						4	82	3	17	76%
						Parent 1	8	3	3	87.3%
						2	19	1	7	57.9%
						3	19	1	2	84.3%
Relative Clauses (i.e., who, when, which, that)	T$_1$	11	91%	9%	0%	Teacher 1	7	0	0	100%
						2	12	0	0	100%
						3	11	0	1	91%
	T$_2$	1		100%	05	4	8	0	1	87%
						Parent 1	1	0	0	100%
						2	5	0	0	100%
						3	2	0	0	100%

Subject	N	Omitted in Sign	Incorrect	Correct
T$_1$	79	63%	11%	26%
	(18 of 50 different)			
T$_2$	48	17%	0%	88%
	(10 of 50 Different)			(33 SE; 50% ASL)

Session 6: Luetke-Stahlman & Moeller (in press)

Subject	N	Omitted in Sign	Incorrect	Correct
Teacher 1	88	3	0	97%
	(23 out of 50 different)			
2	94	0	0	100%
	(28 out of 50 different)			
3	166	6	0	96%
	(34 out of 50 different)			
4	84	2	0	98%
	(31 out of 50 different)			
Parent 1	17	0	0	100%
	(29 out of 50 different)			
2	58	2	0	97%
	(25 out of 50 different)			
3	66	0	0	100%
	(26 out of 50 different)			

	Subject	N	Omitted in Sign	Incorrect	Correct
Verb Tense	T$_1$	126			
Present		68	57%	10%	32%
			(verb: 37%; -P.T. 51)		
Past		57			10%
Future		1			100%
	T$_2$	51			
Present		137	35%	19%	46%
Past 94.1%		14	0	93	3%
Future		0			

Subject	N	Omitted in Sign	Incorrect	Correct
Teacher 1	72	0	1	99%
	20	0	0	100%
	4	0	0	100%
2	59	2	0	97%
	42	0	0	100%
	12	0	0	100%
3	122	8	0	93%
	48	0	0	100%
	3	0	1	67%
4	86	0	3	97%
	41	0	0	100%
	9	0	0	100%
Parent 1	47	4	3	85%
	0	0	0	100%
	2	0	0	100%
2	67	3	1	94.1%
	4	1	1	50%
	18	1	0	94.5%
3	91	1	1	97.8%
	9	1	1	88%
	27	0	0	100%

ASL influence on oral utterances: 12/78 non-English oral utterances or 15% — No ASL influence on any oral utterances for any of the 9 subjects.

motivated to do so. Data analyzed in regard to question forms, declarative sentences, relative clauses, personal pronouns, and verb tense reveal that SEE-2 users can encode these forms of English. Further, when the precise SEE-2 is not utilized, the meaning of utterances most often remains intact. It is the author's suspicion that comparable results could be obtained from cueing and SEE-1 teachers and parents as well. Although the invented pedagogical systems are not perfectly contrived, there are those who are using them with consistency and completeness.

Research is now needed which illustrates that sign to voice ratio can improve over time and that such improvement can be maintained (Luetke-Stahlman & Moeller, in preparation) and that students exposed to SEE-2 obtain literacy skills equally or better than incomplete language users (Luetke-Stahlman, submitted).

REFERENCES

Boatner, E.B. (1965). The need of a realistic approach to the education of the deaf. Paper given to the joint convention of the California Association of Teachers of the Deaf and Hard of Hearing and the California Association of the Deaf, November 6, 1965.

Bornstein, H., Sauliner, K., & Hamilton, L. (1980). Signed English: A first evaluation. *American Annals of the Deaf, 126* (1), 69-72.

Gustason, G. (1981). Does Signing Exact English work? *Teaching English to the Deaf, 7* (1). Published by Gallaudet College, Department of English.

Gustason, G., Pfetzing, D., & Zawolkow, E. (1972). *Signing Exact English*. Rossmoor, CA: Modern Signs Press.

Kluwin, T. (1981). The grammaticality of manual representations of English in classroom settings. *American Annals of the Deaf, 126*, 417-421.

Luetke-Stahlman, B., & Moeller, M. P. (submitted). SEE-2 intervention with parents: Baseline.

Luetke-Stahlman, B., & Moeller, M. P. (in preparation). SEE-2 intervention with parents: Progress and retention.

Marmor, G., & Petitto, L. (1979). Simultaneous communication in the classroom: How well is English grammar represented? *Sign Language Studies, 23*, 99-136.

Quigley, S., & King, C. (1985). *Reading and deafness*. San Diego, CA: College-Hill Press.

Raffin, M., Davis, J., & Gilman, L. (1978). Comprehension of inflectional morphemes by deaf children exposed to a visual English sign system. *Journal of Speech and Hearing Research, 21*, 387-400.

Trybus, R., & Karchmer, M. (1977). School achievement scores of hearing impaired children: National data on achievement status and growth patterns. *American Annals of the Deaf Directory of Programs and Services, 122*, 62-69.

Washburn, A. (1983). SEE-1: The development and use of a sign system over two decades. *Teaching English to Deaf and Second-Language Students, 2* (1). Published by Gallaudet College, Department of English.

Wrightstone, J., Aranow, M., & Moskowitz, S. (1963). Developing reading test norms for deaf children. *American Annals of the Deaf, 108*, 311-316.

Original article:

A SERIES OF STUDIES INVESTIGATING SEE-2 USE

Barbara Luetke-Stahlman, Ph.D.
Learning, Development & Special Education
Northern Illinois University
DeKalb, IL

Many educators in the field of Hearing Impairment (H.I.) have claimed that hearing impaired students have been failed by educators (Boatner, 1965; Moores, 1986; Trybus & Karchmer, 1977). Allen (1986) found that hearing impaired students read at about the fourth grade level and that national data from 1974 and 1983 reveal that this ability level has not improved in the last decade. This predicament is usually attributed to the fact that the majority of hearing impaired students do not enter school programs with the language base that their hearing peers have acquired (i.e., age appropriate language skills). One would assume this to be the logical case since it is rare that a diagnosis of hearing impairment has occurred and been appropriately aided before the child was a year old -- and often occurs when the child is much older (see Davis, Shepard, Stelmachowitz, & Gorga, 1981; Swigart, 1986). Secondly, the vast majority of hearing impaired children cannot completely comprehend the spoken language input used by the majority of the people with whom they interact. To make spoken English more comprehensible to hearing impaired students, systems that manually represent the English language were invented. These systems included Seeing Essential English, SEE-1 (Anthony, 1971), Signing Exact English, SEE-2 (Gustason, Pfetzing, & Zawolkow, 1972), Signed English (Bornstein & Saulnier, 1981) and Cued Speech (Cornett, 1967). But while the systems have been in use for over a decade now in educational settings with hearing impaired students, there is little research available to assist educators in deciding the usefulness of one particular instructional input mode as compared to another.

Recently, several strands of research have been initiated in an attempt to discern the usefulness of Signing Exact English (SEE-2). These studies, many of which are on-going, are summarized below.

Educational Ramifications of Using Various Sign Systems

This major research project (Luetke-Stahlman, 1987a) addresses the question of whether hearing impaired subjects who are exposed to a variety of different instructional communication inputs which attempt to completely encode a language score significantly higher on six tests related to English literacy than do subjects exposed to incomplete input. These tests included four Woodcock-Johnson tests (passage comprehension, picture vocabulary, antonyms, and synonyms), a sight word test, the Northwestern Syntax Screening Test, and a speech intelligibility measure. After a pilot study was completed, a study was designed which included four groups of 69 students aged 5 to 12: oral subjects from private and public programs, ASL subjects from two residential schools (over half had deaf parents), SEE-2 subjects from two public school programs, and subjects using a form of signed English from public and private settings. The latter group used some word endings but there was a great deal of teacher variance as to

how conceptually input was signed. All teachers who used signs were videotaped and curriculum surveys were collected. An analysis of covariance was utilized (covariates were aided and unaided averaged hearing acuity, and age). Subjects exposed to a complete language input (oral English, ASL, SEE-2) (henceforth referred to as "complete" group) scored significantly higher (p < .01) on two measures of literacy than did subjects exposed to signed English. "Complete" subjects also approached significance (p < .06, p < .09) on two other measures. No one group scored better than another on the speech intelligibility measure (scores here correlated with aided PTA).

In a second study (Luetke-Stahlman, 1987a), Cued Speech and SEE-1 subjects were added to the "complete" subject pool. An ANCOVA was again utilized. The "complete" group (n = 69) scored significantly higher than the "incomplete" group (n = 55) on the Passage Comprehension test (p < .001), Synonyms (p < .008), Antonyms (p < .001), Picture Vocabulary Test (p < .04), and Northwest Syntax Screening Test (NSST) (p < .001). The "complete" group also scored significantly higher on the speech intelligibility measure (p < .04). There were no significant differences on the literacy battery among the "complete" groups. The project is on-going with data currently being collected from PSE and residential oral subjects.

The Castle Study

Olsen-Fulero (1983) suggested that the most obvious explanation for the pervasive use of request with hearing children is that questions function as devices for turn-taking, a critical element in successful conversational interaction. It is striking, therefore, how little evidence exists concerning the characteristics of questioning among parents of handicapped children, and, in particular, parents of hearing impaired children. The purpose of this study (Luetke-Stahlman, 1987b) was to describe questions used by hearing parents of hearing impaired preschoolers. Analyzed data was compared to that of hearing parents of hearing children whose MLU was equal to that of the hearing impaired subjects.

Middle-class hearing parents and their hearing (n = 12) children and middle-class hearing parents and their hearing impaired children (n = 5) participated. Two-year-old hearing children were matched by mean-length-of-utterance (MLU) to three and four year old hearing impaired preschoolers. A language sample for each subject-dyad was videotaped as each parent and child interacted in spontaneous, unstructured play sessions. A standard set of toys (i.e., a Fisher-Price castle, people, vehicles, and animals) were present in an otherwise empty room. The language samples were transcribed and coded for language elements of interest (i.e., ____, questions used, meaning encoded, etc.). Interjudge reliability percentages were obtained from a second transcriber and coder. All questions were tallied and frequency counts obtained on (a) types of question asked (i.e., wh-, reversals, and unmarked queries); (b) the cognitive and context demands of the questions.

Results indicated that the two groups of parents (of hearing and of hearing impaired children) did evidence some significant differences in questions asked of their preschoolers. The parents of hearing impaired children used significantly shorter sentences ($p < .007$) and a greater number ($p < .09$) of unmarked questions (questions which did not include question words or in which word order was not inverted). These differences in input, already observable with three- and four-year-old children, alert professionals to promote early parent intervention programs. Parents of young hearing impaired children need to be exposed to the linguistic input that will provide for successful conversational interaction with those around them. The fact that greater differences were not found among these parents, however, indicates parents using Signing Exact English are capable, for the most part, of asking questions which are highly similar to those asked by hearing parents of their hearing children.

The research is currently being expanded to include parents of hearing impaired children who are using Cued Speech and oral English. Differences which occur in the communicative process will alert educators using various systems to work with parents to acquire appropriate question-asking skills.

Understanding ASL-Using Adults

Educators and parents often express concern that SEE-2 users will be alienated from Deaf Culture because of the differences in SEE-2 lexical signs, prefix and suffix and signed markers, and adherence to the grammar of spoken English. The purpose of this pilot investigation (Luetke-Stahlman, 1987c) was to determine the extent to which young hearing impaired subjects can demonstrate their comprehension of adults' use of American Sign Language.

Subjects were hearing impaired students, 7 to 13 years of age. One group attended a public school program ($n = 7$) where they received little, if any, exposure to Deaf adults or ASL. A second group had attended one of two residential schools for at least three years ($n = 18$) and were exposed to Pidgin Sign English and ASL. Many Deaf adults worked in the schools and dorm facilities.

In small groups, subjects were shown three stories signed by Deaf actors, taken from a television program which aired in the late 1970s called "Rainbow's End." The stories were three to five minutes in length and were not captioned. Immediately following each story, subjects were asked to complete three to eight written comprehension questions about the story they had just seen (e.g., Was Atlanta a good runner?). These questions were initially written by the author and rewritten by both a public and a residential teacher. Readability measures showed the set of questions to be at the first grade level.

Preliminary results must be viewed with caution. The data collection is still on-going and some important variables (i.e., reading level of subjects, aided and unaided hearing acuity, etc.) were not controlled. However, results at present are that the mean of the age of the subjects in the two groups is equal ($X = 10$ years). SEE-2 subjects answered a mean of 6.29 questions correctly while residential subjects answered a mean of 3.8 questions correctly. At the very least, it appears that SEE-2 system users can comprehend Deaf adults telling stories (without context) in ASL. Further research of this nature

is desired, however, since bilingual, bicultural assimilation is a primary goal in deaf education.

Parents Use and Improvement of SEE-2

Luetke-Stahlman and Moeller (unpublished) have completed two studies that descriptively analyze hearing parents use of SEE-2. Parents use manually coded English sign systems, such as SEE-2, because they believe that hearing impaired children's literacy skills will improve if they receive signed input that grammatically corresponds to spoken English. Yet, relatively little is known about how effective hearing parents of hearing impaired children are in providing simultaneous spoken and signed input. The few studies that have been completed (Swisher & Thompson, 1985; Bornstein, Saulnier, & Hamilton, 1980) report discouraging results. These studies suggest that parents often provide an impoverished sign code (compared to their spoken input) and fail to advance beyond a beginner's level of proficiency, even after as many as three years of sign exposure and use. Luetke-Stahlman and Moeller (1988) hypothesized that parental difficulties in signing accurately might be related to the limited approaches currently available for teaching parents to communicate via sign. Many teaching programs for parents are didactic in nature, concentrating on building sign vocabulary and basic manual expression -- an approach which may not be that well-suited for training parents to communicate with young children in the home.

In a major research effort, two phases of study were initiated to address this concern. In the first phase, five parents of profoundly hearing impaired children, who had been using SEE-2 for at least three years, were videotaped on two separate occasions while interacting with their children. A standard toy (the Fisher-Price castle and various props) was used in all interactions. Oral and signed segments of the videotapes were transcribed. Transcripts were then subjected to multi-dimensional analyses, including: *grammar accuracy* and *complexity* (MLU, grammatic deletions, and number of utterances where speech and sign message correspond exactly); *semantic content* (meaning categories represented in the signed messages, and determination of whether sign deletions distorted message meaning for the child); and *aspects of functional communication proficiency* (parental attempts to involve the child in pretending; types of questions used by parent to stimulate child and frequency of parent's attempts to introduce novel vocabulary items to the child).

The primary findings of this portion of the study were as follows.

1. Four of five parents produced MLU's in their signed messages that were significantly below that of their children. The average MLU for signed + spoken utterances for parents was 3.0 (range 1.3 - 4.3) compared to an average MLU of 4.5 (range 3.9 - 5.2) for the children. This finding has obvious implications: To stimulate language acquisition, it is of paramount importance that parents sign to a degree which simulates (not underestimates) their child's ability.

2. On the average, parents deleted 24.4% of syntactic features in their signed messages. However, there was wide individual variation, with one subject deleting on 7% and another deleting over 49%.

3. Complex grammar features, like conjunctions, reflexive pronouns, passive verbs, etc., were rarely, if ever, used by parents in the study. Parents had a tendency to use simplistic grammatical forms when communicating with their deaf children.

4. On the average, parents in this study produced signed messages that corresponded precisely to the spoken message in 53% of their utterances. This finding is similar to that found by Swisher and Thompson (1985). Again, however, there was a wide range (from 14% to 85%) in parental performance.

5. Parents used a wide range of semantic notions in their signed and spoken messages. However, complex notions, such as coordination of thoughts, causality or epistemic (contrasted phrases using "but") rarely appeared in parent messages. This again suggests that parents were adhering to simple messages, whether or not this was appropriate for their child.

6. Semantic notions that were most frequently deleted in the signed portions of messages were: question markers, time, quantity, and possession. In these instances, the missing meaning which was conveyed by morphological markers was only spoken and not signed.

7. Parents varied considerably in their ability to engage their child in pretend interactions. One parent, who was especially weak in structural aspects of her sign, was the strongest in interacting playfully with her child. This result suggests that the goals of intervention for this parent may need to be quite different from that of others in her group.

8. Parents varied in their use of didactic, convergent questions vs. thought-provoking or open-ended questions. Three of five subjects were found to be in need of reducing didactic, cognitively undemanding questions, and increasingly open-ended, cognitively-stimulating utterances.

9. In over 1,000 parental utterances, there were only three examples of a parent attempting to introduce and/or define a new word for the child. The parents talked about only the information for which they knew signs. This finding also has important implications for intervention.

10. Although, overall, some intervention needs were similar across subjects, there was considerable individual variability in performance and priority needs. This suggests that parent sign programs, like children's programs, need to be individualized. The authors also found that analysis of parent sign abilities was a rich resource for planning individualized intervention.

The second phase of this study involved provision of an individualized intervention program. Each parent met with one of the investigators and was given feedback on their performance from phase one of the study. The analyzed information was used to set individual goals for each parent. The investigators targeted goals in each of the areas of syntax, semantics, and pragmatics. The parent and investigator discussed the behaviors needing attention, and examples and illustrations were given before the parent was again video-taped. A single subject design was utilized such that the authors could clearly identify intervention results. The parents received three intervention sessions and a fourth session was included three months after the end of the intervention period. This last session allowed for the evaluation of the parents' retention of goals worked on in the intervention sessions. Results of the intervention study may be summarized as follows.

1. All parents in the study made rapid improvements in MLU and correspondence of the signed and spoken message. Following intervention, the parent MLUs ranged from 5.3 to 7.3 morphemes, which was higher than their child's MLU in each case. The group averaged 74% accuracy in correspondence of speech and sign following intervention. This finding, which resulted from minimal intervention, is encouraging in comparison to previous studies.

2. Parents benefited from being made explicitly aware of the following:
   a. seeing a tangible, written transcript of their spoken and signed input;
   b. strategies for introducing the child to unfamiliar words;
   c. strategies for using words for which the parent did not know a sign; and
   d. suggestions for encouraging divergent thinking and pretend interactions.

3. Parents exhibit individual strengths and weaknesses that may better be addressed by consideration of their unique needs. When such an approach was implemented, parents demonstrated excellent long term retention of learned principles.

4. Parents had difficulty changing semantic aspects of their messages in response to minimal intervention. Parents may require structured lessons to learn ways to incorporate complex meanings in their signs (e.g., cause/effect relationships, clauses using *but,* etc.). Parents may need help in appropriately estimating the level of semantic complexity the child is able to receive.

While much of the research reported within this article is still in progress, encouraging results are apparent already. Teachers and parents *can* sign high percentages of what is spoken if motivated to do so. Teachers and parents *can* achieve specific goals involving the form, content, and use of spoken and signed communication and retain improvements over time. Social and academic benefits to complete language or system use need to be documented. The wave of research involving empirical investigation of the available spoken and/or signed inputs to hearing impaired children is long overdue and should be encouraged.

REFERENCES

Allen, T. (1986). A study of the achievement patterns of H.I. students: 1974-1983 In *Deaf Children in America.* A. Schildroth & M. Karchmer (eds.) San Diego: College-Hill Press, 161-206.

Anthony, D. (1971). *Seeing essential English* (Vols. 1 and 2). Anaheim, CA: Educational Services Division.

Boatner, E. B. (1965). *The need of a realistic approach to the education of the deaf.* Paper presented at the joint convention of the California Association of the Deaf. Hartford, CT.

Bornstein, H. & Sauliner, K. (1980). Signed English: A brief follow-up to the first evaluation. *American Annals of the Deaf, 126*(1), 69-72.

Bornstein, H., Saulnier, K., Hamilton, L. (1980). Signed English: A First Evaluation. *American Annals of the Deaf, 125*, (3), 468-481.

Cornett, R. (1967). Cued Speech. *American Annals of the Deaf, 112*, 3-13.

Davis, J.M., Shepard, N.T., Stelmachowitz, P.G., & Gorga, M.P. (1981). Characteristics of hearing-impaired children in the public schools. Part II - Psychoeducational data. *Journal of Speech & Hearing Disorders*, 46, 130-137.

Gustason, G., Pfetzing, D., & Zawolkow, E. (1972). *Signing Exact English.* Rossmoor, CA: Modern Signs Press.

Luetke-Stahlman, B. (In preparation.) *Can SEE-2 children understand ASL-using deaf adults?*

Luetke-Stahlman, B. (1987a). Educational Ramifications of Using Various Sign Systems. (Presented at CAID convention, 1987)

Luetke-Stahlman, B. (1987b). Educational Ramifications of Using Various Communication Inputs: A Further Investigation. To be submitted to the *American Annals of the Deaf.*

Luetke-Stahlman, B. (1987c). A comparison of parental input to hearing and hearing impaired preschoolers. In R. Slavenas (ed.), *Reflections of learning research.* DeKalb, IL: Learning Research Laboratory, Department of Curriculum and Instruction, Northern Illinois University.

Luetke-Stahlman, B. and Moeller, M.P. (Unpublished). Teaching Parents to Sign SEE-2: Progress and Retention. Submitted *American Annals of the Deaf*, April, 1987.

Moores, D.F. (1986). *Educating the Deaf: Psychology, principles, and practices.* Boston: Houghton Mifflin.

Olsen-Fulero, L. (1983). Style and stability in other conversational behavior: A study of individual differences. *Journal of Child Language, 9*, 543-564.

Swigart, E. T. (1986). *Neonatal Hearing Screening.* San Diego: College Hill Press.

Swisher, M.V., & Thompson, M., (1985). Mothers learning simultaneous communication: The dimensions of the task. *American Annals of the Deaf, 130*(3), 212-217.

Trybus, R., & Karchmer, M. (1977). School achievement scores of hearing impaired children: National data on achievement status and growth patterns. *American Annals of the Deaf Directory of Programs and Services, 122*, 62-69.

Wrightstone, J., Aranow, M., & Moskowitz, S. (1963). Developing reading test norms for deaf children. *American Annals of the Deaf, 108*, 311-316.

A STUDENT AND HER DEAF MOTHER LOOK AT THE MAINSTREAMING EXPERIENCE

My Year in the Hearing Class
by Stefanie Ellis

Stefanie is the eight-year-old hearing-impaired daughter of deaf parents.

When summer ended, I had no idea that in the fall, I would attend a hearing school all day. I was filled with mixed feelings, scared and worried. I felt uneasy when I sat down in my own chair, looking at the kids who were staring at me. Some kids, whom I knew, made me feel more comfortable. By the end of the day I felt awful. I hated my new class. I wholeheartedly missed my old deaf classes. I went to Taft Hearing Impaired School for about seven years. I felt like a stranger in this school full of hearing kids. I was very upset and I didn't pay any attention to my interpreters, Julie and Pam. When I came back home from school, I felt awful and at times I cried. I told my mom how I felt and what had happened at school. My mom tried to console me. That helped for a while but it didn't satisfy me. I was still miserable.

At dinner time everyday I kept thinking how I disliked school so much. That made me scared and uncomfortable. My parents explained a lot of things; they felt I should stay in this program. They told me why I should stay, because I would learn much more here than what I could get from the deaf classes. I still wasn't comfortable. A lot of sad thoughts occurred in my mind.

Nearly everyday I didn't want to go to school. I told my mom I didn't want to go to school. I felt like I would rather stay home where routine was the same. I went to the deaf school for some help and comfort. Mostly, I went to the Principal of Taft H.I. She really helped me go through this. Later, my parents were worried about me and my reactions. They decided to have a meeting with my teachers and the principal. It really helped. My teachers and everyone else were consistent and firm, saying I should stay in the hearing class all day because of the GATE program. I suddenly realized that they were right. I didn't belong in any of the upper levels at the deaf school.

The next day, I felt great. I went to school and I'm sure the class was amazed when I entered with the big smile pasted on my face. I'm very willing to continue my education at Big Taft, the hearing school. That school really helped me develop more intelligence. Also, the kids are so friendly, you could make friends with them in less than fifteen minutes!!

You know, watching interpreters isn't too bad, after all. I got used to it. At first, one of my teachers went too fast, and my interpreters couldn't catch up, so I missed part of the subject. But my interpreters would just listen, then catch up. It was really easy for me and my other deaf classmates.

Right now, the teachers are just fine and great. But science and math -- yuck! I'm so glad I learned a lot this year. I love it at Big Taft. I really do.

The Ups and Downs of Mainstreaming

by Gayle Ellis,
Stefanie's mother

Last fall, my daughter Stefanie, who was then eight and a half years old, started her first year mainstreaming full day at Big Taft, the hearing elementary school next door to Taft Hearing Impaired, as a fourth grader and, just recently, in the new GATE program for both fourth and fifth graders. In the past, she took Math and Science at Big Taft, but this time, it was for all subjects which meant that she would no longer be in the deaf program. I must admit that I felt such confidence that she would do it with no trouble or hassle because her former special education teacher would be her instructor part time. This same teacher had currently taken up this new program with another teacher sharing a contract. Thus, she surely would make this particularly new change easy for Stefanie and the two other deaf boys in the hearing class. And with the help of very good interpreters all would be well.

But I was wrong. Was I ever in for a surprise to discover the misery and unhappiness Stefanie turned out to be feeling. Upon figuring out the reason why and also, when asking her, I came to realize that this transition was similar to a cultural shock for her. She was very frightened among so many hearing children in class. There were over thirty students; she was accustomed to only six or seven students in a deaf class. Furthermore, there was just too much for her to handle and she was acutely uncomfortable. Everything, in her exact words, was "different and so strange." She felt that they were so unfamiliar to her. Missing her deaf friends was one of the more important reasons. She did not mind if it was just for an hour or just for one subject such as Math. When she came home from school everyday, she would let go of herself and sob such heavy tears.

Stefanie had also reluctantly learned to focus her eyes solely and constantly on the interpreter all day and she was not used to this. I felt even I couldn't do this. It is like staring at a little black dot for hours. It is, no doubt, very tiring for anyone's eyes. She, as I recall, was upset seeing her former teacher only talking and not signing to the class. Thus, she felt her teacher no longer had the same feelings for her.

The pace was another area of concern. The speed of this class with hearing children listening and working was new to her. She had to learn to keep up with them and it was difficult. Stefanie had to use her eyes a lot more than ever in order to keep up with them. Total class participation then was probably nil. She was struggling hard. She was ill-at-ease, very uptight and depressed. That was scary for me. I was worried and I wanted the best for her. Yet, I didn't quite know how or what I could do next.

Besides, I remember explaining as best as I could that she is very fortunate, being able to come home every day from school whereas I was sent away from home to a private deaf Catholic school. My husband, who is also deaf, had attended a variety of rather complicated hearing schools without an interpreter but remained supportive of Stefanie's new class. It took some time last fall before she finally was convinced that she was better off staying at this excellent school. My husband and I contacted GATE teachers, the principal, and the mainstreaming consultant, to set up a meeting to discuss whether we ought to remove her from this class and return her to the deaf program. Both teachers, however, were adamant, insisting that this move was best for her. We finally agreed to a trial period.

However, early in the first month, I came to visit the class. I discovered to my joy and relief that nearly all the hearing children were signing to Stefanie. Some were rather clumsy for they had just recently been shown how to use sign language. In addition, they learned about the handicap of deafness through films, lectures and reading in a course they had in health. I noticed immediately their concern and eagerness for deaf students. It was as if they were all equal. The outcome of it all was that Stefanie progressed quickly and, amazingly . . . she finally began to feel comfortable.

Her workload, of course, had increased dramatically and yet she managed as the time went by. In addition, when she brought home her work, she was studying so many interesting subjects: social science, history, novel projects . . . to name a few. It was exceedingly more than I had expected. To see her able to be taught at this level was a relief since I knew they were essential for her. Her interest grew and she seemed to enjoy the challenge. She of course, from time to time did have a problem or two especially in math which is not her favorite subject. But, all in all, I had recognized and even now, see a new side of Stefanie. I feel quite gratified that her grasp of the "hearing world" has become agreeable and

pleasurable. She herself, had proven that she could do it. She has a new freedom from self-doubt and uncertainty. Stefanie does feel quite content among her own deaf friends, she continues to keep in contact with them during recess and/or lunchtime breaks.

I understand, at long last, that if a deaf child has, either fortunately or not, achieved academically at or above grade level, it makes sense for him or her to be placed accordingly, typically in a mainstreaming program with the support of excellent interpreters. However, I do still keep my eyes open to absolutely make sure that Stefanie continues to be comfortable and untroubled as well as receiving the appropriate education. Her participation in the class discussion is exceedingly important, too. Frustrations, anxiety, and isolation, a few of the common problems among deaf youngsters when mainstreaming, are what I was afraid of for her, but things looked good in the end.

Like any other normal parent, I hope to have my children acquire strong positive attitudes about themselves and that includes security, poise, and self-assurance, especially among the hearing students in class. Of this I am sure, since before school was out, Stefanie and her class gave an excellent performance both in talking, singing and signing in a play called "Our Country Tis Of Thee," in such a unique unity. It was simply wonderful to see! . . . The praises should and now are able to go to both GATE teachers, two dedicated hard-working people whose beliefs are strong and whose work reflects a harmonious flow.

RESOURCES

This bibliography is purposely brief and necessarily incomplete. We offer it in hopes that it will provide a starting place for further learning.

1. General Language Acquisition

Moskowitz, B. (1978). Acquisition of language. --*Scientific American*, 239, 92-108, November.
A succinct, clearly stated article reviewing the basic findings in child language-acquisition as a general topic. Best place to start.

DeVilliers, P. & DeVilliers, J. (1978) *Early Language.* Cambridge, MA: Harvard University Press.
A complete text on the topic of language acquisition in children.

2. Language Acquisition by Deaf Children

Kretschmer, R. R. Jr. & Kretschmer, L. W. (1978) *Language Develop ment and Intervention with the Hearing Impaired.* Baltimore: University Park Press.
Included are summaries of child language and linguistic capabilities, information on assessment techniques and language instruction.

Quigley, S. P. & Paul, P. V. (1984) *Language and Deafness.* San Diego, CA: College-Hill Press.
This book includes research information on cognition and language, primary language development, reading, written language, bilingualism and English as a second language, and assessment and language instruction.

3. Sign language research (American Sign Language)

Baker, C. E. & Battison, R., Eds. (1980) *Sign language and the deaf community: Essays in honor of William Stokoe.* Silver Spring, MD: National Association of the Deaf.
This book is a collection of articles by researchers on American Sign Language.

Lane, H. & Grosjean, F., Eds. (1980) *Recent perspectives on American Sign Language.* Hillsdale, NJ: Lawrence Erlbaum Associates.
A collection of articles on American Sign Language.

4. Use of signs with hearing children having language problems

Blackburn, D. W., Bonvillian, J.D., & Ashby, R. P. (1984) Manual communication as an alternative mode of language instruction for children with severe reading disabilities, *Language, Speech, and Hearing Services in Schools,* 15, 22-31.
A review of studies on the use of signs with children with severe reading disabilities and report of a study on two adolescent boys over a five-month period.

Christopoulou, C. & Bonvillian, J.D. (1985) Sign language, pantomime, and gestural processing in aphasic persons: a review, *Journal of Communication Disorders,* 18, 1-20.
A review of studies on the use of signs and other gestural processes with aphasic students.

Poulton, K.T. (1980) Manual communication and mental retardation: a review of research and implications, *American Journal of Mental Deficiency,* 85, 2, 145-52.

For a bibliography of readings on the use of signs with hearing children who have language problems, contact the SEE Center, 10443 Los Alamitos Blvd., Los Alamitos, CA 90720. One dollar postpaid.

5. Other resources

Catalogues of materials are available from:

Modern Signs Press, Inc.
P.O. Box 1181
Los Alamitos, CA 90720

National Association of the Deaf
814 Thayer Avenue
Silver Spring, MD 20910
Precollege Outreach, Gallaudet University Press, Gallaudet Bookstore, and Public Service Programs
The above are four different sources of catalogues. The address for each is:

Gallaudet University
800 Florida Avenue, N.E.
Washington, D.C. 20002

In addition, the National Information Center on Deafness at Gallaudet University can help with inquiries on many topics associated with deafness. That office has available a Bibliography of Selected Readings on Education of Hearing-Impaired Students, prepared jointly by NICD and the Convention of American Instructors of the Deaf.

The SEE Center (10443 Los Alamitos Blvd., Los Alamitos, CA 90720) has information materials for parents and teachers. Contact the Center.